AMERICAN MILER

Ad Astra per Aspera

(to the stars through struggle)

—the Kansas state motto

AMERICAN MILER

The Life and Times of Glenn Cunningham

Paul J. Kiell, M.D.

BREAKAWAY BOOKS
HALCOTTSVILLE, NEW YORK
2006

ISBN: 1-891369-59-8
Library of Congress Control Number: 2005938239

Published by Breakaway Books
P.O. Box 24
Halcottsville, NY 12438
www.breakawaybooks.com

FIRST EDITION

CONTENTS

Sweet are the uses of adversity,
Which, like the toad, ugly and venomous,
Wears yet a precious jewel in its head;
And this our life, exempt from public haunt,
Finds tongues in trees, books in the running brooks,
Sermons in stones, and good in everything.

—Shakespeare: *As You Like It* 11, I, 12

DEDICATION

In late 1986 I had a telephone interview with Glenn Cunningham. I asked, "Who were your heroes?" Without hesitation he responded: "My parents were the greatest inspiration I had. They never knew what defeat meant. They never worried about anything. They would just do whatever they needed to do with whatever they had and let the consequences come. They were always very positive about everything." So, to Rosa and Clint Cunningham, two people I never met, but who were an inspiration to a man who would inspire me, this book is dedicated.

There is someone else of whom, sadly, we know too little. It is Glenn's older brother, Floyd. "He was a wonderful boy," Glenn would say. Floyd died of his extensive burn injuries, but not before he would set an example of courage and dignity that became a motivating force in his younger brother's recovery. So it is to the memory of the lost and noble boy, Floyd Cunningham, that I also dedicate this book.

PREFACE

Having grown up in the depression-ridden 1930s, I have a clear recollection of Glenn Cunningham's running, but only a vague memory of his life's story. His name could be uttered in the same breath with other sports figures of his time: Babe Ruth, Red Grange, Jack Dempsey, Bill Tilden, Joe Louis, Jesse Owens, Bobby Jones, Johnny Weissmuller, Babe Didrikson, Seabiscuit. Some votes were even cast for him as the greatest athlete of the first half of the twentieth century; in 1979 he was acclaimed the Outstanding Track Performer in the hundred-year history of Madison Square Garden. But these names and their deeds fade with time.

Then, in late 1986, an organization made up of physicians interested in sports medicine, the American Medical Athletic Association, was planning its annual seminar around the Boston Marathon. Each year some of us qualified to run in that classic. The name of Glenn Cunningham came up. I remember asking if he was still living. He would be about seventy-seven at that time, not much older than I am now. Contact was made, and I phoned in order to conduct a taped interview and to reaffirm the commitment for him to speak at our post-marathon banquet. I remember my bumbling question/answer interview effort. I particularly recall at the end his directness in suggesting I try again so we could have a better interview. Always anxious to get his message across, he must have felt frustrated with what had become a stilted dialogue.

As for giving a talk to our membership, he readily agreed, eschewed any honorarium, wanted only his hotel and travel expenses paid; specifically, his only real request was to bring his wife, Ruth. He said that she was left alone too often when he traveled to give talks, and he wanted her to be part of this.

The Boston Marathon is always held on the third Monday in April. He arrived at our hotel the evening before, had changed so he could be dressed properly to meet these doctors, who, as it turned out, met him in T-shirts and sweatpants. He had driven with Ruth from Arkansas in their pickup truck. (On the way back home they would stop in Pennsylvania to visit with Gene Venzke, his erstwhile track rival. They had become lifelong friends. He would also visit his college classmate and track teammate Paul Borel in the Washington, DC, area.)

Hired buses took the runners in our group from the Colonnade Hotel to race start, twenty-six miles away at Hopkinton. Cunningham rode out with us. He was most forthcoming at our urgings and regaled us with stories of the past, of his races with Venzke, Bonthron, San Romani, Fenske, and Rideout; of his 1936 second-place finish in the 1500-meter run at the Berlin Olympiad won by Jack Lovelock of New Zealand, a race where the first five finishers would break the Olympic record.

Cunningham had been in an auto accident only a few years earlier, sustaining injuries to his neck and upper back. To speak to you he would have to shift and turn his entire body to face you directly, the only way he knew to speak to someone. What I remember is his body posture when telling of the U.S. Track Team tour of the Orient where he witnessed a rickshaw owner beating the coolie with a stick. Glenn's face jutted forward, his shoulders hunched, his face reddened; he was clearly reliving his revulsion at the specter of one man subjugating and humiliating another. He told of how his teammates had to restrain him after he had grabbed the stick from the driver and was about to turn it back on the oppressor.

He spoke to our group that evening and received a standing ovation. Then a few of us went to a side room to chat. I taped both his talk and then later his off-the-cuff remarks—more specifically, in that informal confab, his unequivocal outspoken ideas about a number of social issues.

We corresponded a bit over the ensuing months. The coming April, our organization planned a seminar in New Jersey around the Waterfront Marathon, which that year, 1988, was the qualifier for the Seoul Olympiad. In January he had written, accepting our invitation to speak again at our seminar. He wrote how he and Ruth were looking forward to seeing all of us again. But it would never be. On March 10 he died.

I soon felt the strong urge to fill what had become a distinct void. Through technical help from a high school audio visual teacher and with the generous donation by Bud Greenspan of archival newsreel clips, I was able to assemble a homemade video telling of Cunningham's track career and what he described as his greatest career, the work with troubled children. I presented it at that seminar and again at our seminar around the New York City Marathon the following November. An honored guest then was Gene Venzke, who would have a reunion with another honored guest, Ruth Cunningham. That began a yearly visit to our home for Ruth when we would have the now annual seminar in Manhattan. There I would present a video on the life of Glenn Cunningham.

The idea of a book has evolved over the years since Cunningham's death. Myra Brown, a friend of the Cunninghams and an author, had begun a book some time in the mid-1960s.

She had interviewed Glenn, family members, old neighbors of the Cunninghams from the early years, his coaches, his running rivals. Even the widow of the doctor who had treated Glenn and Floyd after the burns was found and had written letters in response to Myra's queries. There were letters from former teachers and from high school coaches.

The taped interviews were transcribed. But Myra died soon after writing several manuscript chapters. Fortunately, Ruth saved all those transcriptions and forwarded them to me. Accordingly, I had them electronically reproduced and have inserted parts in different sections without any editing on my part. This way the vernacular, the flavor, the idiom of the people present during those years is preserved. Invaluable help was obtained from correspondence with the Kansas State Historical Society. Paul Borel contributed some precious vignettes, photos, and a poem he had written upon Cunningham's death. Howard Schmertz, who directed the Millrose Games—first handled by his father, the late Fred Schmertz—provided old programs from the Millrose Games, historical data, and some precious anecdotes.

Besides archival photos from her personal collection, Ruth sent me Glenn's handwritten notes, often written on the back of envelopes or on hotel stationery. "He was always cutting things out of the newspaper," she wrote, "and constantly writing down on envelopes and scraps of paper things he ran across when he traveled." She had a whole file of sayings he had copied through the years.

Ruth was the proverbial behind-a-great-man-lies-a-great-woman person, but she disdains any reference to her and even to considering Glenn a great man. I quote her again where she wants me to be sure she is mentioned only in passing, something I find hard to do but have tried to: "I want his running career to be the focus, and of course, to do that, you have to halfway understand the man, his philosophy, what drove him, and his outlook on life.

" 'Great men have great faults' he always said, and I think this is true of Glenn. While I wouldn't say he was great exactly, I do think he stands tall and lived his life well. He was the first to say he was as good as the best, and as bad as the worst—he knew he didn't always measure up himself to the ideals he held and taught as we are told to 'live holy as God is holy'—but we can't—we can only strive for that, and when we do there is nobility in our lives. And I think Glenn did that in spades."

Well . . . Glenn and I never had another interview. Maybe now, with this book, I'll finally get it right.

PROLOGUE

Such was the headline for a letter-to-the-editor published in the *New York Times* shortly after Glenn Cunningham's death on March 10, 1988. Here is what Bob Corrigan wrote:

With the death of Glenn Cunningham on March 10, America lost one of its authentic sports heroes.

I am too young to have seen him compete in his heyday, but as a boy I heard the remarkable story of the athlete who overcame severe burns on his legs to become the greatest miler in the world. Cunningham's duels with rivals Bill Bonthron and Gene Venzke in the 1930's made the mile track's glamour event.

In recent years I learned about Cunningham's devotion to helping troubled children. For most of his adult life, he and his wife guided thousands of abandoned, abused, and delinquent boys and girls to productive lives.

Less than two weeks before his death, I had the opportunity to meet Cunningham, who told me his work with young people had given him far more satisfaction than his athletic achievements. I'll never forget his words: "There is nothing as important as a child."

Those of us—parents, youth workers, teachers, and others —who agree with him can only hope in this era of artificial sports heroes that the Glenn Cunningham story will not be forgotten.

—Robert J. Corrigan, Jackson Heights, Queens

In the nearly two decades since that letter, the mile is still pretty much track's glamour event, while track itself has assumed a less glamorous pose. Bob Corrigan and I met and became friends. A video about Cunningham entitled *The Iron Man of Kansas,* by a now defunct producer, was made. Bob wrote a book titled *Tracking Heroes.* In it he chronicled the lives of thirteen trackmen of the past, among them Glenn Cunningham. Glenn's widow, Ruth, became a dear friend of our family. But still, the story of Glenn Cunningham lies fallow, virtually forgotten, yet to be truly told.

It is, however, a story that *must* be told, told in terms of his running but only as this was an extension of the man, reflecting the timeless values he lived by. It is a tale not only of his deeds on and off the track, but of an attitude, a philosophy and a prescience that wears well for all times.

That he was an authentic sports hero was determined, in part, by the era of the 1930s, the time of the Great Depression. In Cunningham the public found its idol in a man who had been scarred and suffered a loss through trauma, yet whose person literally and figuratively soared above the ashes. He was exemplar of the American Dream.

His work with abandoned, abused, and delinquent boys and girls evolved first from his empathy, augmented by his example—a product of his character. From his empiric understanding of animals and his education (he had earned a Ph.D. in biology, health, and physical education) he presaged the practice of animal therapy; his intuition, the biblical scholarship upon which his philosophy of life was based, foretold the science of cognitive behavioral psychotherapy.

His was a way of life forged in tragedy yet caressed by love of family and friends. Among the basics that his recovery and evolving outlook were founded upon were a joy in physical activity that was reinforced by a love of animals, with whom he learned to play and to communicate. Such was an extension of his love for family and friends, particularly friends and others along the way to whom life had delivered cruel blows. He always defended anyone beset by a bully. He hated bullies.

The story begins in the state of Kansas, a state fittingly bearing the old Roman motto: *Ad Astra per Aspera* (to the stars through struggle).

1

EARLY YEARS, 1909-1917

He was always determined to go to school. Even before he was old enough to hardly realize what the words meant, he talked of going to college.

Glenn Cunningham was born August 4, 1909, in the town of Atlanta, Cowley County, Kansas. Almost fifty years earlier, Kansas had entered the Union as a free state. The president of the United States, elected in 1908, was William Howard Taft, former secretary of war under his predecessor Theodore Roosevelt. In 1908 the Ford Motor Company introduced the Model T. It sold for $850.

Weighing in at seven pounds. Glenn's arrival in their three-room, two-story house was at 6 A.M. His mother, Rosa, had had measles just before his birth, and his sister Letha would later record that he was spotted when he was born. A Dr. Stearns and a neighbor, Mrs. Brannam, helped, and the other youngsters were sent to stay with the Brannams that morning. His father was at the time working for the city.

(At the time, Glenn's birth was not registered. Years later when he needed a passport to go to Europe as part of the U.S. Track Team, his mother had to sign an affidavit with the information regarding his birth.)

His entry was amid the August rains that would allow the September winter wheat planting, with harvesting hoped for the coming June. The census taken in 1910 showed Kansas with a population of 1,696,361. Atlanta's tally would vary between three hundred and seven hundred. In Rolla, where they lived at the time of the schoolhouse fire, the inhabitants numbered three hundred. Where the family would later settle, Cimarron Township (Elkhart), the population was 727.

Glenn was the fifth born and third son to mother Rosa Agnes (née Moore), 28, and father Henry Clinton Cunningham, 32. His older siblings at the time of his arrival were: Margerie, 7; Floyd, 5; Letha, 4; Raymond, 2. There would later be two more children. The family moved often, and the conventional method of travel was by horse and buggy or covered wagon.

Sometime in the 1960s, by hand, unedited, later typed, placing himself in the third person, Glenn Cunningham describes life on those windswept Kansas Plains:

As the little immegrant [sic] *was being delivered into the world by the country doctor, the four Cunningham children, two girls and two boys, were sent out to one of the neighbors to spend the nite. There was no hospital or special nurses in this small town, so the doctor with the aid of a kindly lady neighbor was trusted with the responsibility of bringing this newcomer into the world.*

When the four Cunningham children returned the next morning they were all delighted and pleased to see their newly arrived brother who was snuggled close to his mother's side. They all wanted to pull the blanket down so they could see the little crimson, ugly face; they wanted to touch him and later asked to hold him in their own small arms.

When the mother was up and doing her daily housework again, it was the privilege or duty of the four older children to help care for and entertain this new charge. Especially was this true for the two girls, Margerie, eight, and Letha, four, for the mother was always occupied with the daily household duties; in canning food for the winter and mending clothing and making new clothes as all this work was done by hand in the home in those days.

He goes on to tell of what may have been his introduction to animals.

When Glenn was about two years old the family moved on a farm about two miles out of Atlanta. It wasn't long until he had learned to ride a horse and had a pony all his own. His father would saddle the pony the first thing in the morning and place this little tot in the saddle to ride about the corrals while the chores were being done. The pony was an aged, brown colored animal with one eye out, but to Glenn she was as fine a pony as ever trotted upon this earth. She was especially gentle and seemed to understand that the small charge placed upon her back had to be protected. She would walk about slowly avoiding all obstacles, which might prove harmful to her charge. She avoided the other horse which was in the habit of whirling unexpectedly and letting loose with a powerful kick with both hind legs which would have sent little Glenn across the corral in dozens of pieces had he ever been struck by these flying feet.

In the next passage Glenn tells of his burning desire for schooling when he was only two years old.

When the morning chores were over, breakfast finished and the four older children ready for school, Glenn used to beg to go with his two brothers, Floyd, who was seven years old, and Raymond, who was five, down to the end of the land on his pony to meet the 'kid wagon'. The kid wagon would come along each morning, drawn by horses, and pick up the children of the community and take them to school the same as school buses do today. Once at the end of the lane it was always a problem to get Glenn back to the house. He was always determined to go to school. Even before he was old enough to hardly realize what the words meant, he talked of going to college.

The problem was usually solved by tying the horse to the fence and leaving Glenn to sit on her back weeping hopelessly until his mother would walk down the lane to lead the horse back to the yard. Once the other children were out of sight, Glenn was content to amuse himself playing alone or doing little things about the house and imagining that he was helping his mother. Especially did he enjoy helping his mother carry water from the spring in the creek nearby. After the pails were filled at the spring the mother would walk back to the house with her large pail full of water with one arm raised to one side to help offset the weight being carried by the other arm. Glenn walking behind with his tiny pail, seeing his mother's arm out to one side, would swing his free arm high into the air, imagining that he too was carrying a heavy pail of water like his mother.

In another notation he describes a typical winter's day:

Within the tall, two story frame building which stood out as a land mark for miles around, lived my family—six children, father and mother. We had weathered the night in beds piled high with thick, warm, homemade quilts but now we must get up and do our chores. There were horses, cows, hogs, and chickens to feed and cows to milk. Since papa was sick and confined to his bed with influenza it was up to mama, Letha, my second oldest sister, Raymond, my second oldest brother and me to do the chores while Margerie, my oldest sister got breakfast and cared for Melva and John, the younger sister and brother.

Our beds and bedroom floors were covered with snow which had sifted through the walls and roof during the night. Mama was the first up and built the fire in the round Oak heating stove which stood in the center of the room. We all got up and huddled about the stove trying to get warm as we hastily dressed in what seemed to be clothes of ice. There was no time to be lost and we were soon on our way outside to do the chores. We bundled ourselves up with all the clothes we could get on, but as we opened the door to go out, the fierce, biting wind stung our partially exposed faces. It was not necessary to go through gates or climb through fences as we went to the barn as we were able to walk high above the fences on the huge drifts of snow.

Mama and Letha were doing the milking while Raymond and I did the feeding. They decided to turn part of the cows out of the barn so it would not be so crowded while they were milking. Instead of staying around the barn out of the weather, they turned tails to the wind and went to the south side of the little 30-acre pasture. After digging through the deep snow we finally reached the feed stack. All the stock was fed except the hogs which had gotten out of their pens and were no place to be found. With pitch forks we began prodding around a straw stack and finally found the hogs buried deep under the straw and snow in a perfectly warm, dry place.

Now we must go after the cows which had gone to the back side of the pasture. We trudged laboriously and slowly through the snow. The wind was to our backs and we skirted about the drifts which had piled up over the weeks in the pasture. We soon learned that going down was very easy, compared to facing the wind coming back. We could hardly get the cows to go into the blinding wind. By the time we had them started into the wind toward the barn, we were half frozen.

Until the move to Rolla, Kansas, near the Oklahoma border, the site of the schoolhouse fire, the parents both just worked on farms and rented. Once in Rolla, Clint would have a job with the city. He would work a lot of jobs with the city, mostly street and city cleanup or whatever was needed.

But before and after, there were many moves. Ruth Cunningham provided this account of the family's journeys:

In the fall of 1909, soon after Glenn's birth, the family moved 3 or 4 miles north of Atlanta, and later moved 'down the creek' 3 miles west of town where Melva was born. They lived here two years, and then moved further west about 5 miles. This was where John was born.

In the fall of 1914, Glenn first started school at this location. Probably when they lived earlier on the creek, was where Glenn followed the kids to the "kid wagon" when the older ones went to school. He wanted to go with them, and finally Margerie tied him to a tree, and then called her mother to come get him after they were gone. Going to school was always very important to him, all through life.

In October of 1914, their house burned and they then stayed with Clint's niece and her husband, Lily and Leonard Sanders. (Her parents were Clint's brother, Charles, and Mary Luckstead Cunningham). They lived one mile east and two miles north of Clint and Rosa's, and were there about three or four weeks. Then they moved 4 miles north and east. The children went to school at Zion this year and it was here at Christmas time that John had pneumonia. In the spring they moved again, one-mile east and two miles south where Clint put in a crop, which really never did well.

In June of 1915, they left the Atlanta area and went west to Cunningham, Kansas (no connection with the family). They picnicked there at Clint's Uncle Joe and Aunt Annis' place, [Rosa's sister Annis and her husband, Joe Cole], and stayed there for harvest.

They moved on to Protection, Kansas, and lived that winter on a farm belonging to Al Hodson. The children went to school there that winter.

Clint's brother-in-law, Frank Curry, husband of his sister, Lizzie, was a conductor on a train that went by their place. During the time they lived there (one year) he brought Lizzie (Elizabeth) and their two children, Bill and Bessie, out to visit.

In the summer of 1916 (July) they moved again further west, stopping near Rolla, Kansas in Stevens County. Here on February 9, 1917 was when the schoolhouse fire occurred.

2

THE FIRE

Our biggest concern was that we were afraid my Dad was going to have to pay for the schoolhouse.

In 1917 the president of the United States was Woodrow Wilson, having won a second term months earlier on a platform arguing that he had kept us out of war. But murmurs of war with Germany were now loud rumbles. Germany declared on January 31 that it was reneging on its earlier agreement and was now resuming unrestricted submarine warfare. In April we would declare war on Germany and formally enter World War l.

Around Rolla, Kansas, February 9, 1917, the morning would dawn cold and hard, wind blowing high from the northeast stinging faces and whitening nostrils, its chilling wave sweeping across western Kansas and down into the panhandles of Oklahoma and Texas, bringing nightfall temperatures racing to zero.

Romping down the road that fateful morning, going against the biting wind—they always ran—came four of the Cunningham children. It seems that everyone in the countryside ran, both children and adults; it was their favorite diversion and principal means of travel. It was said that Rosa, the mother, had the swiftest feet in the family. Clint, the father, could lift an eight-hundred-pound water well drilling bit unaided. It was told, too, that he was fifty-one years old before Glenn could outrun him.

Their route down that less than yellow-brick road would take them to school, two miles away.

Floyd, 13, and the oldest would be in the lead, Glenn then 7½ just behind with Raymond almost 10, and Letha, close to 12, trailing. Letha was then the only Cunningham girl in the school; Raymond was described as stocky and Glenn small for his years. The boys all entered the school to start the fire; Letha remained outside and was playing on the swings.

Why they were there early had to do with the Cunningham trait of being punctual. (There is some speculation, too, that there was a small stipend, pennies, to whoever got there first to start the fire.) Furthermore, Rosa had spent the night before at Uncle John Cunningham's home where the paternal grandmother, lying ill, was being cared for. It was left to Clint to rush the children through their chores and through breakfast so that he could visit his ailing mother at Uncle John's.

So they arrived first, and it fell customarily upon the first-to-arrive the task of building a fire in the schoolhouse stove. It was Floyd's responsibility, as the oldest, to start the fire.

Floyd was unaware, however, that the night before the literary club that had met there would leave some burning embers in the stove, and that someone had also put gasoline (to light the schoolhouse lamps for the evening meeting and the lamps of the members going home) in the five-gallon can that normally contained kerosene.

Floyd first placed dried cow chips over what he thought were dead ashes, then poured the gasoline contents of the can into the fireplace, only to be greeted by an explosive gust of flames that struck him full force in the chest and abdomen. Glenn was in another aisle, and the flames ignited his pants. Floyd's and Glenn's clothes were on fire. The furious flames somehow did not catch Raymond's clothing. He reached the door but was unable to open it. The doorknob had earlier come off and was replaced by a homemade latch, which in turn, had caught and wouldn't open. Letha, out in the swings, had been alerted to the mushrooming inferno.

"As they went in," Letha told Myra Brown, "the door locked on the outside, and if I hadn't been out there, I don't know how they would ever have gotten out."

(For years the laws of Kansas had banned doors that opened inward in public buildings, yet at the Sunflower Schoolhouse they still opened inward, as they had since it was built ten years before.)

Asked to describe her feelings outside the schoolhouse at the time of the fire, Letha said, "I was scared. I was just awfully scared. All I could see through the window was those two balls of fire rolling toward the door, looked like my brothers! They were running. They got to the door and couldn't get out. 'Course I ran to open the door. I had been on the swing just outside the windows on the west side of the building. I saw them and then there was such a terrible explosion.

"And as soon as they got out, Floyd hollered to us. He said, 'Roll in the sand.' So we threw sand on them to put out the fire."

With their hands, Letha and Raymond scooped up sand and more sand from the schoolyard and aimed it at the boys. In minutes Floyd's clothing from the shoulders down fell from him. Glenn fared little better. They couldn't get the legs of his overalls over his shoes. They clung to him, burning along with his long black stockings and heavy winter underwear. The flesh on both legs was burned. Sand and dirt were deeply embedded in the flesh of both boys. Letha took off her coat and wrapped it around Floyd.

"And you can imagine what a mess that was in the burns," Letha recounted. "It was just terrible. But we got the fire out, and then, of course, *our biggest concern was that we were afraid my Dad was going to have to pay for the schoolhouse*. Because we just knew it was going to burn because the fire was everywhere. *We ran that full distance home*."

Letha apparently looked back after they had gotten about four hundred yards from the burning building. She would see that Jess Reeves, the teacher, had arrived. Behind him came John West, the neighbor with whom Reeves lived.

By then smoke in the schoolhouse was dying down some and the flames, which had been mostly from burning gasoline, seemed almost gone. The men feared that some boy or girl might still be inside, unconscious. West got down on his hands and knees and crawled up and down the aisles. He found no one. The two men made haste to put out what fire still burned. They thought they had succeeded in saving the schoolhouse and were standing in the yard congratulating themselves when Lee Garmon, a pupil, rode up on horseback, and pointed to the eaves and roof, where fresh black smoke was pouring out.

The Christmas decorations that had been stored in the attic had caught fire, and the building was doomed. Neighbors and other pupils were arriving. All the Garmon boys, Lee and Les and Ben, were there, and their father, and many others. Everyone hurried to jerk loose the desks and carry out books—hand-me-downs mostly, but prized—and other supplies. The stove, oddly, was not very hot. Les and Lee seized it by the footrests and carried it outside. Minutes later it was red hot, fanned by the wind.

Many things were saved, but before the last desk and slate and pencil tablet were out, the roof was blazing and the ceiling had started to fall in.

Down the road the children were still running. Before they reached the corner where the road turned south, they cut across the corner of a pasture to shorten the distance a little. The roads were marked by deep ruts made by wagon wheels, and sandbanks along the sides were often several feet high. The road that morning was difficult and the sandbanks offered little respite from the relentless wind.

A newspaper report covered the fire and the fact that the school would have to be closed:

Hugoton, Kansas *Hermes*
February 16, 1917
Vol 30, No 18
E B Mc Connell, Publisher

Last Friday morning the Sunflower Schoolhouse in the southwest part of the county was burned and two boys received very severe burns. Floyd and Glenn Cunningham, aged thirteen and seven years respectively with two other children, arrived a little before the teacher, Jesse W. Reeve, and undertook to build up the fire. Mistaking it for kerosene, they put some gasoline in the stove and an explosion followed, the burning gasoline from the bursted can striking them on the lower part of the body and legs, they at once ran to their home two miles away but the saturated clothing continued on fire and the burns were deep.

The teacher had arrived in sight of the building and he made all speed possible to get there and put out the fire, with the assistance of a man who arrived on horseback; they thought they had it extinguished when another man arrived and said the roof was on fire, so they at once removed everything loose but could do nothing more to save the house. There was $500 insurance on the house which was about 10 years old, but the keeping of gasoline there may invalidate the insurance; it was in a five gallon can to use in lamps; only about a gallon remained however.

This schoolhouse was in District 36, and the school board

is J. A. Thompson, J. P. Gann and Mrs. Belle Hoffman. Seven weeks remained of the seven months term but for lack of a usable building the school was closed.

What the weekly newspaper could not possibly convey was what was in the minds of the children as they ran home—and the very fact that they ran the two miles home with Floyd and Glenn still coping with smoldering fires.

Just imagine: ". . . our biggest concern was that we were afraid my Dad was going to have to pay for the schoolhouse."

And just imagine Letha's understated terse comment: "We ran that full distance home."

3

FLOYD

They had a hound dog they hunted with. When Glenn's pain became the most intense, Floyd spoke to him faintly. Lie still, Glenn. You must hurry and get well so we can take old Jack and go hunt rabbits.

Margerie was the oldest and had finished schooling; she was at home. But the parents, at Uncle John's, were not there to greet the four fleeing from the fire. Soon Letha and Raymond were on the road again and running, this time to Uncle John Cunningham's to get their mother and father. When Clint Cunningham heard the news, he hitched up his team and they started home.

But before they would get back home, on the way they stopped at "Aunt Em" (Emma) Buchanon's. She and "Uncle Milt" Buchanon, her husband, had the only telephone in the neighborhood. Aunt Em did nursing throughout the community and had helped at Glenn's birth.

While Letha and Raymond rounded up Aunt Em's horse, Clint Cunningham put in a call for Dr. J. Harvey Hansen, 28, only a few years out of the University of Illinois School of Medicine. The doctor was not at home, but the telephone operator located him in Russell and Bergner's General Store, where he had stopped to renew the coals in his footwarmer. This footwarmer, with blankets and the curtains on his Model T Ford, made it possible to endure the bitter winter weather when he called on patients. In that Model T they would drive to the Cunningham home: "It was about twenty-five miles over sandy road to the Cunningham's," wrote the now widowed Alice Hansen from her home in Denver, Colorado in 1965, "but we were ready so it didn't take us long to get there."

Letha would tell Mrs. Brown years later: "When we got there my mother and sister, Margerie, and the doctor's wife were tearing up the bed sheets for bandages because the doctor didn't bring any with him. He came just immediately after they called. . . . This neighbor lady had a telephone, the only one close to us. Her name was Buchannon, Mrs. Buchannon. She had a wooden leg. She got on a saddle horse and came up to Uncle John's to stay with my grandmother so we kids could go on home. And the next morning Raymond and I had such terrible sore throats that they put us upstairs, isolated us. They kept us there for four or five days . . . and then they decided we didn't have diphtheria as they had feared, but from exposure, I suppose."

Even before the parents got back and before the arrival of the doctor, Margerie immediately began removing what was left of the boys' clothes. Floyd's shoes were still smoldering. She threw them outdoors, where they landed on the wooden sled that was used to haul drinking water to the house. At the time no one thought there might be trouble from them, but later, when someone opened the door, they found that the sled had caught fire from the shoes. Neighbors who came to help, as well as members of the Cunningham family, spoke long of the hole in the floor of the sled. "I saw that hole," said Ben Garmon. "It was big. Floyd's shoes had burned it."

Glenn, feeling somewhat more secure now that he was at home, began to be aware of the world around him. He remembered seeing Floyd standing in the middle of the floor vigorously flinging his arms downward. Floyd's burns covered not only his arms, but also more than half of his body. They were deep, third-degree burns that reached into his body cavity. His kidneys were burned. "Cooked," the doctor would later say. As is characteristic of such burns, his pain was not intolerable. Sensory nerves had been destroyed.

"Floyd seemed calm and collected," Alice Hansen wrote further on, "though he was shaking all over I noticed."

Glenn's burns were mostly on his legs. His pain was sheer agony. He cried incessantly.

However gently the doctor worked, Glenn's suffering was nevertheless severe. In all the painful accidents of childhood, he'd known nothing like this, not even when he jumped from the roof of a building, so injuring his feet and ankles that they remained weak into his running days. No doubt the fire added to the damage. In that fall, one transverse arch was broken, and with all his running he was never able to come up on his toes.

Glenn had always been the hardiest, most able-bodied kind of a plains child. He could stand on one foot, put the other foot behind the bib of his overalls, and then straighten up. He could sit down and put both feet behind the bib of his overalls. He turned somersaults, made himself into a ball and rolled over and over on the ground. Acrobatic feats of all kinds were his delight. Other youngsters tried to imitate him, but couldn't; no one ever could.

But on that mean and cold February day, hardiness counted for little. And there was now no more fun, no more play, no more school anywhere in Glenn's world. He was just a little boy, small for his years, in pain that was virtually unendurable. "I was surprised that the doctor showed much more concern for Floyd than Glenn who seemed to be suffering more," Mrs. Hansen mentioned in her 1965 letter to Mrs. Brown, "but he [Dr. Hansen] explained to me as we worked that Floyd was in shock and not so conscious of pain."

One of the first things Dr. Hansen did on arrival was to give the two boys something to relieve their pain. Later when he had dressed their wounds and was ready to start home, he gave their parents more pain medication to be given during the night and until he could return the next day. Privately he explained to Mrs. Hansen that he did not believe Floyd could recover, and that Glenn's recovery was at best uncertain.

Mrs. Cox, mother of classmate Bur Cox, speaking to Myra Brown in the mid-1960s, reminisced about the family and the community: "The family of Glenn Cunningham was a poor family as so many of us were in those days, but we were better neighbors then."

No one then remembered which of the neighbors was the first to arrive at the Cunningham farm that morning. All of the Garmons were there. Eventually all the neighbors came, each bringing his own skill and fitting into the family program like relatives. They did chores. They brought home-cooked things to eat. Somewhere they found some coal. Fires were made with chips, the universal fire-fuel. They were mindful that the boys must not get chilled. Arrangements were made so that they would not be alone and so that their parents could get some sleep. And money was brought. How it was collected no one ever knew. In the whole countryside money was scarce.

Neighbors remember that Floyd lay in his bed and sang. Glenn still cried. Floyd told Glenn stories to lure him into forgetfulness. Mrs. Hansen, who came every day with her husband, added stories from her storehouse of tales she had learned when she studied to become a teacher. Melva, the youngest Cunningham daughter, held on to Mrs. Hansen's skirt as she moved about and listened well. Glenn remembered nothing of her visits—nothing but that he loved her. Notwithstanding the suffering that his arrival always meant, Glenn remembered how he loved the doctor, too. Alice Hansen recalled that ". . . as we would enter the door he would start crying saying 'Oh, Doc! Now, Doc!' before we touched him. But he was little more than a boy. . . ."

The removal of the bandages caused the worst pain. Though they had been soaked in raw linseed oil and eggs before application, they had to be soaked off with water that had antiseptic in it—a method no longer used. Each time a bandage was removed, it brought with it chunks of the boy's leg muscles—chunk after chunk, and day after day, but pools of yellow liquid lay on the bed around him and had to be cleaned. At no time was there any infection. This was serous drainage—blood plasma that had seeped through the tissue and was in the process of drying. It had the odor of dead flesh, and the smell of it filled the room.

During dressings when the pain was most acute, Glenn had to be held against the bed to permit the doctor to work. The Garmon boys and Jeff Cox all helped hold him. So did his father. Glenn would always remember the touch of his father's hands. After Letha came downstairs the second morning, she climbed onto the bed, sat on Glenn's chest, and held his shoulders, the only way to hold him down while the doctor changed the bandages. His reflex response was to bite her and call her names.

As the week wore on, Floyd, still singing some, but less and less now, grew more and more quiet.

Nine days after the fire, Jeff Cox and George Ehrhart rose from the chairs where they had spent the night. They stood for a few minutes, talking quietly before they left for home. Their conversation, recounted and probably to some degree re-created by Mrs. Cox, went something like this: "George," Jeff Cox said, "I don't believe Floyd will live through the night. I don't like this sweat. Or his color."

Ehrhart responded: "It looks that way to me, too, Jeff." Jeff had reached home and Mrs. Cox had come when the doctor arrived. With him was a man named C. C. Hale. Other neighbors began arriving, and Mrs. Cox left. She would not be needed. The doctor asked the neighbors and the other children if they would mind waiting somewhere else while he took care of the boys. Clint and Rosa stayed with their sons. There was no sound in the room except Glenn's sobbing.

When Glenn's pain became the most intense that ninth day, Floyd uttered to him ever so faintly. "Lie still, Glenn. You must hurry and get well so we can take old Jack and go hunt rabbits."

(Jack had been Glenn's cherished dog he'd had since before the family came to southwest Kansas. Jack was a mutt with exceptional intelligence, tremendous courage, and, to Glenn, unforgettable devotion. Boy and dog were inseparable. "We even ate from the same plate," Glenn told Myra. "I drew a line down the middle. Food on one side was his, on the other side was mine. If he got across the line, all it took was a sharp whack on his nose.")

Ben Garmon years later described Floyd: "Floyd never lost his head no matter what the emergency. He was quiet, an awful nice boy." Letha conveyed this to Myra Brown: "The way Floyd kept his presence of mind is—well, it's a Cunningham characteristic."

Floyd's words to Glenn about Jack were near to his last. In 1998 Ruth Cunningham visited Margerie, then 97 years old, in full possession of her faculties, who said this on cassette tape about Floyd's last day:

"I never will forget that morning. Mom fed him his breakfast and I can't remember, it wasn't too long after breakfast that he went to singing *When The Roll Is Called Up Yonder I'll Be There*, and when he got through singing it, he said, 'Ohhhh, there's the angels after me, goodbye everybody, goodbye Mama and Papa, and all you kids, *goodbyeeeeeee.*' That's the way he said it. The folks were right by, both of them were crying and all of us kids was, too." (On the tape Margerie was weeping as she recalled Floyd's last moments.)

Very gently Dr. Hansen had begun his examination. But he had scarcely started when Floyd stopped breathing altogether. It was then ten o'clock in the morning.

On the ninth day after the fire, the boy who would sing and tell stories to lure his brother into forgetfulness as they both lay ill, quietly died.

Two hours later the word of his death reached the Jeff Cox family and others.

"We'd been expecting it," Mrs. Cox conveyed to Myra. "But still it was an awful shock. Like it was one of our own. And the other Cunningham children—they were an awful close family—oh, my goodness, the other children were just right there! There was no other place for them."

The funeral service was held in the yard of their home. In his book *Never Quit* (Chosen Books, 1981) Glenn describes an "overcast day, windy and raw-cold. A couple dozen friends and relatives stood bareheaded outside, listening."

"When the brief funeral service ended," he wrote, "several men lifted Floyd's new pine coffin onto a horse-drawn lumber wagon."

Neighbors and friends buried Floyd in a little cemetery across the state line in Oklahoma. So critical was Glenn's condition still that none of the family went to the cemetery.

Glenn at Floyd's gravestone, fall 1987

4

RECOVERING

Doctors ain't always right

From the *Hugoton Hermes* . . . Friday, February 23, 1917, Vol. 30, No. 19, the headline read BOY DIED FROM BURNS. The first paragraph tells of the local undertaking firm removing Floyd's body the evening of his death and the location of the next day's burial. One sentence reads: "Glenn, the seven-year-old boy, was still living but suffering great pain."

> ### Boy Died From Burns
> The local undertaking firm were called to the H. C. Cunningham home in southwest Stevens county Sunday night to prepare for burial the body of Floyd Cunningham, the thirteen year old boy who was burned in the explosion of gasoline while starting a fire at the Sunflower school house two weeks ago. Burial was made in the Barden cemetery in Oklahoma, Monday. Glenn, the seven year old boy, was still living but suffering great pain.
>
> Floyd was born at Atlanta, Ks December 29, 1903. Besides the father and the mother, Clint and Rosa Cunningham, he had three brothers, Raymond, Glenn, and John; and three sisters, Marjorie Letha and Melva. A short funeral service was conducted at the home by Elder A. C. Martin.

Across the state other newspapers kept their readers posted on Glenn's condition, and in schoolrooms boys and girls bowed their heads each morning and silently prayed for the legs of a boy only a little younger than they were.

A few days after Floyd's funeral, Letha and Raymond began taking over many of the farm chores that had been done by Floyd and Glenn. But, even so, both of them continued to help in the house and with Glenn. Letha had always looked after him.

The days that followed found 28-year-old Dr. J. Harvey Hansen and his 21-year-old wife, Alice, visiting daily and, with the help of the other children, changing bandages. Alice Hansen continued to read to Glenn.

What was still the most painful was the bandage changing. In 1965, Letha, then Mrs. Dean Morgan of Cedar Point, Kansas, told Myra Brown: "And they would have to soak those bandages loose every time they dressed the burned places. They'd just stick tight and they'd soak them with water with antiseptic in it, and that was so terrible painful."

The chronology of the rehabilitation process will always be somewhat a matter of speculation. We do have this marker, however, in the local newspaper . . .

March 23, 1917 *Hugoton Hermes*:

Glenn Cunningham is able to sit up a little; we are glad.

It was probably around this time when Dr. Hansen told Glenn he could get up and out of bed. In the *Iron Man of Kansas* video Glenn Cunningham speaks these words:

Later after I had started my healing process Dr. Hansen came and told me I'd be able to be up for a while and I thought he meant I'd be able to be up and run and be out in the yard and play like I'd always done and when the doctor came on one side and my mother on the other they were going to help me up and I fought 'em off. I said I don't need any help I can get up I know I can and I remember pushing off the bed and there was absolutely no strength in my legs at all, I just fell there in a heap on the floor. They just picked me up and put me back in the bed; I remember crying and telling that I'd walk, I said I know I can.

In retrospect, we can reconstruct the anatomic and physiologic processes at that point. Prolonged bed rest alone would have contributed to significant atrophy and therefore weakness in his legs. Combine this with the damage to, and loss of, muscle along with its blood supply. Add the probable damage to nerve supply, and it is no wonder that his legs were virtually useless at that moment.

The history for the days that followed is sometimes a confused admixture of fact and of apocrypha, approaching near urban legends as they relate to the themes of infection and the possibility of amputation of one or both his legs. In telling of those days Glenn vacillated. In 1965 he would tell Myra that these ideas about possible amputation were the written products of imaginative reporters. But as the years went on, as fading memory and legend may have begun to fuse, he would talk of his adamant refusal of amputation.

In *Iron Man of Kansas* he speaks these words: "When they looked at my legs the doctor thought they probably should amputate my legs because they said if I got infection I not only lose my legs, I lose my life. Even though the doctors said I'd never walk, he couldn't convince me because I just *knew* I was going to be able to walk again."

Some clarification finds root in a portions of a 1965 letter from Alice Hansen, responding to a query from Myra Brown.

Mrs. Hansen first illuminates part of the question about

amputation and infection.

As to consideration of amputation, I never heard of it and can see no reason for it at any time. I've never heard of amputating a burned limb. The body has to throw off the poisons or absorb them when skin is too burned to throw them off don't you think? Glenn never had gangrene or any infection which would have made amputation a necessity. He simply had very deep burns that took a long time to heal and that made deep scars which bound the leg muscles. I do not have any idea where the thought of amputation may have originated.

Nevertheless she gives her thoughts of how the rumors may have come about:

Glenn's mother was very honest but I wonder if this was not a worry she had because of lack of understanding the slowness of healing.

She ends the formal part of her letter:

Once the danger of immediate or early death, as in Floyd's case, was past, I have no recollection of anything but the slowness of healing in the deep burns. . . .

Again my best wishes,

Mrs. J. H. Hansen

But there is much more we can learn from her addendum to her letter entitled *Glenn Cunningham's Life As It Touched Ours.*

In it we get an insight into how young Glenn began walking with the aid of a chair. We learn when it was that another doctor filled in because Dr. Hansen had to attend his father's funeral. We learn, too, about the economics of a rural doctor and the matter of payment for services. Finally we get a little more of Alice Hansen's annoyance at what she considered embellishments by writers and even her try at humor and irony:

When at long last, I'm not certain of the time, Glenn seemed to be out of danger, Doctor made less frequent calls and I didn't go. The patient's good mother took over the dressings and an Aunt did come and I met her. But it was too cold for farming so all the older children and Mr. C. helped I am sure, about the house.

Mr. C. told the doctor he had no cash and couldn't pay him, but if we ever needed money badly to let him know and he would try to raise something.

Well—within 2 or 3 months my husband's father died in southern Oklahoma and there was no money to attend the funeral. So I was sent in a blowing snow and dust storm out to see Mr. Cunningham while the doctor performed a scheduled tonsillectomy in his office, there being no hospital within reach.

Mr. Cunningham gave me $25 and with that and a little more raised elsewhere my husband could drive about 75 miles to Forgan, Okla. that night and take the train to the funeral. I stayed at home alone for the first time and felt little and lonely.

While at the Cunningham's on that errand they proudly called my attention to the fact that Glenn was walking with the aid of a chair, which he pushed before him. He was very happy to demonstrate his progress before me and I was pleased after such a long siege he was making real strides.

Not long after that we left Rolla and so we lost sight of Glenn until Dr. Hansen returned from France to settle in Elkhart after World War I.

We heard that the Cunninghams lived there, too, and before long Mrs. Cunningham, true to her conscience, called and asked if she could do our laundry in payment of the old debt. As I had a sickly baby by then, I was pleased to have her help and both of us were glad to let her pay the debt if she wished.

Glenn, about eleven I suppose, came on a horse to pick up and deliver the laundry and we thought he still didn't walk too easily.

We lived in Elkhart for six years before we admitted we were having too much of a struggle financially since so few could pay their bills, and left.

But before we left Glenn was in high school and beginning to show promise as a runner. Naturally this surprised us.

Humor and irony:

One day my husband was talking with the sports editor of our local paper and they discussed the sports news of the day previous when Glenn had lost a race in Chicago. The reporter mentioned that the Chicago papers had criticized Glenn and his coach for using the "alibi" that they hadn't given sufficient notice of the race time to allow for a good warm-up. And doctor told him then that there was a reason for the truth of that and explained it with the story of the deep scar tissue which had been operated while he was in college and needed rubbing and exercising before a race.

Well, that led to the reporter writing the story to the Associated Press, which in turn led to the greatly exaggerated stories by such writers as Dale Carnegie and Robert Ripley.

I must digress and tell that Dr. Hansen wrote to Ripley and asked where he got his information that the old country doctor in the case said Glenn would never walk again; and said that he was the young doctor just out of Medical School and never said such a foolish thing for there was no reason—that he had been afraid Glenn would die. To all of which Mr. Ripley made no reply other than to send an autographed copy of "Believe it or Not". We usually "believed it not" after that! Time *magazine even interviewed us.*

We find in the weekly paper some light on the exact period of time she was speaking of:

Hugoton Hermes Friday, March 9, 1917 Vol 30 No 21
Sunflower District.

Grandma Cunningham is better, her two daughters from Atlanta, Kansas have been visiting her this past week. Glen [sic] Cunningham is some better. Dr. Hanson was called away to see his father who is ill; he left Dr. Tucker in charge until he returns.

It's time to pause and go back a little just to get the story as right as it possibly can be. Remember that Alice has said that Dr. Hansen had to leave to attend his father's funeral about two or three months (it was more like four weeks) after they first started to take care of the boys. In *Never Quit*, Glenn does talk of this time when a new doctor arrived, a doctor he does not name but someone he did not like. He describes the doctor's manner as brusque and his bandage dressing as rough. A passage from the book reads:

To add to my misery a huge boil—about the size of a baseball—had formed on my left hip. Until now I had been able to get some relief from my bedsores by rolling over on my left side. I still had a large burn on my right leg which prevented lying on that side.

Now I had to remain on my back constantly.

I overheard Father ask the new doctor about the boil. "Does it mean the infection has gotten inside the boy's body?"

"That's exactly what it means."

"What can we do about it?"

"I don't know anything that can be done about it. Just pray, I reckon."

After the doctor left I told Father that I'd heard. "Does that mean they're gonna cut my leg off?" I asked fearfully.

"Naw!"

"Dr. Fergusen said that's what would happen if the infection came."

"Doctors ain't always right."

So what. We find some real frontier wisdom: *Doctors ain't!*

Regarding some conflicting stories, I believe Clint Cunningham could very well have, or would have, said that. Doctors truly *just* "ain't always right." And it's highly probable Rosa Cunningham, based on her perception of what the doctor said, feared the possibility of infection, gangrene, and amputation. No doubt from somewhere Glenn got the idea that they might amputate his leg, even though Dr. Hansen had never said anything about that. Perhaps that was behind his obsession to always be massaging his legs. He spoke of his mother doing it for a long time, and when she stopped he did it himself.

There is another item that might give us pause, even wonderment. It is the power of prayer. Young people throughout the state were engaged in active prayer for Glenn. There are currently studies, positive and negative, about the power of prayer. There is at least one study where participants were given the last names of certain people ill in a hospital setting—only their last names. The ones designated for prayer did better overall than the ones not prayed for by the strangers. Better-designed studies on the subject are in progress today. Depending on your leaning, you can decide whether prayer, among other things, had a positive effect in Glenn's recovery.

March 23rd Sunflower District
Glenn Cunningham is able to set up a little; we are glad.

As the days and weeks wore on, the recovery process consisted of Glenn's failed attempts to stand (on the video he says that he must have fallen hundreds of times), of massaging his legs by the family members and by Glenn. The massaging was something he had intuitively come upon. And then, after so many collapses when he would try to stand, one day he did stand.

His next big achievement was leaning across the seat of a

kitchen chair and pushing it across the floor. He called it "walking." It was a wonderful feeling. Everyone who came to the farm had to see how he could walk.

April 6 Vol 30 No 25

J. W. Cunningham's uncle and aunt are visiting J. W. and Clint. Glen is improving some from his burns.

Somewhere within the headlines just above and right below here, he was able to get outside a bit. He would usually need to hold on to something, but he was ambulating although his walk was "crooked."

Friday, May 4th Vol 30 No 29

Glen Cunningham is getting along fine and able to play.

We should again take a moment to consider the very last word in the preceding sentence: *play*. We are really coming upon something basic; something the early Greeks intuitively appreciated when they assigned to their child god Eros dominion over love and play. Children and animals arrive at play by instinct. Glenn could now go outdoors. This was the world of high plains, big skies, and far horizons: a world of constant physical challenge and achievement; of digging prairie dogs out of their holes when the prairie dogs dug away from him almost as fast as he dug toward them; of rounding up cattle, which might take hours. And, most of all, the world of running, which he loved.

He was still a little boy with crooked legs. The neighbors remember that for a long time he walked lopsided. But that didn't bother him a lot. Besides, he didn't think other people noticed it too much. He didn't.

Around now, as part of his recovery efforts according to Letha as told to Myra, "he used to grab hold of the mules when we took them a quarter of a mile to water. He used to grab them by the tail and he would run behind them holding to their tail because it would give him more support on his legs. And it did do him a lot of good."

And it was all play, play with siblings, and play with his animals with whom he could bond in their mutual love of play.

He could play, but he couldn't run yet. He couldn't wholly straighten out his right leg, and the muscles in both legs were still scant. His ingenuity, however, was full-grown.

Racing—"chasing each other," the children called it—was always likely to be under way somewhere on the Cunningham farm. One day the elder children took out like young antelope for the back of the pasture. John, the youngest Cunningham, didn't go. He was too small. Glenn wanted to go. But he couldn't run. But their father had bought a little spotted Indian pony; they called him Paint. That day, John climbed up on Paint. Glenn seized his tail. John dug his heels into Paint's sides, and away they went in a rush, Glenn swaying and lurching from side to side as he made his feet catch him before he dragged the ground.

How did his legs feel with such unwanted activity? "They felt like daggers were being run through them."

Yet he never thought of quitting. This was running. Fun had come back.

They reached the other children, and when they were ready to go back to the house, Glenn and John went back as they had come out, Glenn immediately behind Paint's rear hooves.

Nor was Paint the only horse involved in the extracurricular activities of the Cunningham children that late spring and early summer. Uncle John had loaned their father Roy, one of his work horses. He was a swaybacked strawberry roan so huge that none of the children could mount him by any usual method. The preferred way was to wait till he was eating. When his head was down, they climbed from the manger onto his neck, and when he lifted his head, they slid down his neck and eventually onto his back.

Roy played a major role in the children's life that summer. And Glenn was right in the middle of everything.

Very soon after he was able to get outdoors, his father put him to work. "I'm glad my father was like that," Glenn said (in 1965). His first chore was cleaning the shovels after they came in from the field. This was sometime in the spring after the fire. Glenn's first field activities included pulling weeds and hoeing. Very soon he was helping with the other farm chores, with feeding, milking, and lighter farm work. He helped his mother in the house. Nothing was too insignificant. "Glenn was awful good to Mom," Letha remembered.

In between chores he would massage his legs. Massaging had become instinctive, habitual. For his entire life he would sometimes find himself unconsciously reaching down to massage legs once so badly burned there was little there to massage.

The children of the plains truly knew how to improvise in their play. Myra (MLB) had this conversation with Mrs. Cox:

MLB: What did the children do? For amusement?

Cox: Oh, they had one another. They did anything they could find. They didn't have any toys. They weren't able to get toys. But they never got lonesome, never bored like children are now a days. They played, made things up to do. I have often told people that our nine weren't near the trouble that three are now. We had a ball team of our own.

MLB: I've heard stories after stories about the racing there was. That was one of the things children and grown-ups were always doing for amusement.

Cox: Oh, yes. Foot racing and running, and if they had an old saddle horse, they'd get out and run a race. Of course, the parents knew where they were. They might not approve of it too much, there was some danger, but they didn't entirely forbid it.

Friday, June 22 Vol 30 No 36
Raymond and Glen Cunningham were callers on Bur and Guy Cox Saturday. Glen is about alright again since his burns last winter.

Glenn and Raymond and the Cox boys had been playmates since the Cunninghams moved into the Sunflower School District the fall before the fire. They continued friends as long as the Cunninghams lived in the neighborhood. In recalling those days, Mrs. Cox said to Myra: "I wiped their noses, if it was that kind of weather, dried their feet, and turned them loose to think up what would be fun to do. They never got bored, and they were never lonesome. At our house they 'wrastled' and 'skinned oats.' They tried all kinds of acrobatics. They raced against each other, and they raced horses. They ran and jumped on moving horses. Jeff had a stable of horses and jacks, and custom mares and jennies. The boys rode all these animals, anything that had four legs."

Early that summer, Glenn and Raymond began substituting knife sleds for hoes when cutting weeds. A knife sled was a wooden affair with wide runners of hardwood that soon attained a high degree of polish as they slid over the ground. The cutting knife was on the underside of the sled and shaped like a huge V with the point to the front and the sides running back and set deeper than the runners. With a horse hitched in front and a seat for the driver, they could move across the field fast. It worked well in sandy soil.

The speed of Glenn's recovery, slow as it seemed to Glenn, nevertheless continued to accelerate.

More and more he sought out things he could do. Years later

his father said that Glenn was the only son he had whom he could depend on to do things right and do them without being told.

More and more Glenn ran. Perhaps holding to the tail of a horse or mule. Letha remembers that the second summer after the fire, Glenn held to a mule's tail when they took the mules to water a quarter of a mile away. "It did him a lot of good." Perhaps he would be holding to the wagon gate. For weeks when he first started holding to the wagon gate, his feet dragged the ground more than he ran.

Whatever the manner of his running, it was for the supreme joy of making his feet cover the ground.

After a while, he was running without holding to anything. Wherever the wagon went, he went, jogging along at its side, down the road in front or behind, to a field for feed, to some neighbor's, to Uncle John's, and later to Rolla for groceries and other supplies. Eventually he could run for miles.

The Cox family and other neighbors marveled at the endurance of so young a boy. Most of all, they marveled at his unusual self-command.

As for Glenn, he began to think, as he had before the fire, that there was nothing that he couldn't do, or learn to do.

Meanwhile, the Sunflower School, closed right after the fire, was being rebuilt. School would start for the other students October 1, but not for Glenn. For the moment, however, please think forward to around 1945 or 1946 when Glenn Cunningham was traveling through southwest Kansas and stopped at the new building that had been erected to take the place of the old school that burned in 1917.

It was a weekend, and there was no school in session. But he went inside, and when school reconvened the pupils found a message written in large letters across the entire blackboard. It admonished all the pupils to remember that just because they went to a small school in western Kansas, they shouldn't think they could not reach any goal they might want to reach. The note further read, "Once I went to school here." It was signed "Glenn Cunningham."

(There is a coda to this vignette: He wrote in large letters. He had apparently done so since fourth or fifth grade. Once his teacher told him he didn't have to write his name so big—he wasn't famous. The family always had a good laugh about that.)

Schoolhouse rebuilt. Photo taken in 1947.

5

CONTINUING TO RECOVER:
1918-1921

The feeling my pets and I had for each other and our happy, spontaneous activity together in which there was no strain, meant a great deal to my legs.

His program began to unfold. The cornerstone was his love of and unwavering delight in physical activity. The physical activity came as play, something he did naturally with his play companions—his pets, driven by his love of all animals, and his ability to bond and communicate with them. He understood animals. They understood him. "The feeling my pets and I had for each other and our happy, spontaneous activity together in which there was no strain, meant a great deal to my legs," he declared.

But even more important was his love for his family, for his friends, and for people, especially those to whom life had given short shrift. He told Myra, "I have always loved people."

(That he loved people is the truth. He felt things strongly. Yet he was a man of extremes. And he was no Pollyanna. Although he could find good in adversity, indeed good in everything, he nevertheless could hate and be unforgiving. Particularly he hated bullies. He was often distrustful, suspicious, and even cynical of other people's intentions. In his stubbornness he was for many years estranged from the two daughters of his first marriage; they only partly reconciled a few years before he died.)

He could harness this stubbornness in thought and deed. Later he had two rules, which he called his "bull-headedness."

"Never falter in allegiance to what you have figured out is right. Never change till you find out you were wrong."

But I'm getting ahead of the story. We should return to the end of 1918:

November 11, 1918, would mark Armistice Day for the "War to End All Wars." At the end of the year, President Wilson sailed for France to attend the peace conference. But a fresh new war had been raging worldwide.

The winter of 1918-1919 was the winter of the great epidemic of influenza that swept the country, killing half a million Americans and uncounted millions more throughout the world. It was the winter of big snows and high winds in southwest Kansas. Glenn had observed his ninth birthday August 4 of the year before. He was still small for his age, still uncertain when his legs might give way on him, but he was almost entirely straight now.

During the worst of the epidemic, Clint Cunningham contracted the virus. It was aggravated by an attack of jaundice, and he was bedridden. Before he was able to be out of bed, one of the winter's worst storms struck. Late that day Glenn and Raymond and their mother and Letha went to the barn to do the milking and feeding. The cattle, horses, and mules were all inside and secure. But the barn was so arranged that to get to the cows that were to be milked, some of them had to be turned outside and brought back for milking after the first cows had been finished.

The snow was already deep and drifting in the high north wind. As most breeds of cattle do in storms, the cows that were let out of the barn drifted with the wind to the back of the pasture. Glenn and Raymond went after them.

With the wind at their backs, they managed fairly well going out, though they got very cold. But turning the cattle back into the storm and starting them toward the barn was almost impossible. The cows refused to move. They began milling and kicking up more snow. It constantly became more difficult for the boys to see. In the pasture were many wild yucca plants, called soapweed in southwest Kansas. These were either lodged full of snow or completely drifted under. Raymond, his head bent down against the storm and running hard, was constantly stumbling into them. Each time he came out, more snow was impacted on his head and in his clothing. Finally his eyes and nose were completely frozen over. He could see nothing. Both boys were becoming dangerously cold. Glenn was able to keep his eyes open. He caught one of the cows, put her tail in Raymond's hands, and told him to hang on. Raymond knew it was an emergency. He hung on. With his dog Jack helping, Glenn maneuvered the cows toward the barn and eventually reached it. Letha and their mother opened the door and the cows went inside. Rosa sent her sons back to the house.

Raymond still could not see. Glenn led him, but he didn't know how he could open the door when they got home. His hands were too cold to turn the knob. He couldn't even knock. He thought maybe if he kicked the door, someone would come and open it.

Jack solved the problem. He leaped through the storm, hurled himself against the door, and scratched furiously. Marjorie heard and came.

Glenn pointed out to Myra that it was not that he had brought the cattle back to the barn and saved his own and

Raymond's lives that meant the most to him. Raymond was two and a half years older than he was, had always been a sturdy boy with more fight in him than almost anybody. In addition to that, Raymond had never suffered a physical handicap. Glenn now had done what Raymond failed to do. It was a pivotal moment.

And for Glenn there were other experiences, even earlier, that displayed his growing skills.

In April 1918, more than a year after the fire, Glenn was given the job of harrowing a field with a four-horse team. He was not yet nine years old and still somewhat bent. Most of the stiffness in his legs and body was gone and the stretching, which had been very painful, was almost over.

One of the horses was a bronc, not yet fully broken and sometimes vicious. Always, when he had reached the field, Glenn hitched up the other horses first, watching all the time for the bronc's feet. When she kicked, she took aim. When he hooked up her tugs, he had to jump and grab the lines, for, he said, "The moment she was fast that bronc took off!"

One morning when he reached the end of the row and was turning to go back across the field, the bronc got a foot caught in the harrow. "Man, she raised Cain!" Glenn remembered. "She did everything."

It was an emergency. It would have been a problem for experienced horsemen. Glenn was still a boy people called "that Cunningham tyke." But he had learned to command both himself and animals. He was able to calm the horses, straighten them out, and finish the field.

It was an ability he was never to lose. Years later, guests reported seeing him stand in the yard at his ranch and command Ishtar, a proud Arabian stallion, to come in from a pasture a quarter of a mile away. They saw that stallion lift his ears, survey the brood mares he was grazing with, leave them with reluctance, and come prancing and cantering in like a schoolchild seeking preferential consideration.

Another of Glenn's pets, and there were many, was a burro. Sometime after he was on his feet following the fire, there came through the country travelers who had a wagon and a pair of burros they wanted to sell. Clint Cunningham bought them. The burros he gave to his two eldest sons, Tom to Raymond and Johnny to Glenn. Glenn and Johnny became fast friends. They became playmates, constant companions. "We practically lived together," Glenn said. "The two of us grew up together. I watched over him, fed him, never abused him and Johnny responded with all of his donkey heart."

Years later, when Glenn came home from the University of Kansas, if he could get close enough to Johnny that Johnny could hear him call, the little burro came swiftly to renew their intimacy.

Still another pet was a kid. When the children of one of Glenn's sisters were small, their father bought a nanny goat. He thought they needed goat's milk. The first kid was a billy goat. He gave it to Glenn. Glenn petted it, fed it, raised it. When the time came that it wanted to butt, as all goats by nature must, Glenn got down on the ground and butted with it. Always the kid came up to him easy. Even when it became an adult, it came up easy. But if it was Bur or Guy Cox or some other boy who got down on the ground to butt, that was another matter. They did not know that the bond that existed between Glenn and the goat made the difference between fun and fight. "He almost knocked them out," Glenn said.

The Cunninghams continued to live in their two-story, two-roomed house for four years after they had settled in, but after the fire there was no more schooling for Glenn until they moved to Elkhart, which they did when Glenn was eleven. That fall he returned to school and once more he was dreaming of college and of becoming a doctor like his grandfather, Drury Cunningham. He was eleven years old and in only the fourth grade. But he had already learned much about the nature of animals. "Animal therapy" would become one of the signatures of Glenn's work with troubled children in the years ahead.

6

ELKHART

There's always work for those who want to work.

We might wonder how a family could move so often and what was in their minds. In an interview on March 25, 1968, Myra Brown wanted the exact words he or his family used during his recovery period, and they agreed that family members remembered Glenn often repeating, as in a mantra, "I'll walk, I'll walk." Glenn was explaining that he got this attitude from his parents, illustrating it with their philosophy relating to the frequent moves:

"I get that [attitude] from my parents. Just like I used to ask my parents, I'd say, 'How in the world would you have nerve to take off across this relatively new country in those covered wagons with a two-wagon load of kids and very little money to go on.' I mean, they just start off, maybe it is only a hundred miles or so, but you only go 20 miles or 25 miles a day with the teams and wagons. There were no roads like they have now, there were just trails, and I'd ask my mother how they would have the nerve to start out and she'd say, 'Oh, there is nothing to worry about.' I'd say, 'What if you run out of money? You'd have to feed the family, feed the animals.' She'd say 'you could always stop and work.' I said, 'How do you find somebody who needs somebody.' And she said, 'There's always work for those who want to work,' and there was no problem."

It was now the spring of 1920. The motivation for the move to Elkhart was the same as for any of the many moves: a better livelihood. There were parallels in both the development of Glenn and that of Elkhart itself. They were both young in a young country. Both had vision, drive, pioneer American values, and an optimistic faith in the future. Both were strongly humanitarian, given to promoting the interests of others, sharing problems, finding ways. Francis ("Brigham") Young, Glenn's erstwhile fellow athlete in Elkhart High School, a successful businessman by the 1960s, still remembered where his roots were when he told Myra: "Walk into any man's yard out there and if you gotta problem, he'll help you. You never get turned away. You never get a cold shoulder. Even if you're a stranger you don't," Brigham asserted. "Maybe you gotta dime; maybe you gotta million. It don't make any difference. Bankers out there can wear overalls. Ranchers can wear dress suits, and feel easy. Glenn is still like that."

In the fall of 1920 Glenn Cunningham, now eleven, first resumed school. He was in the fourth grade. Earlier in the same year, Man O' War had set a world record for the mile and three furlongs at Belmont Raceway.

His teacher was Miss Agnes Heueisen. In a handwritten letter, again sometime in the 1960s, Agnes, by then Mrs. John Stedman of Los Angeles, wrote of how there were fifty-nine others in his class, all younger and smaller than he was. When Miss Heueisen walked back to speak to him that first morning, he was so withdrawn she thought he was shy. Glenn would explain that he was overpowered with awe that he was actually on his way to getting an education.

Agnes remembered how she was impressed with him, that "he

was smart," that he was "so eager to learn and he applied himself in such a busy happy manner." She remembers wondering how it could be that a boy of his age and unmistakable ability was not farther along in school.

She would soon be told by a couple of his friends of the schoolhouse fire, but even then she did not realize how serious Glenn's situation had been. Like all boys, Glenn wore overalls. Thus she couldn't see the scars on his legs. And he never mentioned them. She had noticed, however, that he was continually massaging and exercising them.

To Glenn, studying was exciting, absorbing, stimulating. He learned fast. He loved school. He was never ready for the day to end.

"He took advantage of every interesting opportunity," Miss Heueisen said. But at school, he remained withdrawn. Soon she realized that here was a child who needed "help to realize that everybody is somebody" that he was smart and capable of attaining great things; that he need never stand back for anybody. "As it would with any good teacher," she wrote, this realization determined her course with Glenn.

As time passed she became more aware of his extremely active mind, his understanding of other children, and his kindness toward them.

Nonetheless, his goodwill and kindness notwithstanding, a lifelong pattern was emerging. It had to do with his intolerance of bullies.

One of the other pupils was a skinny little boy, a physical weakling who could not defend himself, a boy the other boys called "a sissy." In the difficulties such children often meet, Glenn always stood up for him. One day on the school ground, for no apparent reason, one of the school's bullies thought things had been going too well for the child and began to work him over. Immediately Glenn was on hand. The bully turned on him, expecting to put two boys away instead of one. In that he was mistaken. "I knocked the stuffing out of him," Glenn remembered.

(About a year earlier, another Kansan, Jess Willard, had the stuffing knocked out of him—the giant Willard was floored six times within two minutes. Years later Glenn Cunningham would dine with the 1919 newly crowned heavyweight champion, Jack Dempsey.)

Harry Williamson (left) and Glenn (right) are guests of Jack Dempsey after the Knights of Columbus Games, March 15, 1936. Waiter Fred Scheibeck had won the Waiters' Race.

As a boy and as a man, Glenn Cunningham was known to have an even temperament, and was universally liked. But those who were cruel to the weak or the small, to animals, or who took advantage of others, always moved him to fast and adequate action. Interviewed by Myra Brown in 1967, here is what one of Glenn's contemporaries had to say on the subject:

"My name is Lester Nusser. I started to school with Glenn in 1927, here in Elkhart. I went to school with Glenn all through high school. One thing I always remembered about Glenn was that if anybody ever picked on any child, Glenn always stood up for him. I remember a couple of times that Glenn did have a fight right down on the school grounds. I remember one noon hour he did. Some of the boys were pickin' on a younger boy and Glenn took it up with them and he stopped it. He always did that."

Then there was the classic situation of either the young inexperienced teacher or the substitute teacher being given a hard time by the students. Glenn had a reaction to that, too, as told by Lester Nusser:

"Glenn wasn't for foolishness. He was awful serious all through school. Not like a lot of the rest of them. He didn't have much patience with the kids that would act silly and annoy the teachers.

"Glenn always stood up for the teacher. There used to be clashes. Other boys used to pick on the teachers. I've seen them many a time. I've seen teachers, women teachers, just lay their heads down on the desk and cry. And Glenn would take it up, I've seen him take it up and give the boys the dickens on how big a fool they'd made out of themselves and they ought to be ashamed of themselves. We had some young women, real nice teachers, and these country boys would get to pickin' on 'em and I've seen 'em just lay down on the desk and cry. Because they couldn't control them, you know, and I've seen Glenn take it on himself to kind of get things straightened out around there, and I've seen him get right up in the classroom and tell them it had gone far enough, and very seldom anybody ever crossed his path. When he had to get in and tell them to stop it, it would stop."

It was a mile from the Elkhart schoolhouse to the Cunningham place. Other children living that far away took their lunches and ate at school. Not Glenn. He went home for dinner at noon. Men in their stores, women shoppers and tradesmen on the street, even his fellow students watched him as he jogged along in a fast trot, twice to the schoolhouse, twice back home, four miles a day, week in and week out. They spoke of it to each other, smiled, and many that Myra could interview still remembered.

All the while Glenn was still thinking that someday he would go to college. He knew, too, that this meant money. He began to think of how he would save money to start a college fund.

Each year before Thanksgiving and Christmas, turkey buyers for big-city markets back east crowded into Elkhart to purchase company requirements. There were then no refrigerator cars, and turkeys had to be plucked, dressed, and packed in ice before being shipped out of town. It meant a fall payroll for all students able to qualify. Glenn qualified, as did Raymond.

And so did numerous other students, many of whom had ridden in from the country on freight wagons to attend school, and sought employment to pay expenses. Like Glenn, these students from the country—most of them high school students—were older and larger than their classmates. Like Glenn, they were usually of high caliber in character and natural ability, and behind scholastically only because of poor schooling opportunity. Like Glenn, too, many lost time from schooling because they had to work. Elkhart High School was producing outstanding athletes in these years (it would eventually produce two Olympic athletes, Glenn Cunningham and Thane Baker). School officials and faculty cooperated in arranging schedules to permit turkey plucking and other remunerative activities.

Pay was ten cents for each turkey plucked. The most skillful could easily finish off forty to fifty birds between the time school was out and bedtime. It meant as much as five dollars a day, which was good pay for those years.

Throughout the fall Agnes Heueisen continued to direct Glenn's progress with care. "He was so deserving," she wrote. "I felt he needed special recognition of some kind. But what?"

By midyear she had decided that his mental capacity and acquired knowledge justified her in recommending his promotion at the end of the year from the fourth grade to the sixth. This she did. She wrote the recommendation across his grade card, the customary procedure in such cases. For reasons never clear, this recommendation was not approved, though Glenn's acumen was not questioned. Yet what Miss Heueisen meant to the thirteen-year-old boy that winter, she would never know. She made him believe in his dreams again, even dreams he never mentioned.

None of the boys on the school grounds nor his family at home knew that already he was dreaming of the Olympics. He had not yet begun to grow much, but he was running that winter with rhythm and increasing speed.

"Miss Heueisen was a tremendous person," Glenn was quoted, "I loved her. As much as my mother, almost. Of all that happened to me that school year the most important was that she was my teacher."

The path, however would not be a straight line. Not only would Glenn miss being skipped, but because the Cunningham caravan would leave Elkhart, Glenn would not even get credit for the fourth grade.

From Glenn's journal: "In the spring of 1921, my parents again turned west and traveled to eastern Colorado where we spent the summer between La Junta and Rockyford, working in the melon and hay fields. In the fall we moved 50 miles south of La Junta into the canyons near the tiny community of Hoop-up."

Southeast Colorado was largely cattle country, drier than Kansas. Accordingly, more acreage was required to graze an animal through a season, ranches were larger, ranch houses farther apart, and there were fewer children in the countryside.

In the entire year the family was in Colorado, Glenn remembers seeing not one schoolhouse, even to the farthest horizon, nor did he study at home. Acquiring an education seemed once more entirely impossible. Even his legs, which had improved so tremendously, continued at times to suddenly give way. He could never wholly count on them.

In Colorado the family seeded melons, put up alfalfa hay, and worked with cattle, working twelve long hours a day. In the winter they cut cedar posts. For months at a time they did not go to town, though they patronized a small general store and post office, where they bought staples for fencing, and similar items.

For relaxation Glenn played a violin that was given to him. He still dreamed of college and of becoming a doctor, but he no longer mentioned it.

7

SETTLING IN ELKHART, 1922 ON

Across the countryside there were still men called "sand-rats." They lived in sand-dugouts because they couldn't do better and attended church dinners because they were hungry

Warren Harding was elected President of the United States in 1920. In 1921 he signed formal treaties for concluding our war with Germany. In 1922 he became embroiled in the TeaPot Dome scandal. The United States was leaning away from joining the League of Nations and tilting toward isolationism. In literature T. S. Eliot published *The Wasteland*.

Glenn Cunningham's never-completed autobiography continues: "The spring of 1922 found us returning to Elkhart, renting a house in the same area as we had lived previously, sometimes known as 'Dogtown.'"

When the Cunninghams first moved from the farm to Elkhart, and stayed that brief time, all of southwest Kansas was then still digging in diligently for a foothold from which to move into productivity. The country was arid. Elkhart had an annual rainfall of only about seventeen inches. A livelihood was hard to wrest from the sandy soil. Country people thought they were doing well if their larders held side meat, corn meal, and "coffee" made from cornmeal that had been parched and ground.

Houses were still primitive. The two-story, two-room house the Cunninghams had had on the farm was larger and better than most country houses, and here and there across the countryside there were still men called "sand-rats." They lived in sand-dugouts because they couldn't do better and attended church dinners because they were hungry.

Thomas Sullivan's dugout on his homestead. Picture taken in 1983.

The Myers family in front of the "dog house" entrance to their dugout, 1915.

Elkhart's first town lots were sold April 29th, 1913. Tents were put up and Elkhart was officially established. Ten days later there would be one hundred business lots sold along with several residential lots.

Land sale.

Photo courtesy of the Morton County Historical Museum

Fifty years earlier roads were only trails, with now and then wagon tracks leading off to a cabin or dugout, rarely to a ranch house; and there were still maps that labeled the entire area "The Great American Desert."

There had been no actual town boom when the Cunningham wagons arrived in 1920, but on their return in the spring of 1922, the town was emerging from its pioneer days. Two years had made a difference. It had a population of about 1,500, with churches, schools, a hospital, a newspaper, a theater, three livery stables, and three banks. There was more money now, but it was still scarce. At one time the total deposits in all three banks amounted to less than half a million dollars. Sometimes on Saturdays, the day country people came to town, banks ran out of ready money and had to send out to local stores to bring in cash.

What once had been only trails were real roads now, though not paved yet or well maintained, and the Santa Fe Railway had laid a branch line as far as Elkhart. It was the only railroad serving three counties. Improved transportation facilities meant increased employment and business activity. Elkhart had become the broomcorn capital of the world. (Broomcorn is a short plant with heads that hold the individual grains, and is harvested in the fall. It was used years ago in the making of brooms.)

In Elkhart lived seventeen men who did nothing but buy broomcorn. Turkeys were grown in great numbers throughout the town's trade area. Each year in season, long trains of wagons hitched tandem came in from the surrounding countryside, loaded with the broomcorn or turkeys to be sent east by rail. Drivers stayed in town all night and went home the next day loaded with coal. Elkhart was immediately across the state line from Oklahoma and only eight miles from Colorado. Stores in twenty inland towns in southwest Kansas, northwest Oklahoma, and southeast Colorado bought supplies in Elkhart.

The Cunninghams settled on land that joins Elkhart on the southwest corner. The house, which still stood in the late 60's, green and freshly painted, was back from the highway a short distance and up a slight slope. Their next door neighbor was Ora Emberton. His was the last house within the city limits and the last house on the highway going south out of Kansas.

The first thing to be done after the Cunninghams had arrived and unloaded was to water the mules. Glenn led them down the slope to the tank. But when they had finished drinking and lifted their heads, he seized a tail, slapped the mule on the hips, and went back up to the house on the jump. The action was commonplace for Glenn. He'd been doing it for years, but Emberton, who had never seen such a thing, thought it was one he'd never recommend.

On arrival, the Cunninghams immediately began to put down roots. Employment for anyone who knew how to work was not

Cunningham Elkhart home before 1930.

difficult to find. In the years the Cunninghams had been on the farm in Stevens County their chief cash crop had been broom-corn. That first summer back in Kansas, Clint seeded broomcorn in the surrounding countryside, baled it at harvest and loaded the bales at the huge warehouse at the edge of town. Broomcorn bales are very heavy. He could handle them. He was fast, skilled, and experienced. And now he was in demand.

He would, however, find a steady job. Harry Walker, Elkart store owner, described Glenn's father's job and also something about Glenn in his 1966 taped interview with Myra Brown: "Clint Cunningham took care of the city streets. Way back in the early days, Elkhart built about seven blocks of paving, I believe it was, right down in the business district. It was a hundred-foot wide street, and it was quite a bit of care. Mr. Cunningham had a wagon and a team of mules, and he would sweep that pavement and take care of it. That was his job. And to show you what kind of a fellow Glenn was, he was the champion miler at K.U., and when he came home he's sometimes take a brush and shovel and help his father. He didn't feel a bit swelled up. He was just that kind of fellow."

Soon after the Cunninghams came to town they discovered that Dr. Hansen who had been discharged from the service had come back to the area he had served as a young doctor before going to Europe as a part of the American Expeditionary Forces during the World War l. This time he had set up a practice in Elkhart. An outstanding Cunningham characteristic had always been that they paid their bills however long it took. They had not yet paid all they owed Dr. Hansen for his help when Floyd and Glenn were burned. Learning they were near neighbors, Rosa went to call on Mrs. Hansen. The Hansens had a little girl now. The girl was "fretful" and required much of her mother's time. Rosa insisted that she do the Hansen laundry to make payment on what they still owed the doctor. She told Mrs. Hansen they would come for the laundry and bring it home. Mrs. Hansen consented.

The picking up and delivering fell to Glenn. He did it his way, riding Becky, a mule. She would always take him on a merry ride for blocks at a time before he could get astraddle her. After picking up laundry Becky would steer to the railroad track beds, leaping over the railroad ties and jostling the laundry so that Glenn would be confronted with a delicate balancing act all the way home. He would also ride her for groceries. Mrs. Hansen remembered that in these days she and the doctor thought Glenn's walking was not yet entirely normal. But they agreed that his riding ability could not be questioned.

Beginning that first summer and fall, Glenn did a lot of driving cattle from one pasture to another, or from pasture to the stockyards on the edge of town. The cattlemen he most often drove for were Emmet Addington and George Mills, big pasture operators. They had pastures in Kansas and in Colorado.

Addington told him he had some cattle in a pasture several miles southeast of Elkhart which he'd decided to sell and would like to have Glenn bring into the yards for him. "While you're out there," he added, "you might as well get that steer and bring him in, too."

"That steer" was well-known locally. "Addington had had him since he was two years old," Glenn told Myra. "He was then probably seven or eight years old. It was time to sell."

Glenn rode Becky, a still heavier mule with more pulling power. He knew he might need it.

"It was late when I got out there," he remembered. "I got the cattle rounded up all right and got them out on the road and started toward town. But I hadn't gone far when *that* steer turned around and headed back to the pasture. I was well acquainted with his kind. I didn't try to head him. I just started after him. And little old Becky—I'd kick that mule in the sides with my spurs, she'd bite the steer, and I'd whip him with my rope. I'd double it up and really lay it on. After a while he got tired. Then I got him turned around and brought him back to the other cattle. *I brought that steer to town!*" Myra observed that in telling this story Glenn was reliving it, just as he was when he told me about the incident with the rickshaw driver in the orient of the 30's. She recorded that his voice was decisive.

"But," he went on, "I had quite a bit of trouble with him on the road and it was after dark when I got him into the yards. Even then he was still determined to go back to the pasture. Half the time in the yards I couldn't see him. But he'd be in there running around. I'd hear him. They had a lot of stockcars there to load into and I couldn't tell where he was. But Becky could. She could see him. Together we got him loaded.

"The next day Addington asked me how I was ever able to get that animal to town. He said that for years he'd been sending fellows out on their best horses the country had and they'd never been able to get him. That was the first I knew he'd had any trouble with him. He hadn't told me before.

"All I told him was that I just drove him in with the rest of the cattle."

Terse remarks, brevity and understatement, above all modesty, that day and for the rest of his life would be Glenn Cunningham hallmarks.

Glenn would return to school the fall of 1922 and would continue schooling for the greater part of two decades. We pick up his account again:

"From 1922 until graduation the summers found me working at many different jobs. My mother took in washings at that time, and I would pick up the laundry and return it, riding my little black ring-tailed mule, Becky. It was some kind of feat once I had untied her, to jump on, hang on, and balance the baskets as she took off on a run wherever we were going, her tail spinning like a windmill. One summer my Father worked for the Bloodharts, who owned a drugstore in town but also had a dairy out north of town. My Father and I cleaned the barns and hauled away the manure. The highlight of the day, however, was when we stopped by the drugstore for a cold, frosty mug of rootbeer, a rare treat for me in those days. At different times I drove cattle for the Addington and Mills Cattle Co., hauled ashes and tin cans out of the alleys, and on Saturday mornings I would be at the Maricle Merchantie to clean the trash out of their bins in back of the store. I drove a truck hauling wheat one summer for Earl White, and one summer, going to the Mill for a sack of chicken feed, Jim Heintz asked me if I would like to work a couple of hours, which I certainly did. I delivered the feed to my home then returned and ended up working 28 days scooping grain in the railroad cars. Another summer I worked 58 days straight, 16 to 22 hours a day and I always remember Mrs. Heintz coming to the Mill to bring Jim's lunch, beautifully dressed as if she were going to a party, with little Joe and Evelyn dressed as neat as pins. Jim and Margaret did a lot for me, and they meant a great deal to me— I will never forget them."

He did not forget them. In *Never Quit* they are prominently noted in the Acknowledgments: "To Margaret and Jim Heintz who saw the drive and motivation to achieve and harnessed it along worthwhile channels by giving me work opportunities when jobs were almost non-existent."

Building the Heintz flour mill, 1919.

Glenn picks up his account again:

"In the fall [1922], Raymond, Melva, John and myself returned to school and during the rest of my school years I became involved with football, basketball and track, as well as singing in the glee club and playing the violin in the school orchestra."

Glenn Cunningham is here speaking of the remainder of his grade school years and then high school. He must have been eighteen years old when he began high school. He would graduate in three years and with high honors. He excelled in football—first as a lineman, then as a running back. He excelled, too in basketball and track. We do know he had a good singing voice but how well he played the violin is lost to history. But it was in track that he would attract attention, then and for many years to come.

Elkhart football, 1928 or 1929. Glenn is in the back row, to the left of Varney

Coach Varney and the 1928-29 Elkhart basketball team.
Glenn is third from right.

8

FIRST RACE AND THAT SHINY MEDAL IN THE WINDOW

So I never got the medal that would have meant the most to me

In the evening of April 17, 1987, at the Colonnade Hotel Banquet Room, right after some of us had run the Boston Marathon that year, Glenn Cunningham spoke to the American Medical Athletic Association's Boston Marathon group about his first race.

Well after a few more years on the farm my parents moved into a little town in southwestern Kansas. Right in the heart of the dust bowl. I walked to school, right downtown. We didn't have hot lunches those days, we had a sack lunch, took about five minutes to eat, then you had 55 minutes to kill . . . so you'd walk downtown, do a little window shopping. This particular day I came to this large plate glass window displaying medals and trophies to be given at a track meet to be held on the weekend. I noticed one little medal only the size of a fifty-cent piece. But it shone like gold. And that medal took my eye . . . it had a card stating that it would be given for the "Class A Mile." After gazing in that window admiring that medal I decided I was going to the track, run the mile, get the medal. Didn't occur to me there'd be other boys in the race. It would be the first track meet I ever attended.

My folks were very opposed to any kind of athletics. In fact my father told us, if you're not getting enough exercise 'you just get home here, I'll find enough exercise for you to do [laughter].' My father was one of these old fashioned individuals—in a very striking way on impressing his values on all us kids. I had to figure out a way to get out to the track out where they were going to have this field day. Everybody goes to town on a Saturday afternoon. So I hitched up the team, my parents got the wagon and off they went. I took off on my pony. I was about to find that you had to qualify for the Class A Mile. You had to weigh 70 pounds or more to get in the Class A Mile.

It was early in the spring I still had on my red woolen winter underwear, a pair of overalls, a woolen sweater, two pair of socks, and a pair of basketball shoes. Got on the scale, checked in at just under 71 pounds, I was qualified.

Then for the first time I recognized the fact there were other boys who'd qualified, all high school boys. I remember this one, about six feet three inches tall. I was just a little old fourth grader, I looked up to this boy and said 'how's the weather up in the clouds?' I noticed his big long legs, my heart just wilted. I thought how in the world will I ever take charge of that fellow. His legs were just about as long as I was tall. I wasn't just satisfied seeing these big long legs, I continued looking on down and wondered how he'd run a mile with nails sticking out of his shoes. I had never seen a pair of spikes before in my life [laughter]. I thought I just about got you now, every time you run a step you're going to be fastened to the ground [laughter]. They finally called for the race, we lined together and we all started running. They all took off there and I mean this big old guy was just beating up the grass with those big old legs of his, the other boys hot on his heels. I was struggling back there. We got to about a quarter of a mile. He got over to the inside of the track, he was out! I didn't wonder why he was out. I'd seen him walking around town smoking cigarettes. I'd known this jingle which said cigarette smoking boys are like rotten apples, they fall before harvest.

So I kept plugging along, picking these guys up one by one, we got to the half-way mark, only two boys ahead of me. I knew absolutely nothing about the rules of running, I didn't know you're supposed to pass on the outside. I didn't know you're supposed to be two strides ahead before you come in. The only thing I did know then was the shortest distance around the track was the closest and for me was to be right in between.

When I got to that string, the finish line, I didn't want that string to hit me right across the eyes so I just ducked under it [laughter]. They said to me you have to break that string in order to win the race, so I just jumped up and grabbed that string. Actually the easiest race I ever won in my life. With the race over I was far more concerned about getting home than I was in picking up that beautiful shiny little medal. Because I didn't want my father practicing his, uh, striking way on me. I jumped on my pony ("Beauty") thinking I'd pick up that medal Monday morning when I went to school. Arrived at school Monday morning, inquired about the medal, they said it had been lost. Actually what had happened they had given it to the boy who came in second because I wasn't there when they had called for the winners.

So I never got the medal that would have meant the most to me. I could cover this room I suppose with medals and trophies but none would mean more to me than that one little medal the size of a fifty-cent piece had I got my hands on it as a little fourth grader. My folks never did learn that I had run in that race, thank God! [audience laughter] . . .

At the time Glenn did not feel kindly toward the people he held responsible for not giving him that medal.

Roy Varney, his high school coach, was located in Guymon, Oklahoma. Interviewed October 2, 1964, he told of Glenn's reaction to anyone he thought had done him wrong, that if someone did him wrong he didn't forget it. Varney added for emphasis: "It was a county thing, a county deal is what it was. He says to this day that he'd rather have that little medal than any medal he's got. And he's never forgot that on Jewell."

Varney described another vignette, of "another superintendent that followed there, after I was already there, a man by the name of McArthur. Glenn was a pretty good student, but McArthur gave him a D in math and Glenn never did forget that, either. That superintendent was just there one year, and he came to Glenn's house, some way or other off down there where Glenn lived to see Glenn after Glenn was in college and one thing and another. Glenn didn't even ask him in. I say he's got that characteristic. If he doesn't like a person, he doesn't say anything about it, only that's *it*."

Harry Walker described another vignette illustrating how Cunningham responded when he felt someone had done the wrong thing. Walker told of a big championship track meet in Lawrence, Kansas: "There was one man, he had a boy and girl. He'd lost his wife and he couldn't make it on the farm, the girl just took over and she just raised those children. I think there was about five of them. And she was one of the ones Glenn had made it possible for them to go on to school, her and her next youngest brother. Mr. Grable had been on relief and wasn't doing any good. He'd lost his farm. And of course, he wanted to go and see his children. So Mr. Cunningham, Clint, learned that a big business man there was a-going, he had a big Buick, and he knew that he had room for one more passenger, see, 'cause he'd heard him say so, so he told Mr. Grable to go down and ask him if he couldn't go with him. And this fellow said, 'Nah, I'm taking a bunch of business men.' Well, somebody got Mr. Grable up there anyhow. Clint did some way, I don't know how. This man was W. C. Washburn. So all the Cunningham clan was there for the race. Then sometime after the race Glenn brought Gene Venzke and some of the other mile runners up into the grandstand and introduced them to his father and mother, and went right on down the line. And when he came to this fellow—Clint had told him about, you know—he passed him right by. He introduced these runners to everybody in the stand that he knew except this one fellow."

Myra Brown summarized Glenn's feeling about that shiny medal:

There was a time when the little medal meant so much to me that I hated everything about the man I held responsible for my not receiving it.

There he was, supposedly a responsible man, a man in the business of setting an example for others. And yet he could do a thing like that!

But you can't tell what it is deep within a man that makes things like that happen. There's a lot of good in everybody. There was in him. I don't want that good to be injured, or hurt in any way. There's some bad in everybody too, dormant maybe. I have faults, as much as anybody.

It's like I keep telling my kids: 'Treat all the tragedies as incidents; and none of the incidents as tragedies.'"

There's something else we can get a hint of in Glenn's reference to his father's old-fashioned *striking* way of impressing his values on the kids in the family. There was a different note in Glenn's voice whenever he mentioned his father's "striking" ways.

We know that Glenn's father was a physically strong, strict, hardworking, and responsible family man. We know that Glenn reveled in working alongside his father. In *Never Quit*, when he is honored at Madison Square Garden in 1979, he confides to Ruth as he ruminates over whether he had done enough for the kids he worked with: "I was too much like my father, a disciplinarian, hard working, stubborn." Ruth described Glenn's father as warm and welcoming to her when she first came into the family. Roy Varney quoted Dean Morgan, Letha's husband— and it is unclear whether Dean was quoting Glenn or if it was coming from Dean—saying that "Clint Cunningham had a terrible temper."

This brings us back to where this chapter started, to the banquet room of the Colonnade Hotel.

There ensued an informal yet spirited discussion about social issues, particularly juvenile delinquency. I remember Cunningham saying to me that as a psychiatrist I wouldn't like what he was about to say, which was that occasionally corporal punishment was indicated. (I didn't disagree.) He told of how on rare occasions his punishment for concealing or using drugs at the ranch was a good strapping down. The ministering of large portions of discipline and love were the two elements of his program. (His form of "tough love.")

He truly held court with us, telling of his ideas how juvenile delinquency could be stopped in one generation if each family had a strong father figure. You couldn't argue with the finding that in societies with strong family units, there was much less juvenile delinquency. He told how in his family, when his own father spoke, "we never hesitated when he said to do a thing. We did it."

(In a lighter vein, Harry Walker, the Elkhart store owner, taped in 1966, had something to say showing both Glenn's sense of humor and his father's *striking* ways: "Glenn has a sense of humor. Some people can't see it, but he has. One day a fellow asked him how come he could run so fast. And Glenn said, 'Well, I'll tell you. On the farm out there at Rolla there were pretty lean days and Dad didn't have much crop and he sent my brother and me out to catch jack rabbits so we'd have something to eat. And, he said, 'if we brought in a poor one, *Dad would tan us for it.* So my brother and I got so we'd run along beside jack rabbits and feel their ribs to see if they were fat.'")

Glenn's ideas, as posed in that backroom, were sound and simple but also simplistic, leading to polarized debate. He said that he came down hard on drugs and smoking. (Actually, as will unfold, he was a fervent, sometimes fanatical, crusader against smoke and drugs. In the early 1930s he even made a statewide tour talking against the repeal of Prohibition.) Then he confided:

"My father smoked and my father drank. . . . I don't know whether it was because of the burning flesh and the gasoline and everything but smoke infuriates me. And alcohol, I knocked more guys on their ass when they came up to me and pretended they were drunk and they didn't know what they were doing, and if they are drunk and don't know what they're doing, and they just don't want to fool with me because I won't tolerate it a minute.

"One time my father started to discipline me when he had been drinking and I told him what's going to happen. I didn't need to stay there, I was only twelve years old but I could have gotten out on my own and made it."

(The above was recorded on a hand tape recorder. Ruth Cunningham later added that what happened in this critical, pivotal juncture in Glenn's life, is that Glenn actually grabbed the whip out of his father's hands and challenged his father. His father apparently backed down.)

On the other hand, Glenn had learned to see his father in perspective and in a most positive light. He confided this to Myra Brown: "My father was the most patient and tenderest man in the world, if there was need."

I return now to Ruth Cunningham's request to focus on his running career but "to do that you have to halfway understand the man, his philosophy, what drove him, and his outlook on life."

9

ROY VARNEY AND
THE FOUR-MINUTE MILE

I never ran a race and won in my life because I was better than anyone else was. I think a lot of it is enthusiasm. You know it isn't the size of the sting that makes it effective is it? It's the enthusiasm with which the bee uses it that counts. It's that way with our athletics. It's the enthusiasm for which we go into it, in fact in any field of endeavor.

The accomplishment of a four-minute mile was a matter of conjecture and debate for the first half of the 1900s and it became trackdom's Holy Grail quest. Glenn Cunningham's American and world record as of the early 1940s was a 4:06.7 run at Princeton in 1934. He had run an indoor mile (usually run slower) in 1938 of 4:04.4, but for several reasons it was never recognized as an international record.

During the 1987 Boston Marathon visit he spoke briefly of having run a four-minute mile in high school. It was something then that was kept quiet. His coach, Roy Varney, didn't want anyone hurting himself trying for that mark. We do have a handwritten letter from Roy Varney, then of Varney's Home and Auto in Guymon, Oklahoma, dated February 23, 1965, that sheds light on the subject:

Glenn was in his last year of high school. The place we selected was a mile of dirt and sand road. It was hard and not to [sic] smooth, having some rough spots. The reason I had Glenn run on the road was the track was in poor shape. Glenn and I drove around until we thought we found the best location to run. To determine the distance we drove the car until the speedometer came up on zero. Glenn got out, limbered up and I started him using a stop watch for time. I then drove on down the road until the speedometer of the car came up on one mile and caught Glenn's time at exactly four minutes. There was a slight wind to Glenn's back, but I believe the poor conditions of the road would be enough handicap to off-set any advantage he might have gained by having a slight wind to his back.

When Glenn first started running he was afraid to run too fast the first part of the mile for fear he would not be able to finish, since in this run, since he had no competition, he had nothing to lose if he didn't finish so he ran faster to begin with and gave it all he had the entire distance.

So there we have it: he did—or maybe he didn't *really*—run a four-minute mile in high school. It's interesting to note that an error of 2 percent on the odometer would add (or subtract) about 4.8 seconds.

Varney makes a point of Glenn running alone, without competition. Cunningham often would say that he ran to win but cared little for records. He found joy in running itself and in the evolving camaraderie with his competitors.

There was an article in the *Vanity Fair* issue of May 1935 titled BUMPING THE CEILING IN SPORTS—by Paul Gallico, who explored the feasibility of anyone ever running a four-minute mile. He goes a bit into the physiology by explaining how lactic acid accumulates, slowing the body and bringing muscle contraction to a halt. There is a full-page photo of Glenn

Cunningham to the left of the article's first page. Underneath the photo it says: *Glenn Cunningham, the greatest runner in the world.*

Cunningham is first mentioned only in terms of his former coach, Brutus Hamilton. Through a sophisticated formula, Hamilton calculated the fastest the human body was capable of running the mile in was 4:01.66.

Brutus Hamilton

Gallico seemed to agree. He pointed out that when Glenn made his 1934 record he owned a thirty-yard lead. Could anyone doubt that "if Cunningham had been pressed for the last two-hundred yards he would have turned in even faster time." He quoted Cunningham saying that at the end of that race he still ". . . had some running left [in him]."

Gallico would summarize, however, that a four-minute mile was out of the question: "There is nothing that drives a body in which fuel is exhausted," he concluded, "and waste poisons accumulated. Therein lie the limits of human endeavor."

Cunningham, to the contrary, always contended that the four-minute mile could be done. He called attention to those attributes of the human spirit that Gallico ignored: the elements of enthusiasm, discipline, willpower. He asserted that the breaking of records was more a mental than a physical feat.

On the subject of human spirit, Glenn said this to our group in April 1987: "I never ran a race and won in my life because I was better than anyone else was. I think a lot of it is enthusiasm. If a bee ever stung you you'll understand what I mean. You know it isn't the size of the sting that makes it effective is it? It's the enthusiasm with which the bee uses it that counts (laughter). It's that way with our athletics. It's the enthusiasm for which we go into it, in fact in any field of endeavor."

The man who in 1954 first broke the four-minute mile barrier, Dr. Roger Bannister, then a medical student and now a prominent neurologist, penned a wonderfully written book, *The Four Minute Mile*. Explaining why we run, he says, "we do not run because we think it is doing us good, but because we enjoy it and cannot help ourselves." Later he adds: "No one can say 'You must *not* run faster than this, or jump higher than *that*.' The human spirit is indomitable."

It's unlikely that Cunningham was paid anything for his part in that *Vanity Fair* article. The draconian amateur rules of his day would have prohibited such, and he would not be one to make an end run around any rules of purity. But I wonder what he thought when (and if) he saw the back cover of that *Vanity Fair* issue. For there, from prominent athletes of the day such as tennis player Ellsworth Hines and golfer Helen Hicks, were testimonials to the flavor and the energy-restoring, nerve-calming qualities of . . . Camel cigarettes.

10

HIGH SCHOOL AND GLENN'S FIRST WORLD RECORD

But Glenn never knew in any race he ever started whether his legs might give way on him before he finished. So he never took the lead.

Glenn Cunningham speaking to Myra Brown:
Our football team was undefeated, being scored on only once; our basketball team was excellent, and though we had no track team during my Freshman year, we did make up a relay team of Gene Roberts, Don Smith, Virgil Schull and myself that Mr. Malin took to Liberal. Coach Roy Varney and I traveled to Chicago in the spring of 1929 where I lost my only mile race in high school. . . .

In September 1927 Glenn entered Elkhart High School as a freshman. He was then eighteen years old.

He was endlessly seeking arenas of struggle so to become stronger in every way—*Ad astra per aspera* . . . to the stars through struggle.

Elkhart track relay 1928 or 1929. Left to right: Gene Roberts, Don Smith, Coach Malin, Virgil Schull, Glenn Cunningham.

Elkhart High School 1929-1930

Extra! -- Extra!

The Elkhart Tri-State News

ELKHART, KANSAS, 5 P. M., MAY 31, 1930

Cunningham Breaks World's Record

One Mile Straight

Time 4:24 7-10

Welcome Home!

Glenn Cunningham

Elkhart's World's Record Breaker for One Mile at Stagg Stadium, Chicago Saturday May 31, 1930
Time 4:24 7-10

Compliments of The Elkhart Tri-State News

And his college fund bank account was also growing.

In high school, two men, both forever etched with the spirit of early southwest Kansas, became most pivotal for Glenn.

One was James E. Heintz. Another was Roy W. Varney, a graduate of Kansas State Teacher's College, Pittsburg, and Glenn's high school coach, later an Oklahoma businessman. Varney "understood boys and conditions" and guided Glenn's development with consummate skill.

Glenn's acquaintance with Heintz had begun the summer he was fifteen; it was during wheat harvest. "I've hired lots of men and lots of boys, but Glenn was the best," Heintz remembered. "He got more done, and he went ahead, took responsibility. He was worth more and I paid him more. I paid him fifty cents an hour, which was good pay in those days."

Before school opened, Glenn's father, influenced in part by his son's earning capacity, began to urge him to quit school and get a job.

Learning, however, had not been unimportant in Clint Cunningham's background. Before coming to Kansas, his own father, Dr. Drury Cunningham, had "read medicine" in the office of a physician and surgeon of some standing in Illinois. Such was then a common method of studying to become a doctor. Glenn remembered the times spent browsing through his grandfather's fine medical library.

Ora Emberton, the neighbor they found when they came back from Colorado, said that "everybody thought well of the Cunninghams. They were honest, industrious and peace-loving. No son of Clint Cunningham's ever went without wearing a shirt." (This is reminiscent of my first meeting Glenn. He had changed to a clean newly laundered white shirt to meet the T-shirted doctor.)

But many in Elkhart also remembered that, on some things, Clint had "a queer quirk."

School athletics was one of them, something Glenn learned early. Education, another. Clint Cunningham couldn't see the use of either.

But as a very small boy Glenn had begun to find ways to meet difference of opinion. Ways often learned from his father and mother: "I lived at home until I was twenty-one, the fall I entered the University of Kansas," he said. "In all that time I never heard my parents argue. They had differences of opinion. They stated these differences. They stuck to them. They seemed always to grant each other the privilege of being different.

"My goal of getting an education had not changed. My college fund was still growing. I always tried to conform to my father's requirements. *We never hesitated when he said to do a thing.* But when there was a difference of opinion on a major matter—well, school was a major matter. I made my own decision.

"I decided that if my parents had the privilege of being different, I had too."

Even when he was ready for the eighth grade, his father tried to get him to quit and get a job. Again Glenn went back to school.

"Physically," according to Jim Heintz, "Glenn, at this period, was small-waisted, barrel-chested, weighed around a hundred and seventy-five, I guess. A pretty fair-sized boy. But he was powerful. If he shook hands with you, just gripped your hand, it was like a vise had closed down. [When saying good-bye to him the one time we met, I wrote about my right hand being "engulfed in the catcher's mitt that was his right hand."] Gosh, if Glenn had ever turned loose on a guy he could have beaten him to a pulp. But that he would never do. And he had the mental capacity to match.

"Eventually, Glenn took part in all the high school athletic activities. He wrestled, boxed, played basketball, baseball, football, and went out for track. He did it all because he enjoyed it. *That* is important. Not all great athletes can say that. Glenn believed that whatever you want to do you can do, if you try. He had a terrific tenacity.

"And Glenn had the highest kind of morals; I want to say that. Everybody respected him. He wasn't 'uppish,' and he wasn't boastful. Glenn was real, that's all; believe me."

Unlike Heintz, Roy Varney had known Glenn only casually until he was in the seventh or eighth grade. He was just another boy running around the school grounds. Varney didn't know anything about the scars on Glenn's legs or what caused them until he learned from other boys.

But it wasn't long before Varney realized Glenn's enormous potential. In all the activities on the school grounds he was a standout. "He was rough and tumble," Varney remarked. "He could sure handle those boys. And they all liked him. Whatever we put him at he was good. He had played some basketball down in the grades. He practiced that at night. At noon too if he got back from dinner in time. He was having trouble with his ankles when he first came into high school. We took care of that by insisting that he continue to wear high-topped tennis shoes on the court. Except for his ankles, Glenn had what it takes to get going. You couldn't hurt him. He wasn't a fancy player, but he had endurance. He could stay in there and keep going up and down the court. He could pass the ball, and he could make it pretty rough on the boys around him. He played center, jump center we called it, and always, instead of going right back from making a basket, he'd circle the court and come in from behind. One day I said to him, 'Glenn don't be wasting your energy running clear around the court that way.' He just grinned. 'I don't get tired,' he said. And he was right. He could keep that up all the time. You couldn't run him down.

"I got him out for track by taking him out of study hall to practice. The first time he came out he could beat everyone else in school. The only trouble I ever had with him in track was getting him warmed up before a race. And if he ran two races in one meet the second race was always better than the first. It took a mile, two miles, maybe more to get his leg muscles loosened up. He took calisthenics to loosen up his body, including a small bony spur he had in the neck. The first time people saw him run some of them thought he was a show-off, but never at Elkhart. We never got any static at home.

"Glenn had a very unorthodox running pattern. At that time most runners ran the first quarter mile faster than any other. But Glenn never knew in any race he ever started whether his legs might give way on him before he finished. So he never took the lead. He stayed right with the bunch that was running until he felt sure of himself, maybe halfway to the tape. As time passed and his competition got stronger, he kept increasing his speed, but as long as he was in high school he stayed with the bunch until the race was half or three-quarters finished. By that time he figured he had enough in his legs to give her all he had, and he cut loose. Once he began to move out he never slowed down. At the finish he'd be running as though he were doing a hundred-yard sprint. This practice of running the second half faster than the first has since revolutionized the pattern for running the mile.

"I always knew Glenn could run a lot faster than he did. But I never felt it was a good idea to crowd him into running with all he had. I'd seen boys crowded into running to break records who got burnt out in high school. We ran to win, not to break records. And it worked out pretty well. Glenn won every race he ran in high school but one, and that was a race he ran with a fever of 102 degrees, in the Interscholastics at Chicago.

"Usually we did our practice running on a dirt road. The track was sand and dirt and it never was very good. The wind blew the sand out in pits that could easily turn an ankle. Even on the road, Glenn still had to wear his high-topped tennis shoes.

"He used to chase the other boys to get them to warm up, like he did. But they never would. They thought it was silly. Nevertheless, he kept right on getting himself ready to run."

Herman Mills, son of George Mills for whom Glenn drove cattle, commented, "Glenn used to beg me to run around the section with him—but four miles! That was a way too far for me. Once some of us started running at the high school, which is about a mile from Sloan's Corner. When we got there everybody else sat down, tired out. But Glenn made a big circle and away he went back to town."

Under Coach Varney, the Elkhart High School had runners for all the usual distances. In addition, they had a relay team.

"In 1928-29 we had a pretty good relay team," Francis "Brigham" Young recalled. "We had four boys: Herman Mills, who ran the dash, Lon Hurley, Glenn and me. Lon and I were in the same class in high school. Glenn and Herman graduated in 1930, a year after we did. Up at Ford, a little place of about 300 population close to Dodge City, there lived a boy by the name of Clyde Coffman; he was quite a pole-vaulter. He got to be very good. In 1932 he went to the Olympics in Los Angeles with Glenn. [Coffman had won a berth in the decathlon.] In our high school years, Ford had a one-man track team, and Clyde was it. Sometimes we'd go by and pick him up. He and Glenn are still close friends."

"One time when we were in Liberal for a meet—Liberal's over

east of Elkhart—the Coach came to me and he said, 'Now, Francis, you'll try the pole vault today. I don't think you'll do any good.' (Which I couldn't.) 'And I'll let you run the 220 on the medley relay, and your quarter on the mile relay.' (Which I always ran.) 'And then you'll try the half mile, because I'm going to have Glenn do another distance. He's going to run the two-mile, besides the mile.'

"Well, I ran the quarter mile. And when the time came to run the half-mile, which Glenn always ran—Why, gee! Suddenly from about fifty yards on, I was leading everybody. But by the time I got to the last 220 yards I was tuckered out. I guess Glenn knew it, for I looked over and there he was just outside the track, jogging along and looking at me. He'd been there all the time.

"'Make your arms pull you, Brigham,' he kept saying. 'Make your arms pull you. Raise your arms. Make them pull you.' And he wasn't even in the race. But there he was telling me how.

"Glenn was always helping like that. I've seen him all over the track and inside the track and practically clear around the track, telling you everything he thought would help you. He'd fight tooth and toenail against you in a contest and he'd expect you to win if you could. If you did less than your best he'd be disappointed. But whoever won, he'd go down with you while you drank a Coke at the drugstore. He never drank anything stronger than milk, but he went down with you. There was just never any animosity in our races.

"A lot of credit for the way we were goes to Coach Varney. He used to tell us that it's not all in winning, that you give everything you've got to win, but everybody can't win. Somebody's got to lose. He put that into us. I have been a loser. But sometimes I've been a winner. I was nearly six feet tall and I weighed 125 pounds, but sometimes I was good.

"Once when we went to a state meet at Emporia, we won the meet and we won the relay race. After the races, someone came around to me and said, 'Brigham, we looked every where for you, all through the bunch that was running, and we couldn't find you anywhere. Then someone said, "Hey, Elkhart's winning!" And it was you!'

"Gee whizz! I was winning for once, so they couldn't find me."

Football was the last athletic activity that Glenn went out for in high school. His parents were opposed to all athletics, but most of all to football. They thought Glenn would get hurt. To Rosa the game seemed not only dangerous but also brutal. No son of hers, she said, would ever play football with her permission. Clint held firmly to the belief that if Glenn played football he might be forever crippled with a broken back, or perhaps killed.

Jim Heintz, as I've noted, played a pivotal role in Glenn's life. His was a hands-on approach. Myra Brown and Mrs. Cox conversed on the subject:

"Glenn was not able to carry though on this ambition [to become a doctor] because funds were lacking. And his father felt, when the time came, that he needed Glenn's help, financial help. Glenn was making nine dollars a day in Jim Heintz' mill in Elkhart. That was a big wage. And the family needed it. Glenn always helped his family and he was always proud of them, *but they didn't want him to go on to school.* Mr. Heintz said that Clint Cunningham, Glenn's father, came to him at the mill one day. Clint had a job that he had obtained through Mr. Heintz' influence, so it was natural that he would go to Jim Heintz with problems."

Heintz was interviewed sometime in the mid-1960s. Once Elkhart's ice man, then owner-operator of Elkhart Flour Mill, he was then executive vice president of the First State Bank of Elkhart.

In the summers of 1927 and 1928 Glenn worked in the flour-mill. "We had long harvests in those days," Heintz recalled. "I told Glenn he could work all the hours I did and no longer. For three weeks during harvest in 1927 we averaged eighteen hours a day, including Sundays. That meant nine dollars a day for the boy, sixty-three dollars a week. Glenn didn't care if it was scooping wheat, pitching hay, or pitching wheat bundles. I had him back in the boxcar, which was a big job for two men. He used to couple up those cars, change the spout, jimmy the cars down, do all those things. I'd get a man to help him, but the man would stay an hour or so, and I would go back to see how things were going, and he'd be gone. 'Glenn,' I'd say. 'Where's your man?' And Glenn would say, 'I let him go. I could do better alone.'

"One night we were still at it at nearly two o'clock in the morning, when here came his parents to see why he hadn't come home. They thought something had happened. When they got there we were both up in the car scooping wheat and laying it back. We got it loaded, Glenn shut the door, and there stood his father. We told him we'd be through in about ten minutes.

"So Glenn ran home, and at five o'clock here he was back again—and I was back too. Harvest was good and the grain was coming in fast. We were both pretty good 'hosses' in those days. Though I never could do all the things Glenn could.

"I was the Elkhart mayor then. I got Clint the job of street commissioner. He was a good worker.

"One day Clint dropped into the mill to talk to me about Glenn. He said he was taking Glenn out of school and he wanted me to help get him to agree with it. Everyone in town knew the trouble was football. Glenn had never gone out for it. He wanted to play but he didn't want to go against his parents' wishes."

At this juncture in the interview Heintz laced his fingers together, vividly recalling that long ago day. "No-o-o-o! No-o-o! No, Clinton, you can't do that!"

It wasn't the attitude Clint had hoped for and he didn't like it. "I—" he had begun, setting his feet more squarely in front of him.

Heintz started again, emphasizing his words with a finger that he pointed at Clint, and speaking with some sharpness. "You can't do that to your boy, Clint. Glenn's an athletic genius. He has something to give to the world. *He can't drop out of school.* You must *do* something."

At times, Clint was what the countryside called "quick-spoken." Rosa, firm in her decisions tended to be calm; she was the family balance wheel. Clint began to sputter. He didn't think Jim Heintz or anybody else had a right to tell him how to raise his boy. He guessed Jim didn't know how much it meant to him just to spare his son to go to school. He guessed Jim didn't know what it would mean to him if Glenn broke his leg, or an arm, or his back, or if he got killed.

"I'm a poor man," he stammered. "I'm a poor man. Who do you think would pay for it if he got hurt? I'm a poor man, Jim."

The Cunninghams didn't have much money, but neither did a lot of other people.

Jim's dander was beginning to rise. "It's not that you're a poor man that's bothering you, Clint. It's that you won't let Glenn participate in athletics."

Clint bridled. "If you know so much about my boy, just you take him and raise him."

Heintz got to his feet. "All right, Mr. Cunningham. If he breaks a leg, I'll fix it. And if he dies, I'll bury him. Send him to me."

And before very long in came Glenn.

"Glenn," Heintz began, "Your father and I have had it out

about you continuing in school, and you're my boy now. From now on you're free to do whatever you want to do, play any game you want to play, and if you get hurt I'll pay for it. Whatever happens, it's up to me to take care of you. No one else is going to say what you can do or can't do."

Glenn grinned.

"After this go-in with his father, Glenn knew what he could do," Heintz finished.

But even so Glenn had not yet fully decided to play football. He still didn't like the idea of going against his parents' wishes.

Yet every day during the noon hour he was out on the school grounds as soon as he got back from dinner, kicking the football around and passing it. The team wanted him to play; Varney was always trying to get him out for practice.

But when he asked Glenn about it, Glenn just looked at him.

One noon hour the coach found him standing alone at the schoolhouse door waiting for it to be unlocked for the afternoon session. That day Elkhart was scheduled to play Syracuse High.

Varney studied him.

"Glenn," he said. "Want that suit?"

Glenn looked at him and this time he talked. "You'd feel funny if I'd take it, wouldn't you?"

Varney knew his boys. He knew Glenn. "I didn't even look back," Varney says. "I just said, 'come on.' I unlocked the door, got him a suit, and that afternoon he played. The other boys in the line told him what to do, and he got along pretty well, considering. It was the first football game he ever saw. He would not even allow himself to watch when he couldn't play."

After the game, Varney got the town's newspaper to write him up "pretty well," and later he and Mrs. Varney went down to talk with Glenn's parents. Mrs. Varney thought the coach might have seemed a little underhanded, but it would be a difficult confrontation. Clint dwelled chiefly on the possibility that Glenn might be killed if he played such a game. Rosa said again that no son of hers would ever play football with her permission. Varney remembers that all Clint would finally say was, "Whatever his mother says," and all Rosa would say was, "Whatever his father thinks."

As the Varneys left, Glenn spoke privately to the coach. "I take it that if I can't play with their permission, I can play without it." And so a pioneer decision of sorts was reached.

Glenn's skill on the football field blossomed rapidly in the three games he played before his parents learned that he had even become a member of the team.

Later, Herman Mills, who played quarterback, observed, "I think we took care of the situation satisfactorily. Glenn's father soon found out that Glenn could take care of himself."

It wasn't too long before Clint and Rosa were going all over the state to track meets and football and basketball games as special guests. Both liked the competition, liked the roar of approval that always rose from sidelines when Glenn came out on a football field or basketball court, appeared on a track, or broke a tape. The tremendous admiration for Glenn that existed wherever he was known—admiration he had not sought and that sometimes embarrassed him—and his standing as a person throughout southwest Kansas gave both of them tremendous satisfaction. The day came when Clint sought out the coach to apologize for the attitude he and Rosa had taken the night the Varneys came to call.

Glenn's fame continued to spread and gathered speed. People from surrounding towns and the countryside began coming in increasing numbers to watch games or track meets when it was known that Glenn would appear. If there was a grandstand, it was a standing-room-only affair. All over town small boys began jogging along the streets, day and night, planning to become milers. This activity was to continue for years.

One day after his parents had been attending athletic events for some time, a stranger approached Clint at a track meet at nearby Ulysses. Clint liked him immediately. "See that boy?" He nudged the stranger. "That's my boy." He nudged him again and pointed, "See that woman up there in the stands? That's his mother."

Both men laughed. Clint was all but strutting with pride.

Most small towns did not have grandstands in those years. Crowds banked along the sidelines, moved up and down with each play or race. At one of the games, Glenn suddenly appeared racing at top speed, just inside the sideline from where his parents stood.

"Here, Mom," Clint shouted, seizing the hand of the excited woman at his side and all but dragging her down the field to see how Glenn had come out. Then he looked down at Rosa. But she wasn't there, and he was holding tightly to the hand of a woman he didn't know, a perfect stranger!

The first year Glenn played football, Varney played him on the line. The second year, which was his senior year, Glenn played fullback. He was nineteen in August before he played his first game, twenty before his final year. Elkhart had a fully accredited four-year high school, but Glenn finished the course in three years. If he hadn't he would have been twenty-one throughout his final year, and so barred from high school athletic competition.

Lester Nusser, who went through high school with Glenn, remarked, "Glenn was always a person to remember. I ran around with him a lot. He and I were on the same football team—and track, we were together on that too. Of course, he went a little farther then the rest of us did.

"Here's the way he was. If anything was right, he was for it. He was never overbearing, always nice to get along with. If you needed a little advice, anything to pick up your morale, help of any kind, you could get it from Glenn. If some child on the school grounds was getting picked on, he always found a way to stop it. Glenn could lose his temper, as far as that was concerned. He just about had to sometimes. There were clashes, bound to be.

"I remember a couple of times when he fought, both times over a child. Once he and I were sitting by an upstairs window at school when some boys down on the grounds began making fun of a boy, before a girl. That's what started it. Glenn watched them. When he saw it had gone far enough, he got up and went down. It didn't take him long.

"Glenn played it straight with everybody. If others played fair, he was for them a hundred percent. But he wasn't for foolishness."

"You bet, people had respect for Glenn," Herman Mills added. "When we were kids, going dancing, and together for athletics, that sort of thing, we got to know each other pretty well, got to know what the other one stood for and if he would back it up. Glenn always backed it up. You could depend on what he said.

"And another thing, folks out here weren't snooty. Aren't now. There never was any line between town kids and kids from the country. It didn't make any difference whether they had money or not. How their fathers made a living didn't matter. It was what they were and what they produced that counted. Elkhart was a typical western town. It still is. When you grow up under this kind of influence it makes a difference all your life. It did with Glenn.

"Glenn was serious in high school. But don't get the idea that he was so serious he never had any fun. He'd make faces. He had time for some of that. He'd grin, act bored which he never was and pretty soon all over the room everybody would be grimacing. Glenn dated girls in high school, but not much. There wasn't much to do, maybe go on a picnic. There wasn't much money to spend. Still all the boys and girls liked him. I never knew of anyone that didn't like Glenn."

Clarence "Doc" Crawley was Kansas state boxing champion in the 1930s, and one of Elkhart's outstanding athletes when he was in high school. Glenn said, "Doc never expressed himself easily in words, but his actions spoke eloquently. He had the very highest kind of a character. He was a tremendous athlete with good sense all the way through. Doc was just as solid as they come."

Doc stated, "Glenn never thought he was a better athlete than the rest of us, like he knew it all. I'm trying to think of the word. It's humble, I guess, he was that. There never was any feeling of rivalry toward him. He didn't cheat and he had no use for anyone that did. He trained all the year round. If other boys went out and broke training rules, he'd get all over them. He sometimes disagreed with other students and I will say that he was very emphatic about his beliefs, like on smoking and drinking."

Glenn pointed out, "We had athletes in school with tremendous potential who would drink the night before some event and the next day they'd make one good play and that was it. They were too tired to make another."

Lester Nusser is one of the boys who has his own recollection of how Glenn met the question of liquor and tobacco. "Anyone in Elkhart will remember that a lot of boys in town began to think they had to smoke and drink a little on the sly. Glenn always tried to talk them out of it. I've seen him do it a hundred times. When he talked to boys, or girls too, for that matter, it kind of soaked in, like it was their father talking to them. They took it seriously. He said things so they could understand."

"Brigham" Young remembered, too. "In these years there were no school buses. Athletes and coaches went to meets and games in private cars. Lon Hurley's father had a dairy and owned a Hudson car. When Lon was going we went in style.

"But sometimes we went in my old Ford. Glenn and I always went in my car. Varney was in the other car. Some of the boys liked to smoke. One time when we were coming home from Boise City, Oklahoma, we ran into one of the awfullest blizzards. The wind and snow were bearing right down on us. One of the boys lit up a cigarette, and Glenn, cold as it was, rolled the car windows down, said he wanted some fresh air."

"I told him to ditch it," Glenn recalled. "He didn't. That's when I rolled the windows down. When he got done smoking he wanted to roll them back up, but I said no, this place stinks. We'll leave them open. I just froze those boys all the way home. They all soon learned that when they went with me they didn't do those things."

Varney remembered a bag of rabbits that unexpectedly became his property one hot day during wheat harvest. He and Glenn were working in the harvest field for the same man— Varney on the combine, Glenn on a grain truck hauling wheat to the mill. Following common practice, the field, which was large, had been laid off in "lands" to facilitate cutting. The land being cut had been narrowed to a small triangle when Varney stopped the machine to empty accumulated grain into Glenn's truck. He looked over at the triangle of uncut land, knowing that all the small animals that had lived in what was now only wheat stubble were still in there. They would sure make good eating, he thought. Aloud he observed quite casually, almost as though he didn't expect to be heard, "I sure would like one of those jacks.'"Glenn went right on shoveling wheat back from the spout. He said nothing but grinned to himself. The combine was soon empty and Varney left for another round. When he got back Glenn had gone to the mill with his load of wheat. Varney pulled up to an empty wagon and looked to see if it was ready to load into. There, to his astonishment, he saw three rabbits running around loose.

"Glenn had caught them," Varney said. "He had been listening."

The speed of an adult jackrabbit is up to forty-five miles per hour.

All Glenn's life rabbits have played an important role.

Years later, when he had begun the lectures that took him all over the United States and sometimes abroad, he occasionally spoke of the role chasing rabbits in the pastures had played in his training as a miler. He said that older rabbits grow wise in the way of escaping pursuers by running in a straight line and so outrunning them, but rabbits that are inexperienced, even the young jacks, change direction and can be caught. When they lay back their ears, roll back their eyes to look behind, and discover a pursuer close on, they dodge. In such moments he had dodged, too, reached a hand down to feel for their sides, and if they were fat enough he took them home for a family frying pan. That was his story. And it began to get around.

Later he arrived in a town where he was scheduled to make an address. A group of former athletes met him at the depot. Immediately they went into a huddle and began to exchange recollections—all but Glenn and one other man. Finally the other man spoke. He said that he had heard of a track man, a miler, who had a most unusual way of training, and went on to tell the story Glenn had told on the lecture platform. Glenn looked at the cinders that flanked the railroad track. When the story ended no one spoke. Finally Glenn looked up. Every man was looking at him.

He grinned. "I still do it," he told them.

Myra Brown wanted to corroborate this story. She had a penchant for accuracy and truth. She checked on it when interviewing one of the boys Glenn and Ruth cared for on the ranch. She retold the story of Glenn Cunningham running down rabbits for dinner. "What about it, Johnny?" Myra asked when she had finished. "It seems a little unusual. Do you know of anything like this?"

Johnny was surprised. "Why Mrs. Brown," he said, "we do it all the time."

When Glenn was a high school freshman the only school races were the intramural races held in the spring at the Elkhart Track and Field Day Exercises. But beginning with his second year, Elkhart High School became a member of the Kansas State High School Activities Association, and its teams began appearing at meets throughout the area. How many races he ran in high school years, Glenn lost count. But he ran at every opportunity, and there were many opportunities.

This second year in high school, 1928-1929, he appeared at the Kansas State High School Track Meet in Emporia, the major sports event that closed the high school year. He won there. The following year, as a senior, he ran again in the Kansas State High School Track Meet, held that year in Manhattan, and again he won. His record for the mile: 4:28.3.

In April of his senior year, he appeared at the Kansas Relays in Lawrence. Those relays included both high schools and colleges. Relays were always a group of boys working together. Glenn liked them. Comradeship always meant very much to him.

At Lawrence, Dr. Forrest C. "Phog" Allen, the unforgettable

basketball coach for whom the Allen Field House was named, observed Glenn; so did H. W. "Bill" Hargiss, then head football coach who later became Glenn's track coach at Kansas University. Hargiss played a decisive role in Glenn's decision to make Kansas University his school. Glenn said that in basic fundamentals in all sports, Bill Hargiss was the best grounded; a highly superior coach, well organized. "Without question," he adds, "Bill was one of the greats."

A third man in Lawrence was also impressed with Glenn. He was then track coach, a man noted for his scholarship, a deep and serious thinker in many fields of interest. At the University of Missouri he was an outstanding all-around track and field athlete; in 1920 as a member of the U.S. Olympic Team, he had competed in the decathlon. If any aspiring athlete wanted to work toward chosen goals, he could count on help from Brutus Hamilton. Of Glenn, Hamilton said: "He will be the strongest miler ever to step on a track. His great strength, his courageous attitude, and his strong heart and lungs make up for his lack of normal legs."

The greatest impression made on Glenn those two times he was in Lawrence for the Kansas University Relays, however, was the university campus itself, often called the most beautiful in the United States.

En route to California during the California Gold Rush in 1854, Dr. Charles G. Robinson, who later became the first governor of Kansas, camped along the Kansas River on land that is now Lawrence. At that time he pointed out that the beautiful flat-topped hill that rose steeply from the bottoms along the river and flowed out into the west and southwest would be "an ideal site" for a state university. Five years later when he came back to the state as a western head of the New England Emigrant Aid Society, Dr. Robinson named the hill Mount Oread after the

Mount Oread Seminary at Worcester, Massachusetts, and built his home there. Later he gave this home and his land to the university. Mount Oread, often called "the Hill," still holds as the name of the campus.

Even as with Dr. Robinson, the beauty of this hill made a deep impression on the young athlete from Elkhart. Its magnificent trees and plantings, the grass that laid its velvet over the hill's gently undulating top, the ravines that cut sharply down its sides, the great building that represented the kind of learning Glenn had dreamed of since he was two years old, the magnificent view of the wide countryside where a finger of rain or a thunderhead might move up from the Vinland Valley to the south, mark the town with its loveliness, cross the river, and disappear in the far blue mist that was the hills of northeast Kansas—all this was magic, and it possessed him. When Glenn went home, Mount Oread accompanied him.

Quite suddenly after Glenn came back from winning his first race at the Kansas State High School Track Meet in Emporia, in May of his junior year, the people in Elkhart began to talk of sending him to Chicago to the Interscholastics. Everybody was caught up with the plan. He'd won the K.U. Relays for Elkhart; he had never been defeated.

Jim Heintz recalls that one night soon after Glenn had returned from the Emporia meet, he stopped at the mill to see him.

"Glenn, are you going to Chicago for the Interscholastics?" Heintz thrust the question at him.

"No," Glenn admitted. "Papa doesn't have the money and I don't think I can go."

"Well," Heintz said, "you go up and see the coach. Have him wire your entries. I'm going to see that you get to go."

News of Heintz's decision got around, and very soon Walter

Ford, Morton County Sheriff, came in to see Heintz.

"Jim, you're not planning to send Glenn and Varney to Chicago alone, are you?" Ford asked. "We've got a world champion here in Elkhart. He belongs to us all, and we want in on it."

Heintz thought it over. "Well," he said, "if that's the way you feel about it, Walter. If you want to go around and take up a collection, it's all right with me. But if you can't make it, I'm going to send them up there, myself."

So the ball started rolling. It was agreed among the men about town that it must be a community effort and—since nobody had much money—that everyone would be asked to give no more than ten cents. Otto Hitz, a farmer living in town, "passed the hat," and it is believed that others helped. Jim Heintz remembered that he put in "quite a bit."

All spring Glenn's training had been stepped up, sometimes under Varney's direction and observation, sometimes in pastures, even down the streets of Elkhart.

When the decision was reached that he would enter the Interscholastics, training intensified. The entire area was watching his efforts, a thing he was never conscious of. One of his sisters had married. Her husband's brother-in-law, Wayne Lewis, got out his Ford and rode alongside Glenn, always just a little faster than the pace Glenn set, to drain from his legs and heart and mind the last bit of capacity to run that was in them. For one of the only periods in his life, Glenn began to think of records.

On the train going to Chicago, Glenn began having trouble with a blister on one of his heels. It had formed during his stepped-up training period. He and the coach both looked at it. "It didn't show purple," Varney said. "I thought it was all right."

"When we got to Chicago, Glenn was like a caged lion. We went to the fraternity house across from Stagg Field where we were to stay. He went out on the track and after he'd worked out some, we walked all over Chicago. Normally that wouldn't have hurt him any. But next morning I noticed him shaking a lot. 'What in the world's the matter, Glenn?' I asked him. He said he didn't know, but he hadn't slept very well. I told him we'd better see a doctor. He didn't want to, much. He was crazy he'd not get to run. But I went ahead; I called a doctor. When he got there, Glenn had a temperature of 104½. He said that without any question it was blood poisoning. He would be all right in a few days, he said, but he'd have to go to the hospital. This was Wednesday. The race was Saturday. Glenn didn't take to the idea. The doctor insisted. Said Glenn would have to sign a release relieving him of all responsibility if he didn't. I told Glenn I thought he'd better go. So Wednesday night they put him in a hospital room and got him fixed up. Glenn still didn't like it. The nurses looked at him—and hid his clothes. 'How do I get this temperature down?' he asked one of them. She told him to tank up on ice water."

"I drank ice water every time I could swallow," Glenn related. "And I didn't eat anything but orange juice. I was determined to run."

When Saturday morning came, he got out of bed, weak but still resolute. "I told the nurse to get my clothes. I was getting out of there. She didn't get them. She got the doctor. My temperature was still 102. The doctor said that if I ran in the condition I was in I might have acute dilation of the heart and die on the track. I told him all right, but I was going to run. The coach and I both had to sign my release."

When they left for the track, the wind was high. Glenn had to hold on to Varney's arm crossing the street.

"I went out," Glenn said, "but I didn't warm up. I just laid there on the field till the race was ready and then I got up and ran."

"He started with the other runners," Varney said, "and he managed to stay with them up to about the last hundred yards. Then he began to drop back. Three boys pulled ahead of him."

"I lost," Glenn told Myra, and she could detect the traces of a feeling of failure still in his voice. "This was the only race I ever lost in high school."

"Glenn felt awfully bad about it," Varney said. "We both did. All the folks back home had been counting on him. We decided right away that we would come back the next year. If the community at home didn't raise the money to send us, we'd find a way to finance ourselves."

Glenn still was weak when the train pulled into Dodge City en route home. There they would take "the local" to Elkhart. The local stopped at every station and siding, not only for passengers, but also for milk cans and other local cargo. It gave Glenn and the coach an opportunity to get off and stretch. They both ached from train travel. When they reached Rolla, seventeen miles by rail from Elkhart, they were surprised to find Raymond and Clyde "Tiny" Moore waiting to take them the rest of the way in Tiny's car. Tiny was a fellow Elkhart athlete and close friend. It seemed like welcome relief to go the rest of the way by car, but they couldn't understand why the conductor insisted so strongly that they get back on board.

The road, which paralleled the railroad track, was dirt, but even so, as Raymond and Tiny knew, they'd get to Elkhart before the local, with all the switching it had to do.

But they had not counted on a "stinkin' little shower" that suddenly let down, making the road as slick as though it had been buttered. And neither Glenn nor Varney knew that waiting for the train in Elkhart, the town's band and hundreds of well-wishers from over southwest Kansas, southeast Colorado, and northwest Oklahoma had gathered to welcome Glenn home.

The conductor had known it, and Raymond and Tiny knew it. They still thought they could beat the train into town, and that all would be well. The car slid from side to side over the road. Tiny fought the steering wheel and tried to hurry. But the train had pulled into Elkhart and out, and most of the crowd had dispersed when they finally made their not-so-triumphal entry into town. People didn't know what to think. Some were considerably irked. Some had even gone on the train, thinking Glenn and the coach must surely still be aboard. Some were angry at what they thought was a low-down trick.

Glenn stopped at the mill on the way home.

"I knew he was a sick boy," Heintz remembered.

Full explanations were promptly made, saner minds prevailed, and the gloom faded from what had turned out to be a compromising situation.

During Glenn's senior year he and Varney went through all the necessary preparations for his second trip to the Interscholastics. He played basketball, football, and baseball. And once again the community began to look on with quickening pulse. They had once again raised funds and Glenn was in perfect condition when he and Varney left Elkhart for Glenn's second Interscholastics Chicago trip in June 1930.

Glenn was still in that finely honed condition when he took his place at the starting line in Stagg Field the day of the race. Coaches were not permitted on the field, but Varney managed to get over the fence and stood far down the track away from the finish line. "The crowd was enormous and excited."

Glenn always said that he ran his races from the shoulders up.

Actually his races were creations, a blend of timing, control, sense of pace, razor-sharp attention, and knowledge of his competition. Someone once said they were like music. Like a symphony.

He never knew how large crowds were or realized the roars that rose when he broke the tape. He was completely absorbed in the business of winning.

From its start, it was an outstanding race. "But," he added, "when I hit the last hundred yards I was just beginning to warm up, and I really opened up."

Any person who ever saw Glenn run during the years when he was "America's finest miler" remembers the terrific burst of speed this "opening up" meant. In Chicago that day people in the bleachers stood up. They roared. And still "the boy who would be a wheelchair patient all his life" came charging on. When he breasted the tape, the roar became a din. He was a hundred yards ahead of the runner-up. But he still was not tired. He didn't slow down. He turned around and headed back toward the spot where Varney stood holding his sweat clothes, the crowd still roaring behind him. In the middle of the field a man came toward him with his hand out. Glenn stopped. "Son," he said, "that was the greatest finish I have ever seen in any race, collegiate or high school." It was the great Amos Alonzo Stagg of Chicago, for whom Stagg Field was named

Glenn's time that day was 4:24.7, a new world record for high school milers, and the first world record he set.

It was a good trip back to Kansas the next day. When they reached Dodge City, there was Walter Ford, the sheriff, ready to board their train. He didn't tell them but they both knew he was there to ensure their arrival in Elkhart on time.

Glenn did get off the local while it was doing some switching at the little town of Montezuma. He waited until the last car was some distance down the track and slipping faster and faster away, before he sprinted to the rear steps and swung himself aboard. He was a miler and he hadn't gotten his running done yet that day.

When they reached Elkhart the crowd that closed in at the depot to greet them was enormous. Countryside and town, everybody was there from a hundred miles around. "Everybody but me," Jim Heinz lamented. "It was June. I just couldn't close down the mill."

"I think it kind of embarrassed Glenn," Harry Walker, the Elkhart store owner, recalled later. "I don't think he liked too much publicity. But he was a hero to the country, a champion. And he wasn't the least bit stuck up about it. People liked that."

Later Glenn stopped at the mill to see Jim Heintz, as he had so many times in the past.

The next morning the depot platform and the streets about town were littered with confetti and debris. Clint Cunningham was still street commissioner. At five o'clock he was down with his pickup prompt as always, cleaning up. And Glenn was with him.

"Some people were critical because I was out that morning," said Glenn. "They didn't feel it was fitting that I should clean up after the celebration of my breaking a world's record for the mile. But I always helped my father. I liked to work with him. I don't know why they should think I had changed in any way. I feel the same way now."

11

COLLEGE AND
THE BEGINNINGS OF FAME

I loved to go to school, always loved school. . . .

To bring us up to the present, given Glenn's involuntarily checkered scholastic history, some of what Glenn Cunningham said at Boston in April 1987 should serve as a quick review and take us to his college years:

When I went into the sixth grade my father said you had enough learning, you stay home, work, help support the family. I loved to go to school, always loved school . . . went back to work all the way through junior and senior high school, finished my high school in three years 'cause I'd never know when my father would get up one day and say this is the day you start staying home, work, and help support the family.

A few of you here are old enough to remember the Crash of 1929. I had been saving my money, I had planned on becoming a medical doctor, my grandfather was a pioneer medical doctor. I used to browse over his old medical books. The crash came, I lost everything I'd deposited in the bank. I worked in the summer of 1930 and believe it or not, I earned seven dollars and sixty-five cents.

The summer of 1930 was Glenn's last summer at home with

his parents. That fall he would be enrolled at Kansas University, the only school that, ironically, did not offer him a scholarship. But maybe not so ironic . . .

Officials from most of the leading colleges and universities in Kansas and nearby states approached Glenn about enrolling. Varney, a graduate of Kansas State Teacher's College, Pittsburg, felt that Glenn should attend a school with high national prestige. He made no recommendations. Several schools in California wanted him:

"I went off to go to California," he said to us in Boston, "teammate of mine [Lon Hurley] wanted me to look it over, I went out there and California was like nothing to me. I hated it; they had a hydrant with every plant, it was all green there but they had to have a hydrant and I couldn't get back to Kansas fast enough.

"I'd never been approached by a coach from the University of Kansas to go there. That's why I decided I was going to go. I arrived there, got a job and worked through four years."

What he revealed about his thinking at the time should give us a clue to both a stubborn drive for independence and a general mistrust of people's intentions. He shows this in what he confided to Myra Brown as to why he was without a scholarship: "I could have had but if I had accepted I would have been obligated and again, I did not know what the obligation might come to include."

There were also powerful people who wanted to direct him. For example, at that time there lived in Elkhart a man by the name of E. H. Fisher, a graduate of Purdue with a degree in civil engineering, a letterman in baseball who, for a brief period after graduation, had played professionally. Some years earlier when the Santa Fe Railway had extended its line from Dodge City to what is now Elkhart, Fisher had been employed as a construction engineer. The railroad completed, he laid out the town and named it Elkhart after Elkhart, Indiana, where he had lived as a boy.

The summer of 1930 Fisher focused his attention on Glenn. In every possible way he tried to get Glenn to think seriously of going to Purdue.

Although Glenn appreciated such interest, he knew that in one way or another favors must be repaid. He didn't know what the years ahead might hold. "Why mortgage the future?" he thought.

Kansas had always been his state. The University of Kansas had been the only school in the state that had not approached him in some way about enrolling. He liked that. The idea of schools bidding against each other for athletes had never appealed to him. He thought of the beautiful campus in Lawrence. He thought about the men on faculty he had known.

He was negative about a scholarship despite the precarious status of his finances. How had he earned money up to now and what became of it with the market crash?

We do know of his working in the summers, even during the school years. We know, too, of his turkey-plucking jobs. And at one time, before 1929 debacle, his college fund had grown so that he thought he had enough to see him through four years at a good university.

But then, on October 19, 1929, Glenn's last year in high school, Wall Street's stock market crashed. By December 31, the value of stocks had declined an estimated fifteen billion dollars. The biggest depression in American history had begun. For a time around Elkhart, as elsewhere, it was thought that the difficulty would soon pass, though farmers, stockmen, merchants, all businessmen began to quietly tighten their belts. It wasn't long, however, before men in increasing numbers began to be in financial difficulty, men Glenn had known for years, friends, men who had employed him during during high school years and paid him well, even those who had helped send him to Chicago. Glenn actually began to loan these men money out of his college fund, certain he could get it back when times got better. "When you need it, Glenn," they would say "Let us know when you get to college."

But times would get no better. Accumulations of lifetimes began to be lost. Many men with families would never be able to make a comeback. Glenn's college fund had dwindled steadily. Banks failed. At length his bank closed its doors. Eventually he would be paid a small percent of what was still left in his college fund—but never all of it. Most of his friends who had borrowed money from him would eventually pay him, but that will be the story of another career, one to begin almost two decades later.

So Glenn actually loaned money to many of the people who had once helped him, only to arrive at college with seven dollars and some change in his pocket.

And as if times weren't bad enough, there would be an additional unique problem for Kansas and the surrounding areas. General weather conditions that are the forerunner of protracted drought began to build up in the Southwest. The Dust Bowl that centered in northwest Texas and would reach into Oklahoma, New Mexico, southeast Colorado, and Kansas was on its way. In Morton County (Elkhart is the county seat), as elsewhere throughout the stricken parched land, soil loosened in plowed grounds and grasslands in the violent winds that prevailed. It rolled along the ground in clouds so dense a tall man could not always see his feet. The dust was like powder. It penetrated houses sealed against it. It lifted and swept high into the air above fields and valleys and rivers, some of it not to come to rest till it found ships at sea plowing through the Atlantic. Since this was topsoil, the soil that determines yields, farms, as far as productivity was concerned, literally blew away. When farmers were at last compelled to move, their farms were already gone. This drought was to last throughout Glenn's four undergraduate years.

Dust storm over Elkhart

Photo courtesy of the Morton County Historical Museum

He would arrive in Lawrence with exactly $7.65. His entire wardrobe was limited. He had only one pair of socks, but they were good ones, silk. He washed them out every night. He did his own laundry. All over the campus were students who might not have the money to pay for their laundry when it was returned, and it was not at all unusual for college men to own but one pair of socks.

Two students, Ed Hall and Gerald Menzi, found employment at a fire station where there were sleeping quarters but no provisions for meals. Boardinghouses, meals downtown, were out of the question. The only choice was to buy groceries and cook their own meals. Which they did. At the end of the school year they calculated that a meal that year had cost each of them exactly nine cents.

(An ardent reader and admirer of Thoreau and Emerson, Glenn Cunningham's life before and after college resonates with Thoreau's March 11, 1856, *Journal* note: "That Man is the richest whose pleasures are the cheapest.")

Their meager diet apparently did no harm. Hall became a sprinter and longjumper; in Glenn's final year at K.U. Hall ran with him on an unbeaten mile relay team.

From the beginning, Phog Allen, director of athletics and an osteopathic physician, maintained an intense interest in Glenn. Phog Allen thought that at times Glenn did not have enough to eat. Glenn admits that there were occasions when he went without meals, but it wasn't for the lack of money. It was just that he needed the money to do something for someone else. According to Pete Bausch, another athlete on the Hill, "Glenn more than any other athlete was just squeaking by, financially."

Glenn found employment that first fall at the stadium, mending and cleaning equipment, handing it out, scrubbing floors, and so on. He was paid forty cents an hour and he worked five and a half hours every day; "darn good pay at the time," he quipped. The first semester he carried fifteen hours. Studying, going to class, training, work at the stadium just about took his day.

But one more incident from Glenn's first year at K.U. should first be told. As the first semester neared its end, Glenn received two official communications. One was pre-enrollment papers indicating his intention to continue his schooling in K.U. during the second half-year. The other was an announcement that, beginning with the new semester, pay for work done at the stadium would be reduced from forty cents an hour to twenty-five cents.

At that time Glenn was not only using his influence, which

was already considerable, to find jobs for deserving students from southwest Kansas to make it possible for them to stay in school, but, cramped as he was meeting his own expenses, also *actually footing* some of their bills.

"I was budgeted down to a pretty fine point," he said. "I had to have every penny I had been making. Any reduction at all and I'd have failed some of these kids.

"My record in track at K.U. was still to be made. I thought the work I was doing was worth forty cents an hour. And I thought I had the capacity to make a record in track that would be of value to K.U."

He did not fill out the pre-enrollment papers. He began thinking of the desirability of attending the University of Nebraska. He kept his thoughts to himself.

Shortly, one of the coaches came in to see him. Glenn knew this coach to be fair-minded, a man he could talk to. When the coach asked why he had not sent in his pre-enrollment papers, Glenn told him. The coach listened carefully.

"I think it can be arranged," he said. Shortly Glenn was notified that his pay would continue at forty cents an hour.

When the second semester ended, Glenn took a position with an insurance company in Topeka, filing.

When he returned to Lawrence for his sophomore year, work at the stadium was resumed, again at forty cents an hour. All the students he had helped during his freshman year were back, and this year additional students had come. Eventually there would be eighteen boys and girls from southwest Kansas who owed their college education to Glenn.

"Glenn could get jobs for himself—and for others, for that matter!—that were not easy to get," Phog Allen remembered. He said that it was Glenn's personality, "his influence with the

Student Loan Fund that helped."

As another footnote to this helping out of others is a story, albeit a negative one, about his brother John. John had also done some running in high school. Glenn tried to encourage him to come to K.U. But Glenn caught him smoking and actually told the coach to kick him off the team. Naturally that alienated John; they were estranged for some time, only to reconcile many years after.

Glenn with his parents and brother John, circa 1931

How Glenn accumulated money and was able to help others is still somewhat of a mystery. The timing is unclear but another source was proposed in the interview with Harry Walker. Walker said that a Mr. Smith told him (Walker) that whenever he (Smith) found a piece of land that was very sandy during those dry years that was for sale, he'd send the details to Glenn. Glenn, in turn, had an uncle over by Rolla who was a witcher. The uncle would pitch his forked stick into the ground in question and, depending on what the stick indicated, would then make recommendations. The cost of the land was very little. Much of that land later sprouted gas wells. Glenn did eventually accrue gas revenues. Some of that money either went to his college costs and toward his postgraduate costs and purchase of the ranch at Cedar Point in the late 1930s.

Glenn's room soon became a place where other college men congregated. He had a rule: If students came they must bring a book. His room was his study, and his time was budgeted. Some of the big fellows, football players, two-hundred-pounders, took his rule lightly. Glenn was never overweight. When he ran his first race for K.U. during his sophomore year he weighed 179 pounds. But the big boys soon discovered that he could enforce his rule. They not only brought their books—they used them!

From the beginning there was a good deal of discussion among coaches and trainers about Glenn's legs.

M. Leon Bauman, the wrestling coach also served as assistant to H.W. Hargiss, football coach and head trainer for all athletes. Dr. Bauman learned a lot of what he used as a trainer from Phog Allen.

The head track coach was Brutus Hamilton, already considered "top flight as a person and top flight as a coach." Hamilton had come from Westminster College at Fulton, Missouri. Such was his standing at Westminster that two outstanding athletes at that school, Jim Cox and Ed Hall, followed him to K.U., where Jimmy Cox became assistant trainer to Leon Bauman. "Jimmy worked on my legs about an hour every day," Cunningham told Myra.

These were the men who took Glenn in hand when he reached K.U. and watched over him with increasing satisfaction through the years that followed.

"There wasn't a great deal we could do for Glenn when he came," Hargiss said as he sat in his living room with Myra Brown and reached back into a past rich in experience. "Both his legs were scarred to the bone, one with scars that reached to his hip, and one transverse arch in his foot that was broken.

"As a football coach, I had been primarily interested in him as a football player. He'd been a better football player in high school than he was a trackman, that is, in the beginning. And he was a fine basketball player. It wasn't until about his final year in high school that he came into excellence in track. His track career really began when he broke the world's record for high school milers at the Chicago Interscholastics.

"When he came to the University of Kansas we discouraged him about playing football. He'd have made a fine halfback or an end, or any place you put him. Glenn would excel in anything. In my opinion, Glenn could have been the world's champion middle-weight boxer, though he never boxed professionally. Glenn was terrific.

Cunningham and Coach Hargiss, circa 1935.

"But football! We were worried about his legs for football. We encouraged him to concentrate on track. We knew he had the ability for that."

Glenn was having excessive pain in his legs that first fall in K.U., a factor that probably carried considerable weight with the men who made this decision against football.

"I could hardly get on my feet to go out for track," Glenn remarked to Myra in the same interview with Hargiss. "I went out, but not regularly. I had been hit in the mouth by a baseball in high school. All eight front teeth were loosened. For a time the pain there was intense. The teeth all ulcerated. Eventually they tightened and most of the soreness left. But my legs still bothered me. It wasn't until ten years later that a dentist discovered that my ulcerated teeth were the cause. My legs being my weakest part, that's where the trouble showed up."

It was important to have Glenn firmly in the hands of a trainer. Glenn's first trainer at K.U. was Leon Bauman.

In a conversation Myra had with Dr. Bauman, he made the assertion that the basic work had already been done in Glenn's legs before he reached Lawrence. This basic work consisted of the massaging he and members of his family had done immediately after the burns had healed. "It is essential," Dr. Bauman said, "in burns as deep and extensive as Glenn's were that the massaging and stretching be done early. This is most important. In such cases there is always the possibility that fibrous tissue will develop in skin, muscle and tendons, contracting them and pulling them into a distorted form. A muscle once destroyed is never replaced by muscle tissue, only by fibrous tissue. What is left of sound muscle must be developed before contraction takes place.

"Although the basic work had been done in Glenn's case," he continued, "it was necessary to maintain the condition in his legs that he was maintaining when he came to K.U.

"And it was also necessary, then and later, to remember when he was on the training table for passive exercise, or to apply tape to his ankles or legs, that his skin and muscles were extremely tender. When an athlete develops a 'charley horse,' as often happens, it may be only a muscle spasm; on the other hand, it may tear a muscle. With Glenn, special care had to be given because of this possibility.

"Glenn must be given a great deal of credit for realizing early what had to be done and for sticking to his routine until he developed what muscles he still had in the scarred areas and other muscle to support them. Working to restore himself, to gain muscle balance and good tone meant a tremendous amount of self-discipline. This was his major pattern when he came to K.U., and it has always been his major pattern."

Bill Hargiss added: "The dedication of the boy has been reflected in the man in every field in which he has ever been active."

In a paper read before the National Collegiate Coaches Association in 1933, when Glenn was a junior in K.U., Hargiss presented in considerable detail the training program that was followed with Glenn, beginning at the time he enrolled in K.U. and continuing throughout his undergraduate years, and in addition Glenn's mental equipment that contributed to his continuing success. After Glenn's graduation from K.U., Hargiss continued to function as his ex-officio coach as long as Glenn ran in competition, and the same program continued to be followed. This period included the years when records for the mile were falling continually.

The coach offered this paper to Myra Brown. He said, in part: "To start with, every vital characteristic was carefully studied;

particularly his heart and lung condition, his nervous system, mental attitude, height and weight, muscular development, and form and style of running.

"Mentally, Cunningham has every essential for success. Scholastically, he is an honor student, but he does not believe everything he reads or hears. Good natured and even temperament, yet he has a mind of his own, and can be stubborn in his opinions until convinced otherwise. He has a will and determination to succeed that is almost undeniable. Never boastful, yet deep in his mind Glenn feels that there is not a man living he cannot defeat in a foot race. His willingness to learn and to improve make him an easy subject to coach.

"The training program for Cunningham has been one of under-distance running. Practically no over-distance running; seldom does he run three-quarters of a mile continuously in practice, yet I believe he can run two miles in less than nine minutes. When he works, he works hard. The work is varied with these objectives in view—speed, knowledge of pace and ease of effort, and improvement of form or style. For speed work he runs several 220's. For knowledge or judgment of pace, 440's, and for form and ease of stride, 660's and 770's.

"A typical mid-season training week is as follows: Sunday, a long walk. Monday, a rope skipping, shadow boxing, bag punching and calisthenics. Tuesday, 660's with fifteen minutes rest between, the first one with heavy basketball shoes and sweat suit in about 1:30; the second one with track suit and spikes in about 1:23 or 1:24. This is the hardest work of the week. Wednesday, judgment of pace work, about four 440's—62, 63, 61, 58. At the conclusion of each lap he swings into a fast walk for about 440 yards. Then with a one-minute rest, he swings into the next 440. He finishes this practice period with a 220-yard sprint. This work is done in a sweat suit and heavy basketball shoes. Thursday, work is light and for each of form, occasionally he wears spikes in this work. He usually runs the curves of the track and walks the sides or straightaways. Occasionally this day is used for starts and finishes, especially on indoor track. He starts in the middle of a group of runners near a curve and permits jostling, guarding himself from both pole and wall sides of the track without a break of stride. Friday, no work at all. He doesn't even suit up. Saturday, races. In traveling for races out of town, his training is confined to calisthenics and walking. He never goes on track to practice.

"At least thirty minutes before the start of the first race, he begins to warm up. This is one of the hardest work-outs of the week. First jogging and calisthenics, then wind sprints and 440's. Altogether he will run between two and three miles in his warm-up. He then lies down with his knees up for about five minutes before the start of the race. In meets where he runs more than one race, the second is always the easier and better race.

"He has a pretty definite pace figured out for all races and this pace is very even throughout, with the third and fourth quarters faster then the first and second.

"Off the track Glenn is a most religious trainer. There is no diet prescribed for him. He eats plain, simple food and not in large amounts. He eats very slowly. Drinks only milk and water, never coffee or tea; has never had a drink of alcoholic liquor of any kind; does not drink any fountain soft drinks; has never used tobacco in any form. Fruit and vegetables play a prominent role in his diet, but he eats meat, preferably beef, once or twice a day. About three hours before he runs he eats the biggest meal of the week, including a thick broiled steak. He sleeps regularly and aims to get at least eight hours sleep each night."

Coach Hargiss added the following relevant details for Myra's edification:

"We were pretty thorough with Glenn that first fall when we started him out on physical therapy. We even sent him up to Dr. Eddie Elbel in physical education. Eddie made many tests for heart reaction and response to vigorous exercise. Had him running up four flights of stairs in the gymnasium, up the stairs in the stadium, etc. We had a heavy barbell. Glenn'd drop down, get hold of that thing, throw it up on his shoulders and push up. Then he'd do the squats. To strengthen his legs.

"One of the most vigorous things he did and did for the longest time was rope skipping. That too was fine for his legs.

"And we had a punching bag down there. Glenn could just rattle that thing. It strengthened his arms. With distance runners, or any athlete, many times their arms will get so they can't use them before their legs play out. You gotta be strong all over. Now here is something I know to be true: I had used all those weights we had on the wrestlers and the football boys, and when I got to be track coach I used them on all my track boys too. I used weight lifting, heavy things, lots of it, parallel bars, horizontal bars, I used all of them.

"I never told all this to other coaches because at that time all the track personnel and trainers frowned on gymnastics, particularly on weight lifting, because they thought it made athletes muscle-bound. That was the generally held opinion that coaches went along with in those days. I even had that told to me by the head of the department of physical education in Harvard University's Summer School of Physical Education.

"And, by golly, there's another thing coaches turned thumbs down on in those days. That's swimming. Yet Jack Lovelock trained more in the swimming pool than he did on the track.

When he was at Princeton and he and Glenn each broke the world's record, he spent most of his time in the swimming pool.

"Well, that's what we worked with and how we worked.

"In all Glenn's racing in the years that followed, he held to the practice of the tremendous warm-up. He set the pattern, I think. It was a matter of the adjustment of the body, of the heart and lungs, and the metabolism of the muscles. The long warm-up eliminated the phenomenon of the second wind. This second wind, so-called, is just a phenomenon of the body catching up. Of eliminating carbon dioxide through perspiration, and through the lungs, to make ready for more oxygen. In other words, if you start out in a hard race without warming up—gee, I don't care how well trained you are, if you start out without warming up you're just not going to run very well; because of this business of the body adjusting to it.

"Glenn's normal heart rate was somewhere around 58 or 60, and his heart rate at maximum effort was around 160.

"But it would return to normal in ten or fifteen minutes and this is an indication of what I'm trying to say. When he started out in an actual race his heart had already picked up speed, he'd already eliminated the possibility of the so-called second wind. Because of his long warm-up, his muscles, his nerves, his elimination through lungs and skin, all were at highest efficiency. He didn't have to wait for them in the race.

"I don't think that I had very much to do with working out this racing plan that Glenn had, or that Brutus Hamilton had, or anyone else. Glenn had found it out all for himself. It's something every track athlete or any athlete going into extended physical exertion, does now-days, all of them.

"Now here's another thing about Glenn," Hargiss continued,

"and what went on down in our training quarters. Doc Riley, director of athletics at the Kansas City Athletic Club, had a professional fighter, a boxer up there. I think he'd won the Golden Gloves. He'd bring this professional boxer down to our training quarters to work out with this boxer, kept pestering the boys around there to box with him, spar him a little bit. Finally he got to concentrating on Glenn."

Hargiss laughs here.

"Now Glenn was a boy of very even temperament. This was about the first time I ever saw him kind of snap his eyes. This boxer Doc Riley had down there, was a light heavyweight and he wouldn't stop pestering Glenn. Glenn was busy with his training program, skipping rope, working on weights and bars, and so on. And finally he got tired.

"'All right,' he told the boxer, 'let me have those gloves!'

"Well, Glenn just about knocked the stuffin' outta that guy. He never boxed with Glenn again."

When Glenn Cunningham entered the university, the Big Six Conference had a ruling that no freshman could participate in college athletic events. (In addition to the University of Kansas, the Big Six included Kansas State University-Manhattan, the University of Nebraska, the University of Iowa, the University of Missouri, and the University of Oklahoma.) But with the beginning of his sophomore year, the ruling no longer applied to Glenn. By now his legs were giving him less trouble. Accordingly, training under Brutus Hamilton intensified.

The football season opened and he began accompanying K.U. football teams to make cross-country runs between halves of games with whatever member of the Big Six Conference

K.U. might be playing. These cross-country runs—which were the foundation work for middle-distance runners—were all two-mile dual team runs made on the track around the football fields. They became the first running Glenn did for the University of Kansas, and every race he ran he won, except one. This record earned for him a medal for being the outstanding two-miler in the Big Six Conference. His best time was 9:38.1.

These runs were extremely popular. Attendance at games was standing room only.

Glenn began to meet a variety of contestant types he had rarely encountered in his high school years: braggarts, show-offs, poor losers, boys who had not yet entirely grown up. Asked about poor losers, he told these stories:

"We had a boy in one of our conference schools, the Big Six. He was a senior when I was a sophomore, and he'd just been sweeping through everything in the conference. Apparently there was no competition at all for him. We went up there. We ran on the track, two miles between halves in a football game. When we got there, my coach, Brutus Hamilton, went out to talk with his old coach who was coaching this boy, and this kid happened to be there. And he said to Brutus, 'I hear you have a pretty good boy out there.' And Brutus said, 'Well, he's fair.' The kid said, 'I'll show you how good he is this afternoon. He won't even finish on the same side of the track as I do.' Brutus said, 'Oh,' mildly, like a man playing poker.

"So we both went out to the track to warm up.

"The papers had built this guy up a lot. They said, 'Why, he can finish that last quarter of that two miles so fast it'll take another quarter of a mile for him to slow down after the race is over.'

"Well, I knew it had never taken me a quarter of a mile to

slow down after any race. If I ran a fifty-yard dash I could be stopped in a few steps because I couldn't go that fast. I was really worried because I didn't know too much about this big competition at this time. This was the first and only time Brutus ever went out on the track with me. He said, 'Glenn, if I want you to speed the pace up, I'll just motion you on out. If I want you to slow down, I'll motion you back.'

"Naturally, I hoped he would motion me back, because I thought I could beat him on the sprint; I had pretty good speed. But he had built himself up as a speed demon.

"Later Brutus told me that when the race started you could really see the cockiness dripping from him. He jumped into the lead and took off, and I followed him for the first lap. The pace wasn't too bad and I was right on his shoulder all the way. When we came by the next time, boy, was he pleased and arrogant, so confident. When we came by the next time, Brutus motioned me out into the lead. I thought, oh, well, I'll take it for one quarter and then I'll drop back. The next time when we came around the kid was still so pleased and arrogant, so Brutus motioned me out a little bit faster, and every lap after that I kept thinking I'd get to drop back and follow pace, but every lap Brutus would motion me out faster. 'Speed 'er up! Speed 'er up!' he'd say.

"About the fifth lap, he told me, this boy's cockiness began to change. He got real serious, and by the end of the mile and a half he was hurting, and boy, on the seventh lap it was just sheer agony for him.

"By the end of the seventh lap, as we came around to start on the last lap, Brutus said, 'Give it all you've got, Glenn.' Man, I really hit that back stretch. The crowd stood up and started cheering. I thought to myself, 'here he comes.' But I was afraid to look back. I was afraid he would be there, so I just drove down the straight-away with all I had. As I broke into the last turn I thought I could hear his feet beating down right behind me. Man, I drove down that track. I don't think I ever traveled a hundred yards as long as that one was, and every step I could hear him right behind me, right at my shoulder.

"When I stepped across to break the tape and turned around to shake hands with him, he was clear back, just coming into the last turn. He wasn't even on the same side of the track I was on, which was what Brutus had decided must happen.

"All the time what I heard was that darned number they had pinned on my back. It had gotten loose some way and was flapping in the wind. With all the roar of the crowd and everything, I couldn't tell what the noise was.

"The cheering was because I was pulling away from this fellow who had never been beaten before. The crowd was really going wild. Of course, Brutus didn't tell this till afterwards.

"I was tired when this race was over and I walked off the track, picked up my warm-up suit and instead of putting it on, started to walk away in the direction of the point where we had finished the race. And that moment the wind sprang up a little and flipped that number and once more it sounded like someone right behind me. Then I knew what had happened."

With the closing of the football season, Glenn went south to begin his first season in competitive running at the Sugar Bowl in New Orleans. It was an outdoor mile, and he ran it on New Year's Day. He no longer remembers his time.

Next for Glenn came the Big Six indoor meet in Kansas City at Old Convention Hall. Glenn gave this account: "In those days they didn't run boys like they did when I got up there. I ran the mile and then I ran the half-mile and then I ran the two mile. To me it was nothing. Each race I just ran fast enough to win the race and that was all there was to it, although I think I got a new record on a couple of them. And I know Shulte was the coach in Nebraska and he was very much impressed as well as everybody else, and he got out there, they didn't have a loud speaker. They just had an old megaphone and he was part Indian and you could hear him for a mile and he got out and the meet had just ended and he put his arm around my shoulder and walked over where he could speak to the crowd and told what a remarkable performance it was, one that they had never seen before and might never see again, or something like that."

At this point in the taped interview, Myra asked Cunningham whether he had ridden with Phog Allen that day. He hadn't. But at the time, riding with Phog Allen was a thing of inestimable value. Paul Borel, ninety-two, a track teammate and classmate, wrote me of his shared memories of events with Glenn. Among them was "the lengths we would go to in order to ride with Phog Allen, director of athletics and famed basketball coach, who always had the best car, a Buick, when lean budgets dictated that coaches transport the track team to meets held away."

Next Glenn came north to run the Bankers Mile in Chicago, sponsored by the *Chicago Daily News*. Like all big winter meets back east, it was an indoor mile and his first big one.

At this meet he first met "the big boys" of the day. There were Ray Conger, an Iowa great, Glen Dawson of Oklahoma, Frank Crowley of Manhattan College, New York, and others, all top runners who were just finishing their careers.

"And I was a country boy as green as they get. When I reached Chicago I got off at the LaSalle Street station, got a cab and started for the Windemmer Hotel where a room had been reserved for me. The driver drove all over Chicago. The doorman at the hotel asked me what he had charged me. I told him and he said, 'He took you sightseeing.' It was five times what it should have been, and money was money.

"Oh, but it was cold that day, and I was facing the lake. Coming from Kansas, I had not been around a lot of water much and the wind was high. The lake was really churning.

"I weighed 179 pounds stripped, which was pretty heavy. When I went down to the arena I wore heavy sweats to help me to get warm. I went out to the track, as usual, to warm up. Just jogged. Up in the gallery there was a bunch of hoodlums, and they got to razzing me, bundled up as I was. Every time I'd go by they yell, 'Hey, fats! When's the fat man's race coming up?'

"When they finally called the mile, my legs, which were always sensitive to temperature, were still cold. I went out, but I didn't want to take off my sweats till I had to. Finally I did take off my uppers, but I was just starting to un-zip the rest of my warm-ups when the starter called, 'Go to your marks.'

"I thought he'd wait till we all got out on the track, but maybe he didn't know I was running. I was just jerking out of the last of my sweats when they popped the gun, and away went the other fellows, all big milers. Gosh, they were almost to the first turn before I got to the track!

"As I went around the first turn that bunch of hoodlums in the balcony began yelling, 'Hey, fats, they went that-away!'

"But it didn't take me long to catch up." And as he put it when asked if he won: "Yes, I managed to."

His time was 4:19.2, not an outstanding record, but nevertheless a record, and a win over America's record breakers.

A gold medal set with a diamond was the trophy for this

mile. "On that first medal I put a chain on it," Glenn remembered, "put a link on it and a chain on it and gave it to my mother. The first watch I got I also gave to my mother." She was for him *the* one person who, more than anyone else, had saved his legs for him.

In the years that followed, Glenn won dozens of gold watches.

As the college school year of 1931-1932 wore on, Glenn began to run and to win a good many significant mile runs. His reputation as a miler burgeoned. Now the 1932 Los Angeles Olympiad was in his sights.

12

1932 AND THE
LOS ANGELES OLYMPIAD

He didn't know that was the worst thing he could have said to me. Trying to talk me out of the race.

Cunningham again traveled to Chicago for the National Collegiate Athletic Association meet. His event, the one-miler, would be held on Saturday, June 11, 1932.

Cunningham mentioned that "the guy [who] never learned anything," a runner for Iowa, was also in this contest.

"That spring he was at Chicago for the Intercollegiate National Meet. He was in the mile, and Brocksmith of Indiana, and I was in the mile and a bunch of others. He came around to see me, he was tall, probably better than six feet tall, and he said, 'Cunningham, how do you feel today?' And I said, 'Oh, it's a little too cold for me. I don't like this cold weather.' 'Boy,' he said, 'This is just what I like. This is the day you and old Brock won't finish on the same side of the track as I am. I'm really going to lay it on you.' He never learned.

"He didn't know that was the worst thing he could have said to me. Trying to talk me out of the race.

"Brocksmith was an outstanding runner. We all went out. I just hung onto him. Brutus had told me to be right on him when we came on the third lap, and 'When you come off the first turn at the lap, take him!'

"Well, I thought it would be my best bet to wait till he came off the last turn, because I did have a lot of trouble with my legs. A lot of times, sprinting would just about kill me. It felt like somebody'd hit me with a dagger in my legs, especially in the thigh where the deepest burns had been and where most of the chunks of muscle had fallen out. Well, I went by old Brock. He tried but he just couldn't hang in there, and I kept on driving all the way in. When I broke the tape I looked back *and there was this other guy* a way back on the back-stretch struggling along. When he came in finally, he said to me, 'Oh, I could've won today, I had it. I just didn't put it out.'"

Glenn won in 4:11.1, breaking the preexisting national collegiate record by six seconds. This, too, was the fastest outdoor mile ever accomplished in America. He beat Brocksmith by only a few steps. In telling of this, his delight lay not in the record breaking but in beating the arrogant Iowa runner. This race apparently qualified him to enter the Olympic trials to be held a month later in Palo Alto, California. He would be vying with other runners for a place on the American Olympic Team.

"The summer of the Olympics I didn't work," he remembered, "I just trained. That was at the end of my sophomore year. There was Jim Bausch, Buster Charles of Haskell Institute, and Clyde Coffman. They had all qualified for the decathlon representing the United States. Brutus was coaching them and I had qualified and he was coaching me so we all worked out there together up at Lawrence, every day. Waiting for the Olympic games."

Newspaper clippings, even Glenn's reportage, do not seem to note the actual results of the Palo Alto tryouts. There is one mention that when Glenn did make the team, he finished in third

GAMES OF THE Xth OLYMPIAD LOS ANGELES 1932

Xth Olympiade Committee
OF THE GAMES OF LOS ANGELES
U. S. A. 1932
LTD.
W. M. GARLAND BLDG., 117 WEST NINTH ST.
LOS ANGELES - CALIFORNIA

WELCOME TO OLYMPIC VILLAGE

The Olympic Village has been built specially for you. It will be your home for the next several weeks.

Here for perhaps the first time in history, the chosen youth of all nations dwell in one community and share a common life.

This plan is in accord with the Olympic ideal "to increase friendly understanding by bringing the youth of the nations together".

The discipline in the Olympic Village is left to you and your friends who live here. Let us all demonstrate to the world that Olympic self-discipline can produce a record of peace and happiness among the two thousand inhabitants of the Village.

It is the desire of the Olympic Village management to render you every possible service for your health and comfort during your visit with us.

We extend to you our best wishes.

Cordially yours,

Xth Olympiade Committee

By *Wm. M. Garland*

President

Jayhawker Olympic Stars

CUNNiNGHAM   COFFMAN   MEHRINGER

These three undergraduate students of the University of Kansas were members of the United States Olympic team last summer. Peter J. Mehringer of Kinsley, Kans., won the Olympic light heavyweight wrestling championship. He starred as a tackle on the Kansas football team in 1931 and 1932. Glenn V. Cunningham of Elkhart, Kans., ran the 1,500 meters for Uncle Sam and finished fourth, the first of the three Americans to finish in the Olympic finals. Cunningham is national collegiate mile champion through winning that race at Chicago last June in 4:11.1, the fastest outdoor mile ever run in America and he has won several important indoor mile runs in the east and middle west this season. Clifford Clyde Coffman of Ford, Kans., was a member of the United States decathlon team in the Olympics and finished seventh. Coffman has been Big Six pole vault champion. He is not competing this year although in school. Coffman, with James Bausch, Kansas City Athletic Club and former University of Kansas star, and Wilson "Buster" Charles of Haskell Institute, comprised the U. S. Olympic decathlon team and all three trained at the Kansas stadium.

These three undergraduates now are added to the list of University of Kansas Olympians which includes Fay Moulton, sprinter, 1904 Olympics; Everett Bradley pentathlen, 1920 Olympics; and Tom Poor, high jumper, and Merwin Graham, hop step and jump, both of the 1928 Olympic team.

place among the contestants, behind Norwood Hallowell and Frank Crowley. (The first three make the team.) Gene Venzke, who had eclipsed the then 4:10 psychological barrier early in 1932, surprisingly failed to qualify. He had finished fourth, just behind Glenn Cunningham.

Sometime early in August, days before running his event held inside the Los Angeles Coliseum, Glenn had a fever of 102 degrees, attributed to acute tonsillitis. This was persisting at the time of the actual event.

Glenn ran the 1500-meter event (about 120 yards short of a mile). All Olympic events, in deference to the international standards, are in meters.

After the usual jockeying for position with the lead changing hands several times, by the second lap Cunningham was uncharacteristically in the lead. Just behind him was Phil Edwards of Canada. Though ahead in the pack, his pace per quarter mile was slower than he had run in his record-breaking Chicago appearance. When the bell sounded for the final lap, Glenn and Edwards were twenty meters ahead of everybody. With about three hundred meters to go, John Cornes of Great Britain and Luigi Beccali of Italy began to make their bid.

To anyone who has ever seen newsreel clips of Cunningham racing, what stands out is his blazing, truly blazing, finishes. He knew how to pace himself so that he'd run the last half of a race faster than the first. But this day it would not be.

Edwards caught and then passed the now struggling Glenn Cunningham. The five-foot six-and-a-half inch chunky frame of Beccali would then, with a hundred meters to go, overtake Edwards. Watching the newsreel clip you can see Cunningham begin to pump his arms. He depended on his upper body to supply the drive to the finish. He had often said he could not always rely on his legs. What you see are arms pumping like pistons only to power wobbling deflated tire wheels that are chugging behind the upper body, failing to respond.

Beccali won in 3:51.2, a new Olympic record. John Cornes was less than half a second behind, followed in another two-tenths of a second by Edwards, and then Glenn six-tenths of a second later in fourth place. The other two Americans, Hallowell and Crowley, finish sixth and eighth respectively. Little noticed was the finish of Jack Lovelock of New Zealand in seventh place. Lovelock and Cunningham would have more epic races in the years to follow.

On August 11 a *New York Times* front-page headline alerted the world to Adolf Hitler: EXPECTED TO BE CHANCELLOR IN CABINET SHAKEUP. At the medal ceremony Beccali had flashed the fascist salute. Mussolini and Hitler would soon be firmly in power. Beccali would later emigrate to the United States, becoming a successful wine merchant.

In all of the interviews and newspaper writings there is no mention by Glenn of his tonsillitis. Nor does Glenn offer any alibi for his atypical performance. The sports editor of the *Emporia Gazette* in a letter to his newspaper described the 1500-meter contest:

"At the three-quarter mark, the Kansas University flash was out in front with a comfortable lead and only Edwards of Canada close to him.

"Then down the stretch it became apparent that something was wrong. The Kansas runner did not have his usual kick down the straightaway. His legs tied up. First Edwards, then Cornes of Great Britain, and finally Beccali of Italy, swept by him, the Italian headed for a great finish and victory."

The article then went on to give Coach Brutus Hamilton's explanation: "Brutus Hamilton, his coach, explained that the

Kansan runner had not had enough time to properly warm up. The runners are permitted on the field only ten minutes before their events. This is not enough for Cunningham, who has trouble getting proper circulation through a pair of legs severely burned when he was a youngster. His heart and lungs had it yesterday but his legs didn't."

How reminiscent this is of Roy Varney's description of Glenn during high school years: "The only trouble I ever had with him in track was getting him warmed up before a race. And if he ran two races in one meet the second race was always better than the first. It took a mile, two miles, maybe more to get his leg muscles loosened up."

Brutus Hamilton, in 1933, now Coach Brutus Hamilton of the University of California at Berkeley, wrote a praiseworthy article appearing in the March issue of *The Amateur Athlete*. From its prose, it could have been titled *Ad Astra per Aspera*. These paragraphs illustrate that very theme:

"Glenn Cunningham is a son of the prairies. He has added to the traditional resourcefulness and endurance of his pioneer forbears a courage seldom equaled. The Kansas prairie is no place for a crybaby. There's work to be done and a boy is soon initiated to it. Cows to milk, wheat to harvest, hay to put up, wood to chop and chores to do. It's a hard life but a wholesome one and furnishes an excellent background for future athletic attainment.

"Like most western Kansas boys, Glenn Cunningham has known much hard work. He can bust a bronc with the best, can corral the unruly herd and can scoop as much wheat as any man in Morton County. He works hard, he plays hard, and woe to the opponent who takes him lightly."

His performance would tail off for the rest of that year. In September his tonsils were surgically removed. In the years to come, however, there would be more wins, more records, and one more Olympiad.

That November, Franklin D. Roosevelt was elected president of the United States, winning decisively over incumbent Herbert Hoover. And a month later Professor Albert Einstein was granted a visa to enter the United States.

13

1933

This nation will endure as it has endured, will revive and will prosper.

March 4, 1933 . . . a bleak cold day, a day reflecting the mood of a Depression-racked nation, found a hundred thousand people watching and millions more huddled around radios, all straining to hear words that might uplift them. Those words would be spoken by a paraplegic polio-stricken man whose erect posture was aided by ten pounds of steel braces on each leg and a generous lean on his son, James Roosevelt, standing to his left.

"I am certain that my fellow Americans," Franklin D. Roosevelt began, "expect that on my induction into the presidency I will address them with a candor and a decision which the present situation of our nation impels. . . . This nation will endure as it has endured, will revive and will prosper. So, first of all, let me assert my firm belief that the only thing we have to fear is fear itself. . . ."

During the two preceding months, the track headlines leading up to the February Madison Square Garden's Millrose Games and its Wanamaker Mile reflected the country's need to find a hero, a hero who also had been struck down, who had endured, and who had revived. These headlines repeatedly alluded to the fire, to "Scarred Legs," to the "Schoolhouse Fire that cost the Life of the Champion Middle Distance Man's Brother [that] Only Served to Intensify His Fighting Spirit." There were photos and cartoons; all echoed the public's need for a hero who had been felled but who had risen and who had—in a sense—prospered.

In the doing, however, writers often abused their literary licenses and engaged in much gratuitous gilding of the lily. There was even a cartoon of Glenn winning that race where the shiny medal eluded him. Rather than the bib overalls, basketball shoes, and woolen socks that he actually did wear, he is depicted as clothed in running shorts and T-shirt. So much for historical accuracy.

From the *Kansas State Star*, July 18, 1933.

Such gilding of the lily probably went unnoticed given the needs of the public. One cartoon even showed a victim being carried away outside the schoolhouse (all of the Cunningham children ran home and only then did they receive any aid).

SEVERELY BURNED IN A FIRE THAT DESTROYED THE SCHOOLHOUSE WHEN HE WAS 8, THE CHAMPION HAS ACHIEVED HIS PREEMINENCE AS A RUNNER ON BADLY SCARRED LEGS.

Bill Hargiss remarked on the literary license writers were taking. "I do a lot of painting," he said. "You sometimes think you can improve on what you've done. Well, I suspect that many of these writers wrote for the effect, rather than for the reality of the thing."

George Currie, a writer guilty of some of the exaggerations, said that the mile was to track what the heavyweight championship was to boxing, the Yale-Harvard game to football, even the Kentucky Derby to horse racing; the Wimbledon to tennis and Waterloo to Napoleon.

And the eyes of the track world were focused on two runners: Glenn Cunningham and the young Gene Venzke of the University of Pennsylvania, world-record holder in the indoor mile at 4:10. HOW GOOD IS VENZKE? one headline read. Writers were trying to build this up into a grudge match because Glenn had beaten out Gene the summer before for an Olympic berth.

The track arena for this media-hyped rivalry of the day would be the twenty-sixth running of the Wanamaker Mile of the Millrose A.A. Games to be held at the old Madison Square Garden.

The founder of the Wanamaker stores in Philadelphia in 1861 and in New York City in 1896 was John Wanamaker. In 1907 Rodman Wanamaker, John's son, was head of the Wanamaker business. At that time the Philadelphia and New York employees decided to form separate athletic associations, with both groups wanting to use the name *Wanamaker*. Mr. Wanamaker objected to the "commercialization" of the store name and suggested that the names of his two Philadelphia-area homes, Meadowbrook and Millrose, be used instead. And so the Philadelphia association became the Meadowbrook A.A. and the New York association became the Millrose A.A.

In 1908 athletic competition ensued between the two associations that also included competition with teams from other department stores. In New York the Millrose Games track meet began in 1908 and continued to 1910 at now unknown sites. From 1911 to 1913 the meet, then open to all amateur athletes, was held in various armories. Because of overwhelming crowds, in 1914 the meet was held at Madison Square Garden, then located at Madison Avenue and 24th Street.

In 1916 Rodman Wanamaker presented a trophy to the winner of the mile and a half, then the most popular event in the games. In 1926 when the Garden and the Millrose Games moved to 50th Street and Eighth Avenue, the event became the now famous and charismatic Wanamaker Mile. In 1969 the games moved to the "new" Madison Square Garden at 32nd Street and Seventh Avenue.

Although the New York Wanamaker store closed in 1955 and all the Wanamaker stores eventually ceased operations, the Millrose Games, including the Wanamaker Mile, endured. It is the oldest continuous sports event in the history of Madison Square Garden.

On February 3 1933, seventeen thousand track fans crowded into the Garden, "thrilled to one of the most exciting meets ever staged in New York," The SRO sign came out an hour before games time, "leaving hundreds in the snow outside clamoring for any kind of admission."

Glenn Cunningham, described as "a thick-set youth from the University of Kansas," staged one of his patented finishes. "The roar sent up by 17,000 track enthusiasts, filling Madison Square Garden with a deafening din, acclaimed the downfall of the king of the indoor milers [Venzke] and the rise of a new American idol . . ."

Glenn won by six yards, finishing in four minutes and thirteen seconds. The newspaper account said that he jumped past Venzke with an eighth of a mile to go. This was vintage early Cunningham, laying back until he could assure himself that his legs were going to hold up, then pouring it on. There would be more reprises for the rest of the decade. It was the beginning of a long rivalry but also of a lifelong friendship marked by mutual admiration and respect.

A side story of how he got to Madison Square Garden is of some note. Dr. Phog Allen, legendary basketball coach at the University of Kansas, told this in a telephone interview, July 21, 1967:

"On January 20, 1933, at the annual Kansas-Missouri basketball game being played at the Hoch Auditorium in K.U., a big baggage trunk was rolled out on the floor between halves, loaded with packages and boxes. Everybody in Lawrence knew Glenn was short of clothes, in fact, that he had only one pair of pants and a coat that didn't match. In that day coats had to match pants. And everybody thought an awful lot of Glenn. They honored him. They followed his racing, etc. They knew he was scheduled to run in the Wanamaker Mile and all of Lawrence knew he could not be allowed to go east and run against Gene Venzke, appear at the banquets that would follow, without being suitably outfitted.

"Glenn Charlton, a local insurance man, was the moving spirit in assembling a wardrobe for Glenn: a tux, shirts, underwear, everything a man would need. The trunk was completely filled with clothes, a complete wardrobe."

There is another item. It has to do with how he saved money; whether on this trip or others to come is uncertain. Roy Varney related how the athletes were paid first-class Pullman fare, but that Glenn traveled chair car and would get off at a station when there was time to stop and run in and get himself a hamburger. So he didn't eat on the train, and he saved that money.

In anticipation of the very next event, the Hunter Mile at the Boston Athletic Association's games, that morning Coach Hargiss made a statement that could apply to practically any of Glenn Cunningham's races: "Cunningham will not be trying to break any records tonight. How he runs," he said, "depends on the competition. He will go to the mark with the idea of winning, and for the love of racing."

The Boston event was actually a tune-up. The big match following the grand Wanamaker Mile challenge was the Baxter

Mile, part of the New York Athletic Club's games at Madison Square Garden. Here he would meet Gene Venzke, Glen Dawson, and Frank Crowley. It was anticipated that Venzke's 4:10 world indoor mark would be eclipsed. In fact much had been written about the twenty-three-year-old University of Pennsylvania freshman's running ten to fifteen yards slower this year compared with his year-ago 1932 performances. One headline read: THE COLLAPSE OF VENZKE IS ONE OF THE BIG MYSTERIES OF TRACK.

Glenn's schedule was to go back to Kansas after the Boston run only to return the following Saturday for the Baxter Mile. Following that there would be six scheduled races taking him into late March 1933.

In an article just before the Baxter Mile, a writer spoke of Glenn's dislike for indoor racing: ". . . the smoke-laden atmosphere nauseates him and he never gets a chance to warm up properly."

Before a gathering of twelve thousand at Madison Square Garden he would win the Baxter Mile of the New York A.C. in 4:14.6. Writing in the February 19, 1933, *New York Times*, prominent and classic sportswriter Arthur J. Daley had this to say:

"The return match between these two milers was an infinitely more spectacular duel than their fight in the Millrose meet was. Venzke was more like the Venzke of 1932, with a long blinding sprint for the entire last lap, a mighty effort that would have wilted any ordinary miler.

"But the Jayhawk star is not an ordinary miler. Where others would have faded before the dazzling burst from the smooth-striding national champion [Venzke], Cunningham clung to the Penn yearling.

"As fast as Venzke went, Cunningham stayed with him in a

final whirl around the boards that pulled the crowd to its feet with a roar of acclaim. Then, just as Venzke shot into the final turn, the Kansan chopped his stride and started to climb. As their spikes pounded into the banked turn, Cunningham had drawn up to Venzke's shoulder.

"As though handcuffed together, they ran for perhaps ten strides. Certainly it was no more. Then Cunningham drew ahead. Venzke tried hard to stay with him but he could not match the tremendous power of the Kansan's sturdy legs. Cunningham's lead was clear cut and as he broke the red worsted, Venzke was four yards behind."

But no one should have counted Venzke out. He was described by Grantland Rice as ". . . a fine type of athlete—quiet, serious, smart, courageous, with almost every qualification a champion needs. He has shown both stamina and speed—plus the heart that a star miler needs."

A few meets later, in the 1500-meter National A.A.U. Indoor Championships at New York City, Venzke managed to just edge out Cunningham in the time of 3:55. Arthur J. Daley again waxed eloquent in his description of the contest. Writing in the February 26, 1933, issue, he penned these passages:

"Gene Venzke finally has beaten his nemesis. Last night in one despairing lunge the Pennsylvania freshman went hurtling through the tape to fall prostrate on the track. But he had defeated Glenn Cunningham of Kansas, successfully defended his 1,500-meter championship and provided the supreme thrill of the forty-fifth annual American track and field title games before a gathering of more than 16,000 in Madison Square Garden."

Both had driven themselves to exhaustion. Both lay exhausted on the track, neither knowing who had won. When it was announced that Venzke was the winner, the applause was deafening—now he had become the underdog who had triumphed, his driving finish having bested Cunningham's.

"The big point," Daley wrote, "is that Venzke's victory very likely has restored in the world's record holder all the confidence that his Olympic failure took away."

The stage was now set for the Columbian Mile, Knights of Columbus meet, New York City, to be held at Madison Square Garden on March 15, 1933.

Venzke may very well have regained confidence, perhaps too much confidence. Before fifteen thousand spectators, Gene Venzke set a torrid pace and was in the lead as the gun sounded signaling the final lap. But now little Carl Coan of University of Pennsylvania spurted ahead, only to be matched by the accelerating Cunningham who had the same idea. Coan was soon passed by Glen Dawson who would come in second, one yard behind Cunningham, with Coan trailing Crowley by two yards. And into fourth place—depleted, his tank having run empty, his strategy of trying to run his competitors into the ground having failed—struggled Gene Venzke. Cunningham's winning time was 4:12.

With many of the competitions, the Cunningham story of the fire and of his impaired leg circulation would be retold. In ordinary times the theme, with so much repetition, would have been relegated to the realm of banality. But these weren't ordinary times. It was the depths of the Great Depression. Repeated along with the fire incident was the universal theme of *Ad Astra per Aspera*: "The present king of milers hails from wide-open spaces," Edwin Dooley of the *New York Sun* wrote, "where hard work is an honorable occupation."

With the March 15, 1933, winning of the Columbian Mile, the newspapers heralded Cunningham's fourth defeat of Venzke in less than a year.

Glenn's best time for the one-mile event that year was a 4:09.8 at Chicago's National Intercollegiate. He won by forty-five yards. It was a new American record for the mile.

That 4:09.8 win caught the attention of Dan Ferris, secretary of the Amateur Athletic Union. "It was the greatest double performance ever," Ferris said. Cunningham had also run the 880, coming in second by an estimated two inches. The winner, Charles Hornbostel of Indiana, equaled the American record for the half-mile.

There was another side story. Hargiss noted that Glenn was unusually hot after winning the mile, that his mouth and lips were parched. A fellow coach suggested that a lemon might help. Hargiss searched vainly through the concession stands for a lemon. Finally he grabbed a taxi for a drive to the Loop where he was able to buy a lemon for five cents. The round-trip taxi fare was $1.40, making a total of $1.45 and creating headlines that read about how a lemon costing $1.45 aided in winning a great race. (Actually, he hadn't won that second race.)

There would be a lot of running left for that summer. Picked along with Glenn Cunningham for a European tour of six countries were George Spitz of the New York A.C., high jumper; Johnny Morris of Louisiana, hurdler; Joe McCluskey of the New York A.C, long-distance runner (Glenn was considered a "middle distancer"); Ralph Metcalfe of Marquette, a sprinter; and Ivan Fuqua of Indiana. Cunningham was selected captain of the team.

Headlines touting the tour alluded to Cunningham's intention to double up on races since his second race of the day was often his better effort. Track headlines now told of his stellar performances, all wins with some new records, and often he would share headlines with "Negro" Ralph Metcalfe (THE K.U. STAR WINS

The U.S. team that toured Europe in 1933 (L to R): George Spitz, Glenn Cunningham, Johnny Morris, Ivan Fuqua, Ralph Metcalfe, Joe McCluskey, John Anderson, Henry LeBorde.

1500 METERS AND NEGRO BREASTS TAPE AHEAD OF 200-METER FIELD, or RALPH METCALFE, NEGRO STAR FROM MARQUETTE UNIVERSITY).

Between July 19 and August 17, Cunningham won twenty-six straight races. He left the tour ahead of time to be on time for the beginning of classes in September. The rest of the team went to Italy and some of them to Japan at the invitation of a Japanese newspaper.

He returned to Elkhart where, on a Saturday, he received the key to the city from Mayor Carl S. McClung. It would be "Cunningham Day," featuring a talk by Glenn giving a résumé of the tour, a "few words" from Coach Varney, three rounds of boxing with brother John as one of the participants, and a band concert at 8 P.M.

RETURNING K. U. TRACK STAR IS GIVEN KEY TO HOME TOWN

Glenn Cunningham shown at Elkhart, Kas., receiving the key to the city from Mayor Carl S. McClung. Cunningham returned from a European tour that was replete with trophies for the famous runner of the University of Kansas. His father and mother, Mr. and Mrs. H. C. Cunningham, are shown at the left and right.   *Photo by Rose Photo Shop, Elkhart*

He resumed college in September with thoughts of graduate school dancing in his head. Both running and racing translated to the pleasures of play. His running was a classroom lesson. He rarely lost to the same man twice, always studying and learning about his opponents. As a son of the Kansas plains, he sought out and thrived on challenge. His intensity in play was metaphor for everything else he did. He could certainly resonate to Dr. Roger Bannister's thoughts as expressed in *The Four-Minute Mile*:

"We run not because we think it is doing us good, but because we enjoy it and cannot help ourselves.

"It also does us good because it helps us do other things better. It gives a man or woman the chance to bring out the power that might otherwise remain locked inside. *The urge to struggle lies latent in everyone.*"

In running Glenn was a child at play. He reveled in it. Awards and prizes, save that one shiny medal, were secondary to him.

It must have been an utter disappointment to him when on December 5, 1933, Prohibition was officially repealed as Utah became the thirty-sixth state to ratify the Twenty-first Amendment to the Constitution. Glenn Cunningham had been an outspoken foe of repeal.

If there were any ill feelings about alcohol's official comeback they must have been more than mollified when an Associated Press poll of 1933 listed him as one of three amateur sports leaders. The other two were Jack Lovelock, who had set the world record in the mile, and Johnny Goodman in golf. Five additional choices were professionals, among them Barney Ross, then the world lightweight champion. Glenn Cunningham received the James E. Sullivan Memorial Medal for 1933. It was a yearly award given to the amateur athlete who by his example and influence has done the most during the year to advance the cause of sportsmanship. The committee was particularly impressed with Glenn's ". . . running two races in every meet and sometimes three against the leading European middle-distance champions. He could have refused and would have been justified in doing so. . . ."

At the very end of the year, commenting in a Kansas newspaper in response to a question asked about the Sullivan Medal, he had his own question: "Why don't they have an award for coaches?" He remarked that the coaches get all the criticism and little of the glory and do most of the work. "I want the credit," Glenn said, "to go in my case to Brutus Hamilton and Bill Hargiss."

Cunningham Gets Sullivan Award

The highest award in American amateur sports comes this year to Glenn Cunningham, senior in the School of Education, from Elkhart. The Sullivan Medal, awarded each year to the amateur athlete who by his example and influence has done the most during the year to advance the cause of sportsmanship, was given to Cunningham for 1933 by the American Athletic Union on a vote of its members. The Jayhawker's great running of middle distance races in America and Europe gained him the honor. Last spring he won twelve of the fifteen races he entered in America, setting a new American record for the mile at 4:09.8 July 1 at Chicago. In Europe during the summer he took part in twenty-six races ranging from 400 to 1500 meters in length and won them all.

The Sullivan Award for 1932 went last year to James Bausch, '32, Olympic decathlon champion.

The following schedule has been presented to the K.U. Athletic Board by Coach Bill Hargiss for Cunningham this spring. Even after approval of the Athletic Board it is not certain that the Kansas runner will enter all meets to which the invitation has been tentatively accepted, but he will doubtless appear in most of them. He will meet Beccali, Italian who won the Olympic 1,500 meter race and is probably the fastest of his competitors, Bonthron, the Princeton star who ran second to Lovelock in the famous 4:07 mile last spring (Lovelock incidentally, was beaten several times later by Beccali), Venzske, the U. of Pennsylvania runner, Hornbostel of Indiana and others of note. It will probably be the greatest constellation of middle distance running stars ever assembled.

14

1934

I do not run for records. I run to try and win and for the enjoyment I get out of meeting the fine chaps against whom I compete, as well as meeting so many other nice people in my travels.

The year 1934 would first bring a glimmer of hope for the Depression-stricken down-and-outers. About two and a half million of the unemployed found jobs, but eleven million were still without work. Relief rolls were estimated to carry between sixteen and eighteen million. The stock market nevertheless saw an upward turn, and industrial production was reviving.

The Dust Bowl, however, was still flourishing, particularly during the summer, with dust storms sweeping through half the nation, limiting crop harvesting and increasing farm prices.

Doing even less well were John Dillinger, Bonnie and Clyde, "Pretty Boy" Floyd, and "Baby Face" Nelson, all of whom were to meet ignominious endings.

But for Glenn Cunningham it was a banner year, a pivotal year. He would have successful indoor and outdoor seasons, would graduate from college with honors, would establish a world indoor record and outdoor records for the mile, and would marry—his honeymoon blending with his captaincy of the U.S. Track Team's tour of the Orient.

Early in the year, before the start of the indoor season in

February, hometown people at the Hotel Eldridge feted Glenn. There officials and dignitaries, along with the local friends, all congregated to honor the Sullivan Award recipient. Among the speakers was Kansas governor Alf Landon. Two years later he would run for president of the United States. In a reverse portent of things to come, Landon expressed the hope that he would be as successful in his races as Glenn Cunningham was in his. (He wasn't. In the 1936 election, the Roosevelt landslide swept him under. He even lost his home state of Kansas.)

When it came time, Cunningham spoke briefly, the length of his talk characterized as being less than the time it took him to run a mile. He gave thanks to his coaches and to support from the "Kansas folks." Furthermore, he said: "I do not run for records. I run to try and win and for enjoyment I get out of meeting the fine chaps against whom I compete, as well as meeting so many other nice people in my travels."

With the Millrose Games' Wanamaker Mile, the first meet on the indoor schedule, the hook for the sportswriters was that the winner would take the Wanamaker trophy home as his permanent property. Venzke had won in 1932, Cunningham in 1933. So, in the press, the purported rivalry between these now fond-of-each-other comrades was rekindled.

It was again a capacity crowd at Madison Square Garden. There were fourteen members of the U.S. 1932 Olympic Team on hand, among them Ralph Metcalfe the "Negro sprinter," Joe McCluskey, Charles Hornbostel, and Frank Crowley. But it was the mile event to be run on the boardsof the Madison Square Garden track—eleven laps, 160 yards to the lap—that the spectators were anxiously looking ahead to.

After the first lap, Eric Ny of Sweden took to the front with Venzke just behind, followed by Crowley. Cunningham was fourth. Then Leo Lermond suddenly lurched forward into the lead. Ny, having overpaced himself, began to fall behind. Disconsolate with his poorly paced tempo, he stepped off the edge of the track at the seventh lap to call it a day.

Lermond's pace was apparently slow, testing Venzke's patience, at the same time inspiring him to jump into the lead at eight and a half laps with Cunningham trailing within striking distance. Then the gun sounded for the eleventh and final lap around.

At that point, as put by Arthur Daley, ". . . the Kansan whirled around Venzke and passed him." He was now going all out, he sprinted, "laboriously it is true," Daley wrote, "but sprinted nevertheless." He finished eight yards ahead of Gene Venzke in a time of 4:11.2, the second fastest time ever for the indoor mile.

Cunningham wins the 1934 Wanamaker Mile in 4:11.2.
Venzke, out of the picture, is eight yards behind.

Later the track-suited young man from the windswept Kansas Plains reached up from the track into front-row box 77 to accept the Wanamaker Cup (valued at five hundred dollars) from the mink-tail-wrapped Mrs. Guernsey Munn, daughter of Rodman Wanamaker. It was his to keep forever, a trophy he'd surely have swapped for that shiny medal he never got.

Because it was broadcast on national radio hookup, Glenn ran that Wanamaker Mile at 10 P.M. To avoid the crowd, Glenn and Hargiss stayed in their private dressing room under Madison Square Garden. Glenn would usually run a little to cool down and would get a rubdown from Roland "Kickapoo" Logan. (Logan was a onetime football player at K.U., then became the assistant freshman football coach at K.U. under Hargiss; he would often accompany them to meets.) That particular evening someone knocked on the locked door. Here is part of the description Hargiss gave:

"And someone knocked at the door, which we had locked, and I went and opened it and here was a rather distinguished looking man standing there and he said, 'Coach, I'd like to see you. I'd like awfully well to see Glenn. But, I'd like to talk to you just a minute.' Well, it just kind of struck me that it was somebody that wasn't a gambler or hanger-on, you know. Well, I said, come on in, and I locked the door. And he said, 'My name is William P. Dunn.' Well, I said, Mr. Dunn, I'm glad to meet you, my name is Bill Hargiss. He said, 'I have a sixteen-year-old boy down in Seton Hall Academy at South Orange, New Jersey. This is a Catholic school and he's in a boarding school there. Sometimes I can get him out on Sunday, but I never can get him out during the week. Glenn Cunningham is his hero. He just thinks Glenn Cunningham is the greatest guy.' And, he said, 'Well, what are you and Glenn doing tomorrow?' I said we're not doing anything in particular. 'Well,' he said, 'You know what I'd like to do? I would like very much to have Glenn meet this boy of mine. I can get him out of the boarding school. And, I live down in New Jersey near Unionville. I'd just like to drive by tomorrow morning and I'll have the boy and we'll go take a ride.' I said, 'Come on back and meet Glenn.' There was another room back there, a training room. Glenn was up there and talked to him, and kind of threw his seat over, he was still on the training table. And, Mr. Dunn told him what he wanted. Glenn said, 'That's swell!' Mr. Dunn said, 'I'd like to drive up here and pick you up tomorrow morning, with the boy and we'll just have a ride around New York City and maybe down in New Jersey.' Glenn said, 'I'd love it! I'd like to meet your boy.' "

They planned to meet at the Hotel Paramount where they were staying. The next morning when they walked through the lobby to the street, a chauffeur met them.

"But, any rate," Hargiss continued, "we went down through the lobby and walked out there and a footman came up. There was a chauffeur there, and a footman. Here was a car as long as this room, a big, black limousine. I don't know, I believe it was a Lafayette or a Rolls Royce or something, a great big long car. And, the footman came up and got us and took us out there and held the door open. And we got in, and we met the boy, and started out. So we drove all around. We drove up to New Jersey. He took us to a beautiful place down in the hills of New Jersey for luncheon. And, we had to have the boy back at Seton Hall at four o'clock. We went back at four o'clock and he took the boy back there and he drove Glenn and me back into the Hotel Paramount. And, the footman got out and opened the door. Glenn got out and we'd gotten so familiar then he called me 'Bill.' Mr. Dunn said, 'Bill, I'd like to talk to you just a minute.

I happen to be chairman of National Hotels, Incorporated. I'm chairman of the board of directors. I have a suite of rooms down in the Hotel New Yorker on the 37th floor that it would please me greatly if you and Glenn would just take those rooms. I'd just like for you to stay there. I seldom ever use them. Furthermore, I want you to take all your meals; anytime you're in there. And you're not to sign any checks. I'll see that you're not even given checks.' So I called Glenn back. He had gone down to get the key, and Glenn said, 'Well, gee, that'd be wonderful, but,' he said, 'Mr. Dunn, you don't have to do that.'"

Later they find out that this Mr. Dunn was president of the Manufacturers Trust Company, one of the biggest financial organizations down on Wall Street. "So, we went down there and, gosh, every time he'd come back there he'd take us for a ride or he'd take us down to his home. And this boy got out and he'd come to the meets."

Hargiss had been telling this story to illustrate Glenn's willingness to meet and possibly influence a younger man in a positive way, even before he knew anything about Mr. Dunn. In fact, many times when in New York City they'd stay the whole week, with one meet blending into another. And there were the boys clubs and similar groups that would have Glenn Cunningham appear and talk to them. Or he would go and work out with them, would put on his track suit and run with them at some of the high schools.

A week later Cunningham was running at the Boston Garden in the Hunter Mile. Having arrived a day before by train from New York City, he would be appearing before twelve thousand track and field enthusiasts. Glenn would win in the "not-so-hot for him time of 4:18.4."

The Baxter annual, exactly one week later, was next. Here, in

New York City, for the first time in a while, he took a second place. First place went to Bill Bonthron. Glenn's time was 4:14. His schedule demanding weekly races and travel might now have been taking a bit of a toll. But a break would arrive before the New York City Knights of Columbia Mile scheduled for March 17.

Another incident around this time—probably after the Baxter Mile, while they were still in town—was not as salubrious as the meeting with Mr. Dunn. Hargiss relates their encounter with someone who foolishly wanted Glenn to lend his name to a cigarette advertisement:

"This was at the Hotel New Yorker. And, Glenn and I were up there alone. And the door knocked. Some fellow said, 'May I come in?' I said, 'Well, yes, come on in.' He said, 'I'd like to see Glenn Cunningham.' I said, 'What do you want to see him about?' He said, 'I'm with the so-and-so tobacco company and I'd like to see Glenn.' I said, 'Maybe you'd better talk to him.'

"About that time there were billboards all over the country showing Olympic and world champions in athletics, and they were particularly hitting the track boys, advertising cigarettes. Well, this fellow came back to see Glenn, lying down on the bed, and Glenn got up from there. I believe he had four five-hundred dollar bills, I believe it was, and he wanted to give Glenn two thousand dollars if he could use his picture in advertising his tobacco company. I grabbed Glenn. I don't know what he would have done to that fellow. But, I just said to him, 'I believe you'd better get out. I don't think Glenn wants your two thousand dollars.' But that one time was about the only time that I ever saw Glenn Cunningham really angry and mad.

"By golly, I think it was two thousand dollars, cash, right there, without a receipt or anything if he could just use Glenn's picture and a statement, or something. One of my other boys, it was after school, but he was a great athlete, and he subscribed to it. Had his pictures. And he said, 'Cigarettes never hurt my wind.' Well, he didn't lie about it. He didn't smoke. Hell, no, he didn't smoke. Never had a cigarette in his life. But he wanted the two thousand. Glenn needed the money too, but he wasn't selling his principles."

March 15, the date then for filing of income tax, was also the date for the Knights of Columbus Mile. It was held again at Madison Square Garden. Its location in 1934 was at Eighth Avenue and 50th Street. It would remain there until it held its final track meet in 1967.

Glenn would compete against Charley Hornbostel whose specialty was the half-mile. And Gene Venzke was again in the mix. Oklahoma's Glen Dawson was another competitor to be reckoned with.

This was not a typical Cunningham race in that he took the lead before the halfway mark. He swung up wide and high on the fifth turn and "barged down into the lead" as he completed the fifth lap. He built on to this lead and finished in 4:08.4. It was a new world indoor record. Venzke's old record of 4:10 for the indoor mile was broken. Only Jack Lovelock's 4:07.6 world record outdoor mile in 1933 was faster.

What was different was that he had no pacers. Usually he depended on the competition to spur him on. And at least one newspaper noted that judging from the applause, Venzke was the most popular of all the milers. "It is hard to understand why the cheers for Cunningham," the reporter wrote, "are usually mixed with boos. It must be that those whose blood runs thin from lack of sporting nourishment resent the very thought of his coming out of the West to beat their Eastern idol."

That reporter's explanation of the mixed reaction to Cunningham and the unequivocal response to Venzke falls short. It lacks the perspective of time gone by. The real reason, I think, was that Gene Venzke had now become the underdog.

Like Cunningham, his second half was often faster than his first. It was usually the third quarter of a race where he lagged, but they did run similar kinds of races. Comparing best mile times by quarters, Cunningham and Venzke would have run dead heats for the first two quarter miles. Comparing best mile races, it was the third quarter that Glenn ran three seconds faster than Venzke did in his 4:10 time.

The wisdom of the day had dictated that the miler should run as fast as he could early when there was little or no fatigue. By running the second half faster than the first, Cunningham had ushered in a new concept in mile racing. "The answer," declared Coach Hargiss, "I think will be found in rhythm." By that he meant the runner could go as fast as possible without undue exertion by maintaining the rhythm of the stride in the first half. This would then prepare the body for the all-out exertion in the second half.

Hargiss was really on to something—maybe more than he realized—when he said the answer would be found in rhythm.

But the rhythm that determined the pace had to be maintained consistently. The enemy of that rhythm, the real villain, that which separated the great from the good milers, lurked in the third quarter of the mile.

It was something that Paavo Nurmi had apparently developed a method to cope with, and so reign supreme during his era, a period that had just preceded Glenn's.

The big difference between Cunningham and Venzke was in

their third quarters. Their last quarters were equally fast.

They were similar too in persona: both were solid and strong in character. Yet Cunningham was becoming too strong, too victorious. The track-racing public needed another little guy who was down. So they were yearning for Venzke to revive. If he could recover, so could they.

It was probably around this time when there was an amusing off-the-track incident that Hargiss took note of:

Buddy Rogers was a K.U. graduate who later went into the movies. He had a nightclub in New York City and invited Glenn and Hargiss to come there after one of the meets. Hargiss made it known to Rogers that Glenn might be hungry after the track meet but he didn't drink. "He gave us a table right up close to the dance floor," Hargiss related. "The leading thing at the Paradise Club was Sally Rand, with her nude fan dancing. He brought Sally Rand and they sat at our table. Well, along came some photographers and they asked me if I wanted a picture taken. I said 'no' I didn't want any picture. But they took some pictures anyway, with Glenn and me and Sally Rand and Buddy Rogers at this table in the nightclub. You know, that thing was in every important daily in the rotogravure sections of the Sunday newspapers. Old Chancellor Lindley had a fit! He flipped his lid. I had the damndest time explaining to him how it came about. He finally subsided a little bit. But that shows what you can get into if you don't look out. Of course, now Sally Rand, so far as I'm concerned, she was an awfully nice person. They had her up with a net with a veil over it and you couldn't tell if she had on tights or—she was supposed not to have anything on, but you couldn't tell it. It was a very artistic dance, this ostrich fan dance. She had those things and she could keep herself covered, most of the time. . . ."

Interviewed around the same time, Glenn Cunningham's account, recorded in the 1960s, injects a positive side of the Sally Rand matter:

"I went to this nightclub nearly every year at the invitation of someone. In fact, I think Walter Winchell invited me to this nightclub one time. And I have a picture of Walter and Sally Rand and I. Sally Rand was a performer there and she was putting her young brother or someone through college. I don't know anything in particular about Sally Rand, other then she was a performer there.

"There were photographers there and they wanted a picture of Sally and me and she said, 'you can take a picture.' And she had me stand—you know she was a fan dancer, she posed with the fan. They wanted some other stupid thing and she said she wouldn't do it. 'This young man is not in this category and I am not going to do it.' She did hold the fans up, part of them covering her and part of them covering me. And I have a picture of them, somewhere. But I appreciate her attitude, wanting to protect other people who are not involved in that type of thing."

No snob about nightclubs, he had this comment:

"Well, you know I was continually being invited out by someone for a steak dinner after the meet. The nightclubs didn't appeal to me in the least. I enjoyed some of those people. You think of this type of nightclub people as being just nothing, but many of those people are just as good as a lot of other people that you would know, that would probably never enter a nightclub."

There were several more meets on the calendar before graduation. After the world indoor record Glenn won the mile race at the Butler Relays in Indianapolis in 4:17.9, slow for him but a new meet record. In an even slower time he dominated the Kansas-Nebraska dual meet in 4:35.5 (apparently he did let others set the pace, running only to win). He ran the exact same time in a win at the Kansas Missouri dual meet. But in the Kansas Relays he must have met swifter competition, winning in 4:12.7 and setting a new meet record and furthermore running the fastest mile ever in Kansas.

Much was made in the papers of Bill Bonthron declining to come west to participate, ostensibly because of his studies. But in the press, accolades were extended to Gene Venzke for making the trip to compete—only to lose to Glenn for the tenth time in eleven tries.

Before the late-spring and early-summer season there would be three races of particular note. Meanwhile Cunningham was finishing his senior year and readying for graduation.

1934 K.U. graduation. Chancellor Lindley is on the left.

A little before graduation he was voted Honorman of 1934. Chancellor Lindley, his pique over the Sally Rand episode assuaged, presented the award on April 12 at the Honors Convention. He reported that the committee voted unanimously to give the honor to Cunningham, who, in their estimation, exemplified best the qualifications of the award. They were character, scholarship, breadth of interests, unselfish service, and leadership.

He was also inducted into their highest scholastic honor society, Sachem. Paul Borel writes that when Glenn was told of the tribute of an induction to Sachem he responded, "What's that?" His scholastic record, furthermore, earned him fifth place in his entire graduating class.

The next mile race of any major significance took place in the Penn Relays. These were always two- and three-day-long contests. For the last day, April 28, 1934, a very special match was arranged. There would be only two contestants: Glenn Cunningham and Gene Venzke. The day before it had rained. Crews worked all that night, having borrowed two of the city's large suction blowers. Applied to the track and infield of Franklin Field, they sucked out the rainwater, restoring the track to its natural solid surface.

There is a unique photo showing the start of the race with only two runners about to vault from their starting positions. Below that is a shot of the finish.

Thirty-five-thousand pairs of eyes watched as Glenn Cunningham, now dubbed the "Kansas Cyclone," was content to allow Venzke to set the pace for the first three quarters. Then came the typical blazing finish that left Gene fifteen yards in the rear. At the finish Glenn had shattered the Penn Relays track record, winning in 4:11.8. This time a newspaper wrote, "even in

defeat Venzke received a big hand while the crowd roared its approval of the Kansas ace."

The next event Glenn was pointing toward was the mid-June Princeton Invitational. That week Glenn, Hargiss, and later Roland Logan had been staying in their New York City hotel. Hargiss again had a story. Apparently they were given tickets to the heavyweight championship bout between Max Baer the challenger and Primo Carnera, the champion. Carnera, a literal giant, had made his way to the top by way of a series of fixed fights. The only problem for him this night would be that Max Baer was a legitimate fighter.

"Colonel John Kilpatrick," Hargiss recounted, "manager of Madison Square Garden, sent down to the hotel ringside tickets for Glenn and me at the Carnera-Baer championship fight out in Long Island Bowl—way out there at the end of Long Island. . . . I think the fight was to go on the radio at nine o'clock or ten o'clock. But, there were several preliminaries so we went to this world's championship, heavyweight fight between Max Baer and Primo Carnera in the Long Island Bowl and there were sixty thousand there. But, we went out by subway and just got along pretty well. But, when that fight was over—now, this was on Thursday night prior to Saturday when we were running at Princeton. And, you know, we liked to never did get back to the hotel. The subways, with sixty thousand people getting out of there—it was two o'clock in the morning, or two-thirty, before we got back to the hotel. And, that was keeping Glenn up pretty late. But, it didn't bother him. Then, on Saturday we went down to Princeton."

(For the record, Baer annihilated Carnera, flooring him twelve times in eleven rounds. One of the fighters in the preliminaries was Jimmy Braddock. A year later, he defeated Max Baer to take the heavyweight title.)

Around this time Glenn graduated from the School of Education with a degree in physical ed. A photo of another graduating senior, his wife-to-be, Margaret Speir, showed her smoking the ceremonial pipe of peace. Such was a regular part of the graduation exercises, symbolizing the cessation of all college rivalries, with the graduates going out into the world at peace with the world and with themselves.

The Carnera-Baer contest was on June 14, 1934. The real main event, however, would be Saturday, June 16. All would pale in importance to what would be called Cunningham's marvelous mile that late afternoon at Princeton's Palmer Stadium before twenty thousand spectators and one electrical clock, courtesy of the Western Union Telegraph Company.

The finals of the track and field events started at 5:00 P.M. and ended at 6:00 P.M. The running events ranged from the half-mile, to the mile, to the two-mile. In the half-mile, Ben Eastman out-spurted Hornbostel. Eastman's time was 1:49.8, a new world record. Hornbostel finished in 1:50.7, also breaking the pre-existing (his own) world record, but second to Eastman's new record.

In the two-mile run, John Follows of the New York Athletic Club just beat out his clubmate, Joe McCluskey, with a lunge at the finish tape.

Yet it would be the mile run that marked the day. Not the race itself, however, but what had happened just before the starting gun that made the finish so remarkable. I have an account that Cunningham told me in 1987, and the account of Hargiss of what happened just before the mile run.

In relatively terse terms Glenn said, "I had warmed up. I was just taking a little spin on the grass and stepped in a hole and popped my ankle. They first told me I better just cancel out the race."

As Hargiss put it, and in his usual manner: "We went down there. Kickapoo Logan [who sometime later became conditioner for the Boston Red Sox] was with me and we had a fine warm-up. Just before Glenn would get into a race he would do a lot of kicking. He'd step, kick, and bend down. And he did one of these kicks, stooped over and he stepped into a hole. It was just as they were lining up. He sprained—oh, he just tore up his ankle. Well—gosh, they allowed us a little time, probably ten minutes. Logan rushed down there. He'd come up from Washington, and he wrapped Glenn's ankle with two-inch adhesive tape. Put it on in a figure-eight as tight as he could pull it."

The usual competitors, Bonthron and Venzke, lined up at the start. Venzke had the pole, that is, the lane at the very inside. Bonthron was one lane over and Cunningham on the outside. Right after the crack of the gun Cunningham leaped ahead of Bonthron. Early on it would be Venzke, Cunningham, and Bonthron in that order with little distance between any of them. But at the halfway mark it switched to Cunningham, Bonthron, Venzke. Cunningham seemed to be running with ease. The gun sounded the final lap as they completed the third quarter, still closely packed.

Glenn en route to the world record. Among the chasers, Bonthron is in white.

Then it was all over as far as the race was concerned. Cunningham began to increase his lead, five yards, ten, then going into the last straightaway fifteen yards ahead, sensing a record, he shifted into another gear and accelerated. Now the spectators, sensing something spectacular was unfolding, were looking first at the Western Union electric clock as if they could will it to slow, then back again to Cunningham to spur him on. At the finish he was perhaps fifty yards ahead of Bonthron. Then they had to wait for the official announcement. When it came the crowd roared its approval. He had finished in 4:06.7. It was a new world record—the fastest mile ever run, indoors or out. Like Max Baer, he had brought a world title back to these shores.

June 16, 1934: Cunningham sets a new world record for the mile in 4:06.7. Ben Eastman, who had just set the record for the half-mile, is at the extreme right on the grass.

(As to the finishing time, Hargiss said that he had timed him on his own watch in 4:05.5 and that another coach had gotten the same time. He also went into a discourse on proper use of a stopwatch, that some judges used their thumb to stop the dial whereas the index finger was much faster and could mean fractions-of-a-second difference.)

"Glenn ran that race on that ankle that had just been hurt awfully bad, and he broke the world record," Hargiss recounted. "Afterward we went into the dressing room, and his ankle had swollen so bad it had broken the tape. The next day he couldn't walk."

At day's end, with new records established, the history of the falling records for the mile run read as follows:

Mile Run

4:15.6 Tommy Conneff, U.S., 1895
4:15.4 John Paul Jones, U.S.,1911
4:14.4 John Paul Jones, U.S.,1913
4:12.6 Norman Taber, U.S., 1915
4:10.4 Paavo Nurmi, Finland, 1923
4:09.2 Jules Ladoumegue, France, 1931
4:07.6 Jack Lovelock, N. Zealand 1933
4:06.7 Glenn Cunningham, U.S., 1934

After Princeton, that next morning they took a plane from Newark Airport to Harrisburg, where they boarded a train for Los Angeles. The next Saturday afternoon would be the National Intercollegiate, and Cunningham would face Bonthron again in the mile run. "I couldn't even put my foot on the floor to walk," Cunningham told me in April 1987, at Boston. "It was terribly painful. I wanted to withdraw from those next two races but the promoters insisted that I get on the track and start the race, go thirty yards and go off the track. But I never quit a race in my life and never intended to. I went ahead and entered, even though I hadn't been able to get on the track for a workout. In fact, I could hardly walk. I tried to run and lost those next two races."

Those last two races were a win by Bonthron in Los Angeles beating Glenn by six yards and finishing in 4:08.9, and, in an A.A.U. meet in Milwaukee, besting Cunningham in the 1500 meter run, winning in a world-record time of 3:48.4. The photo in that race showed Cunningham being beaten by less than half a step. He had also broken the previous world record, this with his ankle still not right.

Although newspaper reports did cite Glenn's ankle difficulties before the races, neither Glenn nor Hargiss offered any excuses. In his lifetime Glenn Cunningham had known much greater pain than that of an ankle injury.

Cunningham was now ineligible for any more college competition. In his three years of college competition he had run in seventy-six races and had won sevnety-one times. The races ranged from 800 meters to two miles. Most of his races were in the one-mile event; there he had won twenty-eight of thirty-one races.

Glenn Cunningham's college career could now be summed up, first in terms of his mile races and recorded times:

1932
Big Six indoor meet, 4:21.9 (new record)
Kansas-Haskell dual meet, 4:35.5 (present record)*
Kansas-Kansas State duel meet, 4:25.0 (new record)
Kansas-Missouri dual meet, 4:23.0 (new record)
Big Six outdoor meet, 4:14.3 (present record)*
National Intercollegiate, Chicago, 4:11.1 (new record)
*As of end of college career.

1933

National Intercollegiate, Chicago, 4:09.8. (present record)*

Wanamaker Mile, New York, 4:11.2

Baxter Mile, New York, 4:14.3

Columbian Mile, New York, 4:12.0

Big Six indoor meet, 4:21.8 (present record)*

Big Six outdoor meet, 4:18.4

Triangular meet (Kansas, Kansas State, Nebraska), 4:17.4 (present record)*

Tulsa A.A.U. meet (second to Glen Dawson), 4:29.3

Kansas-Missouri dual meet, 4:20.3 (present record)*

*As of end of college career.

1934

Wanamaker Mile, New York, 4:11.0

Hunter Mile, Boston, 4:18.4

Baxter Mile, New York, 4:14.0 (second to Bonthron)

Columbian Mile, New York, 4:08.4 (world indoor record)

Butler Relays, Indianapolis, 4:17.9 (new meet record)

Tulsa A.A.U. meet, 4:17.7 (new meet record)

Kansas-Nebraska dual meet, 4:35.5

Kansas-Missouri dual meet, 4:33.5

Kansas Relays, 4:12.7 (new meet record and fastest mile ever run in Kansas)

Penn Relays, 4:11.8 (new meet record, new field record)

Princeton Invitation meet, 4:06.7 (world record)

National Intercollegiate Championships, Los Angeles, 4:08.9 (second to Bonthron)

Big Six outdoor meet, 4:23.3

It was enough running for a little while. He next made the newspapers in the *Boston Sunday Post*, July 1, 1934: CRACK MILER TO WED. Wedding plans were not yet set. In fact he had been somewhat cagey about his marriage plans. At Milwaukee a head-line read CUNNINGHAM SEEKS SECLUSION AT MILWAUKEE. He was described as "surrounded in mystery. . . . Rumors of his impend-ing marriage and injuries caused him to seek seclusion." Gossip had him eloping.

What actually had happened was that County Superintendent A. W. Urquart, a former minister, performed a ring ceremony in Marion, Kansas, uniting Margaret Speir of Peabody and Glenn Cunningham. From Marion they took the Santa Fe to California where they would sail on August 16 for Japan; there Glenn would be captain of the U.S. Track Team. There he would compete in six track meets, running in the 800- and 1500-meter events.

The team sailed on August 16 and were scheduled to compete in Tokyo September 8-9. The *Japan Times*, written in English, covered the events, as did the *Japan Advertiser,* also in English. The Americans won the first day by one point when Ralph Metcalfe, now a third-year law student, overcame the Japanese runner in the last 100 meters of the 400-meter relay. This was September 9, 1934, and two columns to the right was news of the steamer *Morro Castle* being hit by lightning with a heavy loss of life, right off the Asbury Park, New Jersey, coast. Cunningham took the 1500-meter race at their Meiji Shrine Stadium, "an easy victor." Curiously, the photo printed of his win in Japan actual-ly was the one of his win at the Penn Relays the preceding April.

The American team won, Cunningham and Metcalfe did very well. There would also be a tour of the Philippines. Glenn was part of a group that would tour much of the Orient, going to Manchuria, Korea, and the Philippines. Another contingent that included Bonthron and Venzke would tour Europe.

It must have been during this tour that Cunningham became enraged over the mistreatment of the coolie pulling the rickshaw. And it was around this time, too, in 1934, that the U.S. all-star baseball team, with Babe Ruth and Lou Gehrig, played against Japanese teams in Tokyo. Little known until long after Japan's defeat in 1945 was the role of a third-string major-league catcher, Moe Berg, who then was playing for the Cleveland Indians. Berg was also a linguist and was ostensibly present as an interpreter. While there, Berg went to the top of the St. Luke's Hospital, the highest point around, and took panoramic photos of the city of Tokyo. These very photos were thought to be those used in the Jimmy Doolittle raid on Tokyo in April 1942.

"Japan, with Germany," John J. Magee of Bowdoin, the American coach was quoted, "is the most improved nation in sports, and her athletes will be a real threat for the next Olympic championship." He was right about Japan (and Germany) being a threat, but it wouldn't be in Olympic battle. The United States suspected as much, and even Berg may have then actually been employed as an undercover agent by our government.

Much was made of the upcoming meeting between Ralph Metcalfe and Yoshioka of Japan. Metcalfe, who was making more and more headlines this year, would win their 100-meter dash contest in 10.3, duplicating the then world record. The name of Jesse Owens, "the fine negro sprinter and broad jumper from Cleveland," had also begun to be noticed in 1934. Much more would be heard of him and Metcalfe in the 1936 Olympiad.

Early in December, after their return, Glenn's indoor records for the mile and the 1500-meter run, along with his outdoor world mile record of 4:06.7, were all approved at the A.A.U. (Amateur Athletic Union) Convention meeting in Miami. But the convention also established a precedent that no former winner of the Sullivan Memorial Medal could receive the award a second time. Glenn had been among the first ten in the preliminary balloting leaving Bonthron the outstanding candidate for the title.

Cunningham would begin studies for his master's degree in physical education at Iowa University in 1935. His graduate studies would occupy more of his time than in his undergraduate days, limiting his travel and curtailing the number of appearances he would make in 1935 and 1936.

15

1935-1936

This afternoon, Jack Lovelock of New Zealand ran the greatest race I have ever seen or am ever likely to see, and became world champion and world record holder. It is almost impossible for me to describe the race in detail because the picture in my mind is one long thrill of superlative excitement.

Although the regions of the continent toured by the U.S. Track Team housed the very nations that were mobilizing for a full scale war of world domination, the United States was more focused on maintaining neutrality and dealing with its economic problems. As part of President Roosevelt's New Deal, early in January 1935, in his message to Congress, FDR proposed plans for social security. Later in the year, the Social Security Act would become law. Furthermore, as a way of creating jobs for the unemployed, by executive order the Works Progress Administration (WPA) was established.

In April powerful dust storms again would hit the Midwest, destroying crops and homes. In June, Jim Braddock defeated Max Baer for the heavyweight championship and Babe Ruth retired. In September, Senator Huey Long was assassinated. And in November, *Porgy and Bess* opened on Broadway.

Back in Elkhart, sometime in the year, Elkart would do right by its hometown hero. A city park was dedicated in his name,

Cunningham City Park. "No one ever makes a speech here," declared Willard Mayberry, editor of the Elkhart newspaper, "without referring to Glenn as an example of what a western Kansas farm boy, reared under the hardships of this section, can do if he has the right stuff in him."

But the Cunninghams were out of Kansas. By early in January 1935, Glenn and his new bride settled in an Iowa City apartment. In February both entered the University of Iowa in master's programs. (Glenn would get his master's in physical education in 1936.) The 4:04, not the 4:00 mile, was the track world's next goal. With Glenn's ankle sprain persisting, he was not certain he was up to a 4:04 mile, even a 4:10 mile.

In discussing the 4:04, almost out of character, Glenn posed for a silly photo with his smiling wife pointing to the ground as he assumed the starting crouch, the headline reading: MRS. CUNNINGHAM TELLS GLENN HE MUST TOE MARK. This was in a Buffalo, New York, paper in late January; the photo was taken at the 174th Armory, where that evening he competed in the three-quarter-mile event (an event no longer held), which was a warm-up for a race two nights later in Boston, the Knights of Columbus in Boston mile run. This he won in 4:16.4 with Gene Venzke second. But even that race was only a prelude to the premier events to be staged at Madison Square Garden in the coming weeks.

Those races would be the Wanamaker Mile of the Millrose Games on February 2, the New York Athletic Club Meet with its Baxter Mile two weeks later, then the National A.A.U. 1500 meter run the following week. Finally there were the Knights of Columbus races again at Madison Square Garden scheduled for March 16. Here Glenn was entered in both the mile and the 1000-yard run.

Just before the Wanamaker Mile, Cunningham made a visit to Washington, DC. There he was consulting his old friend and trainer, Roland "Kickapoo" Logan, then a member of the George Washington University coaching staff. Newspapers spoke of Cunningham's "ailing leg" and that Logan had aided Glenn in beating Bonthron at Princeton the year before when he set that world record. But now Glenn was expressing doubts over his ability to beat Bonthron.

Besides Bonthron, there was another entrant to be reckoned with, Eric Ny of Sweden.

Hailed as the fastest European runner at the 800- and 1500-meter distances, Ny had been training in snowshoes and skis around Stockholm, where he owned a sporting goods store. It was worthy of mention that such entrepreneurship, allowed under Sweden's amateur code, would have barred him from competition by America's draconian A.A.U. rules. Ny had hosted Bonthron during the American tour in 1935. Because he had proven to be such an affable host to Bonthron, Princeton

University had offered their college facilities for Ny's training.

For Ny, too, there was a score to settle. Unfamiliarity with the indoor board tracks and overwhelming emotion triggered by his hearing the Swedish national anthem played at the last year's Millrose Games had all contrived to produce a dismal performance.

Thus the stage was set for the battle among Ny, Bonthron, Venzke, and Cunningham on February 2, 1935.

Again the Garden sold out, swollen to its sixteen-thousand-seat capacity. Fire department codes allowing no S.R.O.'s turned hundreds away.

The runners lined up with Bill Bonthron on the inside at the pole. Bonthron was now "business-man Bonthron." He was working as an accountant and taking night courses in commercial law. Just to his right was Bill Ray of Manhattan, who would take the early lead. Gene Venzke was in the middle with Glenn to his right. Ny was on the very outside. (If the runner kept his position in the lineup, it was estimated that every six inches that separated one runner from the other going inside to outside meant one more yard of running per lap, eleven laps to the mile.)

Ray's initial lead evaporated by the end of the first of the eleven laps, yielding to Cunningham, but by the halfway mark of the second lap Bonthron had forged ahead, only to give way to Venzke at the end of the third lap. Glenn's time for the first quarter of a mile was 64.8, and for the next quarter 62.6. By the time he had whisked through the third quarter mile in 61.9, Ray and Ny were literally and figuratively out of the picture. At the three-quarter mark, it was a battle among Cunningham, Venzke, and Bonthron.

About halfway into the ninth lap it was Cunningham, Bonthron, Venzke. Gene was running smoothly but Bonthron's head was bobbing and distress was beginning to show. As they neared the finish pole for the ninth lap, Venzke sent the crowd into a roar as he approached Bonthron's shoulder and then whizzed past him on the backstretch. Venzke was the favorite of the crowd. Venzke, whom Glenn would label his greatest competitor, was now side by side with Cunningham, the roar of the crowd drowning out the bell for the final lap as he glided by Cunningham.

With a little more than 150 yards to go, Venzke was still in the lead. But he couldn't hold it. Nor could Bonthron summon up anything resembling a final drive. It was Cunningham, his arms close to his sides pumping raw power as he thumped past Venzke (who would finish second), with Bonthron a more distant third. There was a space of seven yards between Glenn and Gene, but only one second in time separated them at the finish line.

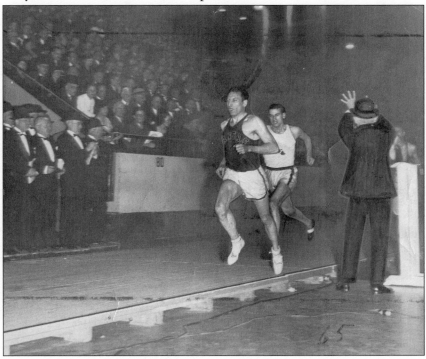

Cunningham finished in 4:11, his second half faster than his first.

(For a 4:10 mile the average miler travels about seven yards a second, so that even one-second difference meant a considerable amount of daylight between finishing places.)

Joe McCluskey, the erstwhile pride of Fordham, suffered his first defeat to Ray Sears in the two-mile run. Charles Hornbostel, having won the 1000-yard event, hours later would win the 600-yard dash, shaving three-tenths of a second off the world record.

Jesse Owens won the 60-yard dash as he "glided" past the fast moving Eulace Peacock of Temple. Jesse's winning time was 0:06.3, one-tenth of a second behind his own world record.

Two weeks later marked the reprise of the New York Athletic Club's Baxter Mile. Sportswriter Jesse P. Abramson's prose spoke of "The greatest mile machine the human race has yet produced . . . before a roaring crowd of 15,000 . . . all-conquering Glenn Cunningham mowed down his rivals with his invincible speed, power, rhythm and stamina to win the twenty-fourth running of the Baxter Mile."

In this race, Ny—the "foreigner"—set a blistering first half-mile, leading Cunningham by twenty yards over the first quarter mile. But Cunningham forged to the front exactly at the halfway mark. At the third quarter he was ten yards ahead of Bonthron and twenty ahead of Venzke. Despite Gene's strong last quarter, he gained little on Cunningham. Bonthron wilted near the end. Meanwhile, Ny had dropped out just a little past the halfway mark. Cunningham's winning time was 4:09.8.

One week later, February 23, 1935, we can hear newsreel commentator Ed Thorgersen's voice-over description of the 1500-meter National A.A.U. race:

"Here's the great Glenn Cunningham of Kansas at the climax of his brilliant performance in the 1500-meter run, the Monarch of the Milers has left the rest of his field far behind, Venzke and Bonthron are out of the picture as he races to the tape to shatter a world's record in the amazing time of three minutes, fifty and five-tenths seconds."

In the newsreel footage, both Venzke and Bonthron are nowhere to be seen, their presence a mere footnote. For Glenn Cunningham: 3:50.5: a new world indoor record for the 1500-meter run.

Jesse Owens set a new indoor long-jump record of 25 feet, 9 inches, and broke the indoor record for the 60-meter dash, being timed in 6.6 seconds.

March 16, 1935, Madison Square Garden was the site of the Knights of Columbus annual event. Because Cunningham was been known most for his one-mile and 1500-meter performances, it is hardly remembered that he was outstanding, too, in shorter races. That night he won the mile in 4:14.4. In this mile race, as in most of his races, he ran against the competition, not against the clock. Gene Venzke again assumed the bridesmaid role.

Cunningham's competition in the 1000-yard race was Chuck Hornbostel, who at the Millrose Games had broken the world indoor record for the 600-yard race, winning in 1:11.3. Hornbostel had also won the 1000-yarder that same evening and two years earlier had established the American record for the half-mile.

It was a close race. Both lowered the old indoor record of 2:12 for 1000 yards. Cunningham won by about a yard. Daniel J. Ferris, national secretary of the Amateur Athletic Union wrote "that Hornbostel-Cunningham classic," citing Hornbostel's sportsmanship and Glenn's uniqueness: "I think Hornbostel lost that race to Cunningham," he wrote, "by being a gentleman and living up strictly to the rule. He never came within a foot of Cunningham, altho [sic] he could have run much closer to him, thereby causing Glenn to break his stride."

Then he spoke about Cunningham, who, by the way, also had the reputation for not running right behind a competitor. Cunningham would break his own stride rather than run up another runner's back.

Ferris said this about Glenn: "It's unusual for a man to run the longer distance after the shorter as Cunningham did in running the Columbian mile after beating Hornbostel. But, then, Glenn defies all track tradition, anyhow. I thought his victory was the high point of the season."

In 1935 there would be more races but then, as it is today, it was the sporting events in the New York area that attracted the most interest and the most newspaper documentation. At the Princeton Invitational in May, for example, Glenn was third. It was won by Lovelock with Bonthron just trailing. Cunningham's time, 4:11.2, was well off his world record made the year before. Glenn had been ill with the flu and later said that he didn't feel fully recovered until well into summer. Saying he might not have beaten Lovelock even at full strength, he was nonetheless outmaneuvered by the New Zealander. He had run the first quarter too slow (67 seconds), then the second quarter too fast (60 seconds) but he was not up to such a punishing pace, and he trailed off to come in third.

At the annual Kansas Relays, Glenn's time was 4:17.5 coming in second to Frank Dawson. But he would win other mile events none under 4:15. Each win was strictly against the competition.

By year's end he held the American record for the indoor 1000-yard event in 2:10.1 and the world record for the indoor 1500-meters (3:50.5).

As a symbolic portent of what Cunningham would later term his "greatest career," his work with children, there arrived a letter from the White House to "My dear Mr. Cunningham," appointing him as a member of the Advisory Committee of the newly created National Youth Administration. The second paragraph read: "The problem of assisting in the adjustment of Youth under existing conditions is one of the most important problems that confront us. I feel that you are particularly well equipped to give us valuable counsel." It was signed by Franklin D. Roosevelt.

It was a lofty quest but all that came of this was Glenn's attending a few meetings, refusing a drink offered him by Eleanor Roosevelt, but also his admiration of her for her ideals.

Cunningham was already assisting youth, and Roosevelt must have gotten word that this was a man who took seriously the example he set. "Glenn was interested in helping young people very early on," his widow, Ruth Cunningham, wrote. "He financially helped several young people from Elkhart to go to KU. There was one family in particular that had lost their parents and the older children took care of the younger ones. He helped them arrange things so that the older girl could come to KU, and then one of the boys as well later on.

"When he was in New York he organized places for children to play sports, baseball and basketball; he gave tickets to kids to come to the races. The opportunities that running had given him, to travel and meet people and the many experiences involved meant a lot to him, and he wanted kids to aspire to high goals and discipline themselves for it. He wanted to give back for what others had done for him, and to inspire kids to reach for the stars. It was just fundamental to him—and was reflected in all of his talks to youth, and reminders to adults in service groups of their responsibility to youth, as well in his desire to bring them into our home."

The new year of 1936 was ushered in when, right on New Year's Day, unemployment insurance, mandating a 1 percent payroll tax, began. In early February, Charles Curtis, vice president under Hoover, and the man who declared the opening of

the 1932 Los Angeles Olympiad, died. The Republicans nomi-
nated Alf Landon, Kansas governor, to run for president against
the incumbent FDR. (He would suffer a resounding defeat by
Roosevelt.) And in Europe war clouds were gathering. The
Spanish Civil War, a omen of the Second World War, began that
July. In this country, however, the Depression was still on and the
country's attention was focused on jobs and the economy. Crops
in 336 counties in the land had been ruined by drought.
Nevertheless, the track world's focus was on the Berlin Olympiad
scheduled for that summer.

A telegram that had come for Glenn dated the past October
18 reflected rather misplaced values. I say it came "for Glenn"
because it was addressed to a George Bresnahan at the University
of Iowa and read: CAN YOU GET STATEMENT FROM CUNNING-
HAM ALONG LINES WHICH ROBERT HUNTER SPOKE TO YOU
ABOUT SEE IF CUNNINGHAM WONT MAKE STRONG STATEMENT
REGARDING AMERICAS PARTICIPATION IN OLYMPIC GAMES
WOULD LIKE TO HAVE IT BY MONDAY IF POSSIBLE.

This telegram was signed: AVERY BRUNDAGE.

Avery Brundage was then president of the American Olympic
Committee. There was growing opposition to America's participation in the 1936 Olympics scheduled in Berlin because of
Germany's flagrant and vicious anti-Semitic laws and acts. Even
the A.A.U. was ambivalent about our participation. But
Brundage, a prosperous general contractor, and a poorly con-
cealed bigot and racist, had his own agenda in terms of his particular company's profitable business dealings with Germany.
Having traveled to Germany in 1934 and 1935 to investigate
conditions, he made his "personal" guarantee that the German
government would allow German Jews to participate in the tryouts for the German team. To that Heywood Broun, legendary

sportswriter, responding to Brundage's whitewash asked "whether tryouts had been held in all the concentration camps."

To combat statements like that voiced by Broun, to neutralize movements like that of the Anti-Defamation League, to blunt attempts at boycotting goods made in Germany, Brundage mounted his own campaign. He was relentless in his pursuit of our participation in the upcoming Berlin Olympiad. He spread the word in a publication he put out titled *Fair Play for American Athletes*, that Communists and Jews had allied in a conspiracy to keep American athletes at home. He declared that we should not let "politics" interfere with the games, a statement he essentially repeated in 1972 at Munich after the Palestinian terrorists' massacre of Israeli athletes.

Whether Cunningham responded is unknown. I do remember his telling me that once in Germany, he was unaware of any persecution of Jews. The Nazis had cleaned up their act for the games, removing any signs of their nefarious deeds. Cunningham's main concern then, before and for the rest of his life was the example he and all of the athletes set, particularly as witnessed by the young people.

The Nazis also used Max Schmeling, onetime world heavyweight title holder. Here in this country to fight the undefeated Joe Louis, Schmeling brought assurances from Hitler that all was well in their land as far as treatment of Jews was concerned. Schmeling would hand Joe Louis his first defeat by knocking him out in twelve rounds that June.

It was Cunningham's intent to run in the New York City events early in the year provided he could arrange his academic schedule accordingly. That meant the trio of the Wanamaker Mile, the Columbian Mile, and the Baxter Mile.

As usual the premier event was to be the Wanamaker Mile of

the Millrose Games. But this year, a week before, there would be a prelude, one that would set up a grudge match for the February 1, 1936 Wanamaker classic.

The week before was the Curley Mile in Boston at the Boston Garden. Some ten thousand spectators had upbraided Cunningham for swerving out from the inside pole to block Joe Mangan's closing rush. Mangan, a law student and inconsistent up to then in his performances, would now be the underdog and the crowd favorite to beat Glenn.

(That the "fouling" of Mangan by Cunningham was deliberate is highly improbable. That was never his style; it was not in his character. A similar episode took place in the 5000-meter race in the 1932 Los Angeles Olympiad. Clearly seen in a video of those games beautifully produced by Bud Greenspan, the American Ralph Hill was obviously blocked from passing and taking the lead by the swerving Finnish runner, Lauri Lehtinen. Lehtinen would take first place, Hill second. Realizing what he had done, deeply chagrined, at the awards ceremony for that event Lehtinen tried to lift Hill up onto the first-place platform, but Hill declined.)

Glenn was now in the crosshairs of the Madison Square Garden sixteen thousand. The crowd even took umbrage at Glenn's unorthodox warm-up where he would prance up and down, snapping his head back and kicking like a ballerina, legs high above his head. They had no doubt seen his limbering-up routine before, a practice essential given his impaired circulation. But now he was the villain, "the man who had done him [Mangan] wrong."

As for his tortuous warm-up, this would prove a problem for gamblers. Bettors would sometimes try to hedge their bets. They couldn't imagine how he could run a race after seemingly tiring himself out during his warm-up phase. The gambling crowd just didn't understand the whole process.

Cunningham was leading for the first nine (of eleven) laps. His time at that point was 3:10.8. Then into the eleventh lap he began to go all out. Mangan was also known for a strong finish, and Glenn was only two yards ahead of him. With fifty yards to go Mangan turned it on so that with only twenty yards left he was at Cunningham's shoulder. Ten yards later he was edging Cunningham. He was able to stave off whatever Glenn had left. All of a sudden Venzke, amazingly strong, caught Glenn with only a yard remaining.

There was only two-tenths of a second between first and third place. Mangan won in 4:11, equaling Cunningham's Millrose Wanamaker Mile record. Venzke was timed in 4:11.1 and Cunningham also in 4:11.1, so close was their finish.

In an editorial sports column by Jack Miley titled BOO, YA BIG BUM! the scribe wrote that Mangan and Venzke were "hysterically applauded as they flung themselves through the tape only a couple of strides ahead of the thick-chested champion. . . ." But as Glenn moved over to congratulate the first- and second-place finishers, "small boys were shaking their fists at him and grown men were pursing their lips to produce low and vulgar noises." Both Venzke and Mangan were embarrassed by the crowd response to Cunningham.

The crowd loves an underdog. Same for the voting electorate. Cunningham was now too good. He had long outlived his little-guy role. For the moment at least, the crowd now had Mangan and Venzke to cheer for. And it had the Baxter Mile to look ahead to, a meet to which both Venzke and Cunningham had committed themselves.

As if ordained, Venzke would win the Baxter event even

HERALD TRIBUNE, MONDAY, FEBRUARY 3, 1936

Inches Apart in Record Equaling Wanamaker Mile

Associated Press photo

Two-tenths of a second separated these three runners at end of stirring race in Millrose Games Saturday night at Garden. Joe Mangan, left, was the winner in 4:11; Gene Venzke, center, was second in 4:11.1, and Glenn Cunningham, left, was third in 4:11.2. Mangan's time equaled record for event set by Cunningham. Picture of same finish was printed in 'yesterday's late editions of Herald Tribune

though Cunningham's second-place time of 4:10.2 was faster than in his Wanamaker effort. Center of attention for all concerned, however, were the Olympic tryouts. Studies for Glenn also were a concern. When asked how he kept up with his graduate work, he answered that on the road he usually took textbooks with him to read. Perhaps a lack of sleep was a factor in his losses. For Mangan, as he would explain to the press, a resumption of a normal sleep pattern may have contributed to his excellent performance. No matter. Despite the press ballyhoo of any burnout with Cunningham or of any enmity between Cunningham and Mangan, Cunningham's running performance would more than revive; and a photo of Glenn, Gene Venzke, and Joe Mangam having tea together would soon appear in the newspapers.

In 1987 I had asked Cunningham about sportsmanship in his day, and this is what he said: "That's the one thing about track. We were always friendly competitors. We were friendly off the track, but on the track we battled each other with everything we had. I think that's the real essence of sports, or supposed to be at least. I was just reading an article about how the fights they have, like after the World Series, have affected college students and minority groups. Those things ought not to happen."

Sandwiched within the New York City events was an A.A.U. 1500-meter run at Madison Square Garden on February 22. Here, fifteen thousand would witness a classic, truly epic, Venzke-Cunningham clash.

This time Cunningham set a sizzling pace. He ran the first half a mile in two minutes. Venzke also possessed the physical tools and the heart needed to mount a final spurt. Cunningham, the reigning world-record holder for the indoor 1500-meter run, always respectful of his opponents, was out to blunt Venzke's anticipated fierce final surge. The finish line, because of the 1500-meter distance, was at the end of the long straightaway rather than the middle. So Venzke just stayed behind Cunningham, gliding in his picturesque running style. Then about forty yards from the taut red worsted at the end of the final span, with an easy acceleration of pace, he passed Cunningham with thirty yards to go. Cunningham, however, rose to the challenge mounting his own sprint. It was not enough. Gene Venzke finished in 3:49.9, a new world record. Cunningham arrived two-tenths of a second later, breaking his own record of 3:50.5 by four-tenths of a second, yet at the same time abdicating the crown to his persistent undaunted challenger, Gene Venzke. Cunningham now had a newly invigorated stronger challenger, one who this time didn't wilt in the homestretch.

The *New York Times'* Arthur Daley wrote: "The thunderous outburst from the crowd had the rafters echoing and re-echoing as the handsome Pennsylvanian burst through the tape. Paper drifted down like confetti at a Mardi Gras."

That night too, Joe McCluskey won the 3000-meter steeple-chase "by a city block" from his clubmate, Frank Nordell. It was the fifth time Joe had won this event, and it was his tenth national steeplechase crown.

The next major (translate: New York City) racing event would be the Knights of Columbus Columbian Mile at Madison Square Garden, its seventeenth annual running. Traditionally it was held around St. Patrick's Day. This was special in that only those runners were invited who had a chance of breaking the world record for the mile. Meet director Frank Brennan had refused to accept any entries except those of Cunningham, Venzke, and Joe Mangan.

Cunningham told us of this race at our 1987 post Boston Marathon banquet. The event was more than half a century past, but the spirit of that evening was still with him. In quoting his words, however, some of the irony and humor that we could hear in his voice may be lost:

They had it advertised, all the sportswriters publicizing this as the greatest mile of all times. It was going to be a new world's record, a record I had established earlier, four minutes, eight and four-tenth seconds indoors. They said this would be at least 4:06. They had huge headlines on the newspapers, three inches high about this new world record. Madison Square Garden was sold out weeks in advance. They were selling standing room and even the aisles were jammed. . . . The sportswriters had it that Cunningham would go out in a fast pace, try and kill these other boys off. And then it would just be a battle the last hundred yards over the last lap of the track.

We got on the track, ol' Johnny McHugh got out there, and he took his stance and . . . 'Go to your mark, set.' *I wanted to make these boys believe I wanted to set that pace so I took a false start, went around that first turn as if I just wanted to burn up that track . . . they called us back, then Mangan and Venzke knew that I wanted to set that pace. The promoter had advertised the fact he was limiting the race to just us three, so the other fellows wouldn't be in there cluttering up the track, we were the three top milers for that year . . . . When Johnny McHugh fired the gun Mangan thinking I wanted the lead jumped in front, Venzke right out after him and I just rode right out slowly behind him.*

What had happened is that no one wanted to take the lead. The first quarter meant to be run in the low 60-seconds was in 1:32, or 92 seconds according to the newspaper account. Cunningham told us then that it was 77 seconds; more likely his number was the accurate one. The half was clocked at 2:34, another 77-second quarter, and the three-quarter mark in 3:51.5. Again 77 seconds. Cunningham telling of this, now fifty-one years later, even gave us the correct three-quarter time of 3:51.

And everyone was jeering and booed, and they threw their hats in the air and did everything but throw the chairs from the balcony out at us. And finally I noticed the boys were watching me over their shoulder down the straightaway; when you go into the turn you take your eyes off the boy at the turn so I had to jump them on the turn which could be suicide. When I jumped them on the turn I picked up five or six yards before they realized what had happened and Venzke followed me out; the race was over, we set a new world's record for the slowest time.

The time was 4:46.8. It would be known from that time forth as the "Slumber-mile-of-the-century."

Glenn spoke at the time to reporters of that Knights of Columbus meet at Madison Square Garden in 1936 pitting him against Mangan and Venzke, the race itself being built up for a new record. He told them that he had sprained his ankle badly earlier that winter: "I knew I couldn't run exceptionally well. I just hung behind Mangan and Venzke from the start. They kept waiting for me to go around them and go out with a good pace. I never did. As we were taking a turn a quarter of a mile from the finish line, I suddenly moved up and went by them. They weren't expecting a pass on a curve. Furthermore, you always concentrate on taking curves correctly in indoor running or you may be thrown off stride. I caught them by surprise.

"Once I got the lead, the race was won. I could sprint as fast as they could. We all sprinted the last 200 yards. And we all came *storming* in in 4:46.8. But I did win the race which was my aim."

From the somnolent to the very awake qualification heats for the 1936 Berlin Olympiad Glenn Cunningham finished first in the tryouts for the 1500-meter event. Also making the team for the 1500-meter run were fellow Kansan Archie San Romani and Gene Venzke. On the boat going over to Germany, Cunningham was voted the most popular teammate. There was an unfortunate matter of swimmer Eleanor Holm Jarrett. World-record holder for the 100-meter backstroke in the 1932 Los Angeles Games—boasting that she trained on champagne and cigarettes—she got drunk several nights during the voyage.

Asked about Eleanor Holm, Glenn said:

"She was kicked off the team for drinking. In fact, she would get drunk around the lounge there and make a mess of herself. Some of the sportswriters tried to circulate a petition among the athletes to get them to sign it to get her reinstated. I wouldn't sign it because I thought that the Committee did the right thing. I had gone out and I had talked to her one day. We stood at the railing of the ship and watched the ocean and I told her about the importance of setting examples for the younger girls. Just as I did with the fellows I traveled with over on the foreign nations as a track team. I kept telling her 'you are representing the U.S.,'

Eleanor Holm Jarrett aboard ship, 1936.

and I said, 'people will get the opinion of Americans in general by the way we conduct ourselves and it is highly important that we conduct ourselves all the way as gentlemen and good sports.'"

Berlin's Olympic Stadium, August 6 1936, 4:18 PM. Down on the track the starter raises his gun and slowly, but in a loud enough voice, enunciates *Feurtig!* (FOOOOR-TEEG, "ready"). Moments later the pistol shot's sound pierces the air and the runners break forth. At first it is Beccali in the dark vest from the inside racing ahead, overtaken soon by Cornes of Great Britain with Fletcher of Germany coming into third place. With each runner assuming the front position, partisan chants from the crowd leave their signature in the air. Cornes holds his lead until just before the end of the first of four laps. Then Fletcher coming down the straightaway passes Beccali and then Cornes. But then Cornes surges ahead once more as they begin the second lap. Suddenly, "here's Cunningham's thick-set figure forging ahead on the back stretch," announces the voice-over in thick British accent. And now you hear chants of "YOO-ESS-AYE, YOO-ESS-AYE, YOO-ESS-AYE." Cunningham leads for a while. Beccali is third, Cornes fourth. Now Ny makes his bid, "the fair-haired Ny from Sweden runs into second place." He is in second place behind Cunningham with the USA chants still ringing. It is now Cunningham, Ny, Lovelock, Beccali, Shaumburg, Cornes. Then Ny comes up on the bend, and into the straight again it is Ny and Cunningham fighting it out, cadenced YOO-ESS-AYEs echoing throughout. Lovelock is now third as the bell rings signaling the last lap.

Ny leads Lovelock, Cunningham, Beccali, Phil Edwards, and John Comes.

Into the backstretch it is Cunningham in the lead with Schaumburg of Germany almost to his right shoulder and Lovelock in black running shirt a stride behind Schaumburg. Then Ny makes another bid, eclipsing Shaumburg. All of a sudden, "Here comes Lovelock," shouts the voice-over, "running like a train." He appears as if shot out of a cannon as he blasts into the lead. Cunningham catches the idea and suddenly spurts past Ny. But Lovelock's sprint has taken him past Ny and Cunningham. As if sucked up in a vacuum, Beccali also whizzes by Ny. They keep these relative distances with Lovelock about four or five yards ahead of Cunningham, and Cunningham three or four yards ahead of Beccali. And they will hold these relative positions for forty-three seconds: Lovelock, Cunningham, Beccali. There is one long cacophonous din. If you look closely, about twenty yards from the end, Lovelock sneaks a look back, seeming to slow down just a bit as he crosses the finish line: "WORLD RECORD!"

The sports editor of the *New York Star,* Arthur Daley, wrote of Lovelock's and Cunningham's contest: "Desperately Cunningham strove to cut down the margin of the running robot from New Zealand. But he was not equal to the task. Little Lovelock, 133 pounds of dynamite [Cunningham weighed 165], scampered around the last curve into the home stretch like a mechanical rabbit staying ahead of a pack of greyhounds."

John Lovelock, New Zealand, 3.47.8 WR

Glenn Cunningham, USA, 3:48.4

Luigi Beccali, Italy, 3:49.2

Archie San Romani, USA, 3:50.0

Philip Edwards, Canada, 3:50.4

John Cornes, Great Britain, 3:51.4 (0.2 second outside the old Olympic record; the first five had broken the previous Olympic record for the 1500-meter run)

Nowhere to be seen in the *Olympia* video showing that marvelous race was Gene Venzke. He finished eighth.

BBC commentator Harold Abrahams (of *Chariots of Fire* fame) would write: ". . . this afternoon, Jack Lovelock of New Zealand ran the greatest race I have ever seen or am ever likely to see, and became world champion and world record holder. It is almost impossible for me to describe the race in detail because the picture in my mind is one long thrill of superlative excitement."

Lovelock was, at the time, a medical student. He was also a student of running. Through his diligence he learned what was for him a strategy that let him sustain a final sprint. Whatever was his secret, it worked. He ran the last 400 meters in 56.8 seconds, and of that, the last 200 meters in 27.2 seconds.

One year later Lovelock would get his medical degree; two years later Cunningham would earn his Ph.D. It almost could have been Dr. Lovelock versus Dr. Cunningham.

At the awards platform Cunningham, smiling and radiating good cheer, stands a step below and to the right of Lovelock, Beccali to his left as "God Save the King" is played. Lovelock has a shy grin. A photo of Cunningham and Lovelock shaking hands is taken. It produces a baseball-like card. Both are in sweatshirts, Glenn's with USA emblazoned over the front, Lovelock in dark black sweatshirt.

Looking at the photo there is one small incongruous detail. It is their handshake. Cunningham had large hands, which he employed in a firm strong grip. You knew it when you were shaking hands with him. Lovelock, however, must have been using the more Continental finger clasp, locking his fingers into Glenn's hand before Cunningham's right hand could envelop his.

Although the 1500-meter race may have been the most exciting of all the events, and for Harold Abrahams "the greatest race I have ever seen or am ever likely to see," the most extraordinary performance was that of Jesse Owens who would win the 100- and 200-meter dashes, the long jump, and would lead off the winning 4x100-meter relay team. But it was a relay team whose coach had capitulated to the "political" when, at the last moment, the only two Jewish members, Marty Glickman and Sam Stoller, were replaced. And Jesse Owens, anxious to get home, had cut short his participation in the barnstorming European events. Consequently, he would have his amateur status stripped, courtesy of Avery Brundage and Dan Ferris. The relay replacements and the suspension of Owens also bore the imprimatur of Avery Brundage, who was a stalwart member of the pro-Nazi America First Committee.

One note of irony: Owens was also anxious to get home to take advantage of some lucrative offers, many of which turned out to be bogus. One legitimate job, one that did pay him some money, was to stump for Kansas governor Alf Landon in his disastrous presidential bid.

A few days after the closing ceremonies at Berlin's Olympic Stadium that August, the Olympic Village became an infantry-training center. A military hospital and an officers' club replaced the largest restaurant and music hall. Some journalists even reported the sounds of machine-gun fire days after the closing. Soon too the anti-Semitic placards, slogans, and graffiti resurfaced. But the athletes were looking more to the 1940 games scheduled for Tokyo, Japan, another nation planning for total war. Little was mentioned in the newspapers about Germany's actions; nor was much said about the Glickman/Stoller episode. It was a time when note was made that an athlete was "negro" or "colored" and even the *New York Times*, a newspaper owned and operated by Jews, was chary in its reportage of German anti-Semitism. Baseball's major leagues were a decade away from integration, our South was many decades away from equality of any sort, and the National Football League's record on integration of athletes was at best spotty and ambivalent.

Meanwhile there was that barnstorming European tour. The A.A.U., in financial arrears, needed to raise money, and business deals were made with European promoters. The tour was successful financially and for the U.S. team in terms of medals and victories. Glenn Cunningham broke the world record for the 800-meter run, finishing in 1:49.7, one-tenth of a second better than the previous record. It was at Stockholm Sweden, the very meet Owens had bypassed.

Soon there would be one more race of note, the Princeton Invitational. It was set for Saturday, October 3, at Palmer Stadium, to be run between halves of the Princeton-Williams football game.

This year it would again be Cunningham and Lovelock; Archie San Romani, Glenn's Olympic teammate and student at the Emporia, Kansas, State Teacher's College; Don Lash of Indiana, holder of the American record for two-miles; and Glen Dawson from Tulsa Oklahoma, an Olympic steeplechase runner representing the Tulsa Skelley Club.

Glen Dawson, as per plan, ran all out the first half followed by Lash, Lovelock, San Romani, and Cunningham. They kept this order for more than three-quarters of the race. Then San Romani turned on the afterburners, blasting past Dawson and Lovelock. Cunningham, taking the cue, sprinted past Dawson but was unable to get more than ten feet behind San Romani.

The 45,000 gathered would thrill to Archie San Romani, "uncorking a terrific last-lap sprint" and winning in 4:09. Lovelock was timed in 4:10.1 and Cunningham at 4:13.

The *Dodge City (Kansas) Globe* wrote of ARCHIE AND GLENN and their friendly rivalry. It spoke of San Romani's success and attributed much of it to Cunningham's interest and counsel. "These are fine Kansas boys," the article read, "giving the athletic world which is somewhat cynical because of the professional stigma on much of it, an example of splendid sportsmanship. Glenn will quit running one of these days. That should be the opportunity for some big university to obtain a physical education director whose influence with youth will bring him greater fame than any world record mile he can claim."

To some degree this reference to his influence would be prophetic. If not greater fame, however, the influence he would bring to bear in later years would give him far greater gratification.

To this end, master's degree in physical education secured, soon after the Princeton race Glenn would enroll in the Washington Square branch of New York University working toward his doctorate in biological sciences and physical education.

His studies a priority, he was quoted in the press to the effect that he would stay in shape but would have to cut down on racing. For Glenn Cunningham, the latter half of his resolve would be difficult to sustain.

Avery Brundage's resolve, however, would pay off for him and for his financial interests. In 1938 when it was revealed that the Germans were building a new embassy in Washington, DC, Brundage immediately lobbied to have his company as part of this project. His proven friendly attitude toward German sports a matter of record, the responsible German parties granted him permission to take part in the building of the new German embassy.

From the games, Germany's monstrous creation had gained credibility, Brundage's corporation had gained business, but the United States—duped and rendered impotent—had gained shame and dishonor.

16

1937

Everyone hurries all day long but they do not get anywhere.

Although he was no doubt diligent in his studies, Cunningham was just as conscientious in his play. In 1937 he would be in more races than in 1936. Outlined now will be the highlights of the year in general and later the high points in his racing.

In sport Joe Louis would become heavyweight champion of the world and hold that title for eleven years. He beat James J. Braddock, the same man who beat Max Baer who, in turn, beat Primo Carnera at the Garden City match where, in 1934, Glenn and Hargiss were spectators two nights before he ran that record breaking Princeton mile. Aviator Amelia Earhart vanished somewhere over the Pacific, and at age thirty-eight, George Gershwin died. Other notable deaths included John D. Rockefeller, Sr., ninety-seven and Elihu Root, ninety-two, former Secretary of State under Theodore Roosevelt.

The Supreme Court upheld the fledgling Social Security Act, and General Motors agreed to negotiate with the United Automobile Workers Union, granting workers a five-cent-per-hour raise. The German dirigible *Hindenburg* caught fire and exploded as it tried to land in Lakehurst, New Jersey, killing thirty-seven of its ninety-seven on board.

Our beginning-to-revive economy would falter and begin to

slide into recession at midyear.

A daughter, Sara, was born to the Cunninghams on May 25, 1937.

Late that year my parents purchased a brand-new four-door 1937 Plymouth for $750.

The track year of 1937 began successfully, if not rather quietly, with Cunningham winning the 800-meter run at Brooklyn's 108th Infantry Armory. It was a typical finish with Glenn closing fast to beat a typical rival by five yards, his game "foe," Gene Venzke. This race was only a prelude to the Knights of Columbus Curley Mile at the Boston Garden. And eyes would be on a new man of interest, Don Lash.

In the same race, listed as former indoor mile record holder, would be Gene Venzke. Rounding out the card were Archie San Romani, who was lately beating his fellow Kansan, and Charles Fenske, Big Ten indoor title-holder from Wisconsin. To create some suspense, the press raised questions about Lash's ability to run on the indoor board tracks, and whether his best running would come in mile or two-mile races. Furthermore, the Millrose Games were a week away and Lash was scheduled in the two-mile race to meet the Rideout twins, who had both beaten him in the New Year's Sugar Bowl Mile.

The newspapers created another issue of suspense. Venzke had won the Curley Mile in 1932, '33, and '34. Glenn had won in 1935 and '36. So if Glenn won, they would tie as three-time winners.

Lash took a big lead at the quarter-mile mark. Cunningham and Venzke ran together, not allowing Lash's unusually fast pace to change their game plans. Lash ran the first quarter of a mile in 58.5 whereas Cunningham was clocked in 64 seconds. At the half-mile mark Lash was timed in 2:01 and Glenn in 2:06. Then

Gene Venzke and Glenn Cunningham
at the Knights of Columbus meet, January 9, 1937.

at the three-quarter mark Lash still led by five seconds. At one point Lash may have been as much as 70 yards ahead. Glenn and Gene meanwhile were staying close together. But with two laps of the twelve remaining Lash seemed to fall back; Cunningham would later say, "I began to step on it two laps from home and never felt so good in my life." Arthur Duffy wrote of Glenn's "great dash" at the end. He won in 4:11.9, a new indoor mile record for the Boston Garden. Lash finished second in 4:13 with Gene Venzke just four-tenths of a second behind him.

Twelve thousand fans gave Cunningham a rousing reception. Other athletes and everyone near him also mobbed him for autographs. All requests he graciously obliged. The item of last year's race where Cunningham was vilified for unintentionally cutting off Mangan was never mentioned in any of the pre-race write-ups. "You will recall when I ran last year that little mix-up I had with Joe Mangan at the finish," Cunningham told columnist Arthur Duffy, "which I assure you was unintentional. You'll also recall the boos I received and it sure did hurt. I was so pleased when I won and the crowd gave me such a hand." Having won the K. of C. mile three times in a row and in breaking the record, he was awarded and given permanent possession of the James M. Curley Trophy. Sportswriters unanimously voted him the outstanding athlete for that Knights of Columbus Boston classic.

Never one to forget someone who helped him, Cunningham heaped praise on Jimmy Cox, who was now Harvard's new trainer: "I probably would not be running if it hadn't been for Cox. . . . He is a wonder with injuries and they certainly miss him back in Kansas."

Back in Kansas, too, was stored the memory of the fire and of the painful recovery, the unexpected recovery, the come-from-behind kind of recovery and ultimate victory. You wonder: Was Cunningham unconsciously reliving this pivotal juncture in his life, particularly in this most spectacular vintage victorious run? Did he relive that period of time through many of his races? Indeed, within his race strategy, was he the director, setting the stage and returning time and time again to those nightmarish moments in his life?

Another winner that evening was the "colored" Jimmy Herbert, who won the 600-yard event. Herbert would also be a Madison Square Garden repeater over the years. And the next week it would be Madison Square Garden again for the Millrose Games and its Wanamaker Mile.

The Wanamaker Mile, over the years, was the charismatic gold standard for the indoor mile. With the record-breaking performance at the reputedly slower Boston Garden track a week earlier, newspapers hyped this year's race as a potential world indoor mile record setter. The hype, however, was more of a hope.

"Running against the opposition rather than the clock, the battleship gray boards rumbling under his pounding feet, his muscular legs whirring like a threshing machine and the roar of 16,000 people beating down on him, through a thin, blue veil of smoke Glenn Cunningham staged a great Man o' War finish at the Garden last nite [sic] to win the Wanamaker Mile and permanent possession of the Rodman Wanamaker Trophy," wrote Kevin Jones in the *Sunday News* (February 7, 1937).

It was a usual Cunningham race with the usual cast. Yet it did not lack excitement. Glenn clocked 4:12.4. Gene Venzke, now of the New York A.C., was second, seven yards behind. Third was Archie San Romani representing Kansas State Teacher's College. The time was slow, 4:14.6. Don Lash was fourth. But he had set the pace for the first three-quarters of a mile. Then Venzke and San Romani angled their way ahead of Lash while Cunningham kept his next-to-last position. Charles Fenske representing the University of Wisconsin held fifth (and last) place throughout.

For the fans and for the newsreels, it was thrilling. The public was really enthusiastic about track and particularly so for the mile race. Listen again to newsreel commentator Ed Thorgersen's voice-over description of the February 6, 1937 Wanamaker Mile as now they are in nearing the eleventh or last lap: "At the far turn coming into the last lap, Don Lash leads with Gene Venzke snapping at his heels. Glenn Cunningham is running third, biding his time, San Romani is fourth, Chuck Fenske is fifth. Lash the pacemaker now gives way before the burning drive of Cunningham. Venzke steps into second place, Lash is third. But it's Cunningham exploding his chilling finale while 16,000 shrieking spectators once again acclaim the mighty Kansan as the undisputed king of the milers."

Lash, the pacemaker, being passed by Cunningham and Venzke.

What you see in this newsreel footage, and in any of Cunningham's races, is not so much speed—and he was indeed fast—but raw power, power coming not only from his legs but from his entire body.

That Cunningham studied his opponents is true. That he needed a long warm-up and felt insecure about his legs is true; but it seems true, too, that he relied on his opponents to set a pace so that he might come from behind and thus relive, and again win, at a time when it seemed he might not. And it's harder to come from behind since the lead runner is at the very inside and the runner behind has to run around him.

Some footnotes to the evening. Herbert again won ". . . the Millrose 600, which went to James B. Herbert, *colored*, of the New York Curb Exchange. . . ."

An earlier footnote was covered in the newspapers: Police were strictly parolling the area, chasing away anyone who didn't appear to have a ticket. One policeman approached an apparent idler and ordered, "Keep moving, buddy." The idler responded "Okay officer, but give me a chance to warm up." It was Glenn Cunningham, still outside with his wife waiting for a friend.

Another runner Glenn would meet years later in an abbreviated old-timers' exhibition at the 1988 Millrose Games was Abel Kiviat. Kiviat had come in second in the 1500-meter race of the 1912 Olympic games (3:56.9, one-tenth of a second slower than the first place finisher). Now (in 1937) forty-five years old, he criticized Lash's poor pacing judgment and predicted Lash would never beat Cunningham in the mile. He was almost right. Cunningham would lose one time to Lash. It would be that year in the Dartmouth indoor mile with Glenn third, Lash second, and San Romani first.

Outspoken, verbal, and frank, Cunningham had a lot to say

when questioned by reporters. He wasn't surprised by Lash's comparatively slow first half mile. He attributed that to Lash having flown to New York only that morning, and after competing the night before. "You chaps who have never done any running write so freely about 4:10 miles that you lead the public to expect a new record every time out." At that point Cunningham mopped his sweat-drenched brow, then continued. "It's not as simple as that. Records depend on pace and friend Lash wasn't in the mood to run himself ragged tonight." He concluded a long discussion saying: "I could have made better time, but I planned this race to win, not set a record."

There was even some prescience to Cunningham's response. Remember that in 1954 when the four-minute mile was broken, Roger Bannister had Chris Brasher and Chris Chataway, his running colleagues, set paces for him.

In the same interview Glenn was asked about some of his rivals. He said that Venzke was the most consistent, that Lovelock peaked for one race better than anyone, but the best miler he ever met? He named Brocksmith of Indiana, the man he beat at Chicago for the Intercollegiate, winning in 4:11.1— breaking the old record and getting by Brocksmith by only a few steps. "Brocksmith could have run a 4:04 mile," Cunningham contended, "if he hadn't had to quit track for business."

What endeared Glenn Cunningham to sports columnists (as quoted from an original article from *KU Connection* April 20, 1940, when Glenn was to compete in his final race at the Kansas Relays) was his humility. One writer said that what he and his peers had "first liked about Cunningham was that he was a great runner who didn't go around telling everyone that he was [and] never made a practice of criticizing his opponents."

One more note: Cunningham told reporters then that he was better indoors than outdoors despite the heavy atmosphere inside. In the Wanamaker Mile, the announcer had asked people to stop smoking half an hour before the race. Cunningham said that he actually felt the difference and was grateful that the crowd had cooperated. "It made me feel fresher for that tough stretch drive."

As in just about every sport, if it happens in New York, it's big and it gets headlines everywhere, particularly in the East. For this particular Wanamaker Mile there was a plethora of articles and commentaries. For the next contest, however, one in a location not exactly a minor city, namely Boston, there were headlines but few articles. And the headline read: CUNNINGHAM SETS B.A.A. MILE RECORD. Cunningham's was a mere Boston Athletic Association record and in the relatively slow-for-Cunningham time of 4:12.3. In a sub-headline that said CUNNINGHAM MILE WINNER, it told that the largest gathering—13,682 paid customers—ever to attend an indoor meet in the Boston area saw three world records broken; one of them was Don Lash's breaking of Paavo Nurmi's indoor record for the two-mile event. Yet it was Cunningham's usual, oft-repeated type of performance that gained notice.

Usual? Here's what the Boston writer said: "Cunningham was content to let Venzke set the pace for the first ten laps and just strode along with the former U. of Penn star until he hit the back stretch of the gun lap, then Glenn started to go."

Surely Cunningham was back in the good graces of the track world. He won most of the time, though not all of the time. So there was always some suspense. Furthermore, it is human nature to focus on an individual. We identify with the flagpole sitter, the tightrope walker, the individual fighting a rare disease, more so than with destruction of thousands, even millions, in famines, hurricanes, and fires.

Cunningham was again the hero, coming from behind, emerging victorious just as Roosevelt had predicted the whole country would ultimately do. But this was a particular time when the underdog was needed by the public, and was needed to win.

A simple definition of a hero is someone who has overcome an obstacle of nature. Cunningham had certainly done that, as had his parents along with the early Kansas settlers. And why do we need a hero? Bernard Malamud answers this in the words of one of his characters in his classic *The Natural*: "Without heroes," he explains, "we're all plain people and don't know how far we can go."

For Cunningham, too, the limit of how far we can go was a matter more mental than physical. He did think that the four-minute mile barrier was strictly a mental issue. He always said that he did not know what the human limitations were, but that we were still a long way from our potential.

Glenn Cunningham was certainly a hero for his time, a time of economic depression.

There was no sign of Cunningham's intention to cut down on racing in 1937. On the other hand many of his races would be in the New York/New Jersey locale. He was attending New York University so there was no extensive travel.

Next race was the Baxter Mile at the New York A.C. games in Madison Square Garden. The Baxter Mile was named for Harry Baxter, still living in 1937 and "hale and hearty" at age seventy-five. Baxter in his heyday was a champion vaulter, a hurdler, a high jumper, a gymnast with a New York A.C. weight-lifting record, even a hammer thrower. The donator of the trophy for the Baxter Mile had done everything but run a mile.

A feature of the 1937 Baxter Mile was the entry of Luigi Beccali. He had won the 1500-meter Olympic race in 1932 and was third in that event in the 1936 Olympiad. Now twenty-nine and an engineer, combining this trip with "business," he was expected to be in good enough shape to seriously challenge Cunningham. His short strides and studious pre-race planning augured well, at least in the press, for a keen competitive effort. Another entrant, Archie San Romani, the fellow Kansan who had beaten Glenn the past fall at Princeton, was also considered a formidable threat for Cunningham. Rounding out the entry field was Mikles Szabo of Hungary, and—undaunted by anyone, anywhere, in any competitive venue—was Gene Venzke.

Also on the card, but in the two-mile race, was the new record holder, Don Lash.

Pre-race press articles focused on whether Cunningham's indoor record of 4:08.4 would be threatened and whose closing surge was faster, Beccali's or Cunningham's?

As usual it was a sellout crowd of sixteen thousand. San Romani was unable to appear because his plane was grounded by fog. He was replaced by Ray Sears. Sears was probably inserted as a rabbit. His job was to set a fast pace. Which he did. For seven laps Sears was well into the lead. Cunningham didn't bite. Not even when Sears began to tire. Finally Venzke burst into the lead at eight and a half laps. Still Cunningham, "the imperturbable one," let the race flow on. But then with eighty yards left—actually only half a lap to go—Cunningham began to drive. At the final turn Venzke was seeing Cunningham's broad shoulders just ahead of him. Glenn won by two yards over Gene. Ten yards behind him came Beccali. Winning time was 4:12.4. Beccali's time: 4:14.2.

Cunningham spoke to the press. He said that he felt very good for this race, that an ankle injury had healed. But last year, in his loss to Venzke in the same race, because of his ankle problem he was unable to get up on his toes and so couldn't depend on a fast finish. Therefore he went faster in the first half, hoping he could get a good enough lead to stave off Venzke's ending thrust. But that was all last year. This year he was content with his race and was gracious in his words about his opponents. He said that Beccali ran a strong race considering it was his first on the boards and that Venzke "is by far the most consistent miler I ever faced."

But he was negative about the presence of tobacco smoke: "It tears your throat out after you've gone half a mile. Your mouth is so dry you can't swallow and every breath cuts like a knife. . . . All I aim to do is win the race—and the slower the pace, the better."

Much was written about Cunningham's consistency. Lovelock was quoted as calling Cunningham "the greatest contemporary miler." He added, "No runner in the world, including myself, can match him over a year or a period of years. He runs in high gear every minute."

Consistency in running, consistency in rearing his children, consistency in discipline, consistency in values, these were all Cunningham hallmarks.

Soon after the Baxter Mile, syndicated columnist John Lardner, son of Ring Lardner, wrote two long articles, really essays, on Cunningham's running style. Apparently Glenn had truly ushered in a new era, the idea of running the second half faster than the first. He explained that the first half was tantamount to a warm-up: "At the end of the first half your heart and lungs and glands are built up to maximum efficiency. And that's the time to apply the pressure."

Before Cunningham, coaches would tell their milers to run as fast as they could right from the beginning and try to hold on as long as possible. Such a strategy often found milers sagging and staggering at the finish line. Cunningham often could tell a timer exactly what his clock time was for a given distance, so keen was his sense of pacing.

Cunningham's ideas were foreshadowed by Paavo Nurmi. Nurmi's running career was ending at the start of Cunningham's. The fabled Finn introduced the "even pace" method, spreading his effort uniformly over the mile course.

Lardner offered some other insights about Glenn's running. One was that he did prefer an indoor setting, but one in which there was no smoking. Outdoor running, however, had its own obstacles like wind resistance and the state of the track itself. Indoor conditions, furthermore, could be modified. For example there could be longer loops, giving the runner a chance to open the throttle a longer way without having to cope with too many turns. Lardner also told of Glenn's scholarly master's thesis at Iowa U. In it Cunningham showed that the mechanical timer was one-tenth of a second more accurate than the stopwatch.

And one more note, good for a trivia question: Glenn's heart rate was forty-eight beats per minute and Paavo Nurmi's was forty-three. Nurmi actually ran in longer races than did Cunningham, his slower heart rate probably an advantage for the distance events.

The next race that the press could summon up any suspense for was the Chicago Bankers Mile. Glenn had done it in 1932, winning in a time of 4:19.2. What was at stake this time was the trophy donated by the late Melvin Taylor. Cunningham had one leg up on it with his 1932 first-place finish.

It was a race that was narrowed down to the two Kansans,

Archie San Romani the "little Emporia Kansas runner" and the "husky" Glenn Cunningham. It was a jockeying for position for about the first half until the little guy took the lead. Then at the eleventh lap, the final lap, Cunningham turned it on as the now screaming crowd arose as one. Cunningham was able to pull up to San Romani's shoulder with half a lap to go. But little Archie had a spurt of his own and Glenn couldn't equal San Romani's sizzling kick, which carried him two yards ahead of Cunningham at the finish. Venzke finished five yards in "Cunningham's wake," as the Associated Press put it. Finishing time was 4:21, considered fairly good for a new undeveloped track, one that had been cut up by spikes in earlier events.

Other times San Romani was referred to as a "slender Kansan Italian," and Cunningham as "aging and ailing." Apparently San Romani had been severely injured as a youngster, with some reference made to his leg being crushed by a truck. As the story went, he was saved from amputation by a childhood plea to the surgeon. Thus the runner with the burned legs versus the runner with the crushed leg.

Of special note was a coast-to-coast Columbia hookup for the broadcast of the Bankers Mile classic.

At this time there was a newspaper write-up telling of Cunningham's training and studying in New York City. The article said that he did not like New York, that he "much prefers the plains of Kansas to the towers of Gotham."

In a statement reflecting his keen observations of New York living and his philosophy of life, he commented that "Everyone hurries all day long but they do not get anywhere."

But New York still thrilled to Cunningham's mile runs and was now looking toward the reprise of the Columbian Mile, last year's notable for the slowest major mile of all time. This time it would be San Romani, Beccali and of course Gene Venzke.

George Trevor writing in the *New York Sun* was under the impression that the Columbian Mile this year would be Cunningham's valedictory appearance. He thought, as did many of track's writers, that Glenn was looking for a coaching job. Such a position would disqualify him as an amateur. Further on he wrote what had been obvious up to now: "They haven't always cheered Glenn," he penned, "these garden regulars, but even when they hooted the Iron Horse they acknowledged him as a master miler. New Yorkers are a queer tribe. They root for the under-dog and boo the odds-on favorite. It's the penalty for being too good. Glenn's repeated triumphs bored the customers. They craved variety and yelled for Venzke to upset the superman."

He went on to explain Glenn's odd-looking warm-up mannerisms and the unfair thinking that he was cocky and had a swelled head. To the contrary, Trevor described Glenn as shy and diffident. "There's a purpose behind his eccentric going-on," he explained. "He tosses his head to loosen up the muscles of his neck; he snorts to clear nasal passages which are too small for a runner; he prances around the track before a race to warm up legs which are covered with scar tissue as the result of burns suffered in a schoolhouse fire; he waits until all rivals are stripped for action before removing his sweat suit in order to keep those scorched legs from being chilled."

No wonder bookmakers hedged their bets when they saw this seemingly exhausting ritual.

Appearing in the same newspaper (the *New York Sun*), Glenn Cunningham dispelled rumors of his farewell to running. As to the evening's events, he was wary of a schedule change for the mile. It was moved from 10:00 PM to 11:00 PM . The later the race the more smoke in the air, and "that always cuts speed," he remarked.

What is particularly noteworthy is the actual number of New York City newspapers functioning at this time, all trumpeting the track scene. There was always the *New York Times*, also the *Sun*, the *New York American*, the *Sunday Mirror*, the *Herald Tribune*, the *New York World Telegram*, the *Sunday News*, the *Daily News*. And a write-up for the Columbia Mile sitting in the Cunningham scrapbook was in the *New York Evening Journal*.

Dated Thursday, March 18, 1937, it told of Cunningham's race in the K. of C. Columbian Mile where he vied with the usual cast of San Romani, Beccali, and Venzke.

Cunningham ran behind San Romani and Beccali for most of the race, at least until well past the three-quarter mark. Then with less than a lap (160 yards) to go he powered his way into the lead. But the others had the same idea. San Romani would later rue his speeding up too soon when he discovered he was a second behind at the three-quarter mark and had "robbed myself of the finish kick I needed to hold off Cunningham." Glenn finished four feet in front of Archie; two feet behind him was Beccali. Venzke was last but only three yards behind Beccali. Glenn's time was 4:08.7, only three tenths of a second off his indoor world record mark. It was also recorded as the fourth fastest mile in history.

The *Daily News* added another slant: "San Romani made a desperate driving attempt to regain the lead, but Glenn refused to give ground. He finished strong as the fans boomed approval from the smoky recesses of the Eighth Ave. structure." Cunningham would have heartily approved, too, if the smoky recesses were entirely absent.

Something else happened in this race. At one point Glenn was forced off the track just before the last lap. Beccali was crowding him. It was a matter of going off the track and losing about half a second, or being forced to run up the back of the front-runner, San Romani. (Looking at the 1936 Olympic 1500-meter footage, there was a point where Cunningham, on the inside, was momentarily forced off the track. In a race the upfront runner would be spiked by the runner behind who, in turn, was avoiding being crowded. The front-runner would always emerge second best if the crowded runner chose to lunge forward rather than sideways.)

The next competition in the New York area was a Senior Metropolitan A.A.U. championship in Yonkers, really a tune-up for the upcoming Princeton Mile a week later. As many as ten thousand track enthusiasts saw Glenn Cunningham win the mile race in 4:14.1, a time that cracked the previous meet record. A feature of that race was the introduction of Leslie MacMitchell, then only sixteen. He finished second, sixty yards behind Cunningham. Glenn had run the second half faster than his first, a 2:09.4 followed by a 2:04.7.

In a postscript, Lewis Burton in a column titled DOTS AND DASHES, wrote of Cunningham's appearance in that track meet at Glen Park in Yonkers. He wrote of Glenn's disbursing of autographs, of the crowds of children that had mobbed him and how he patiently obliged their requests. (The same writer opined that Glenn Cunningham had become a legend along with Babe Ruth, Jack Dempsey, and Bobby Jones.) Finally at the end of his signings, Glenn was quoted: "Phew! I think some of the kids doubled up on me, but when I was warming up I promised some of them that I'd see them after the race. I don't like to break into my warm-up, and I don't like to break my promise. You have to keep the interest of those youngsters in athletics alive. Anything that will help in that way is a service. Shucks, I don't want to be a moralist. I like to do it, even though I know that most of them are thrown away as soon as the kids get home. But as long as I run I'll have to face and like it."

The Princeton Invitational on Saturday, June 20, was a bleak day with a cold raw wind whipping across Palmer Stadium, a wind that would buffet the runners as they approached the open end of the stadium but would lend them winged feet as they rushed down the homestretch. There was also the threat of rain hovering over the field all day. Rain never did arrive—nor did the predicted new world record. It was, nevertheless, a real thriller. The catalyst, by virtue of his semi-absence, would be Gene Venzke. The field also included Archie San Romani—now dubbed heir apparent to the mile throne—Don Lash, and Luigi Beccali.

Venzke's role was crucial. That day he had his own agenda. He was out to break the three-quarter-mile record. His first quarter was 0.58.6, his half-mile time was 2:00.2, and at the three-quarter mark, his private goal line, Gene Venzke's time was 3:01.4, only eight-tenths of a second behind the sought-for record. He had brought Lash even with him at the halfway mark, where they were twenty yards ahead of Glenn and Archie. Somewhere between the halfway and three-quarter point, both Cunningham and San Romani caught on to what was going on. They began to close on Lash so that at the three-quarter mark they were only ten yards behind. As the gun sounded for the last circuit, Venzke quit.

Now the race was on among Lash, San Romani, and his fellow Kansan Glenn Cunningham. At first the two Kansans exchanged the lead, with Lash a whisker behind them. Then into the homestretch with Cunningham holding a very meager lead, both Lash and San Romani, with forty yards to go, galloped past Cunningham. There they stayed together and crossed the finish line virtually together, each timed in the same 4:07.2. The only one ever to beat that time was Cunningham in 1934 when he set the then still-standing world record of 4:06.7. Glenn was only two yards behind the San Romani-Lash duo.

A quiet came over the once screaming twenty thousand assembled. Five minutes passed. Then the judges made their decision. The heir apparent Kansan was the winner with Don Lash second, beating Cunningham and defying Abel Kiviat's prediction that Lash would never best Cunningham. Luigi Beccali, although twenty yards back, finished under 4:10.

The mile run brought the games to an end, fulfilling a promise that the fourth annual Princeton meet would provide great performances and surprises, even though the runners had failed to eclipse the world record for the mile.

After the race, San Romani (a sportswriter wrote that he was the most personable of all the milers) paid homage to Cunningham's consistency. Asked if he expected Cunningham to overtake him he replied in the affirmative and added: "You can always bank on Cunningham passing you in the homestretch. It's a safe bet every time."

The next important race was a week later, important in that it was the only time—Cunningham told us in 1987 at Boston—that he ever set out to actually break a record.

The distance was one and a half miles, one of the race distances no longer held. The world-record holder for that distance was the fabled Paavo Nurmi. Earlier in the day Glenn had won a half-mile race in Passaic, New Jersey. He then sped by auto to New York's Randall's Island for the mile-and-a-half.

What he told us in Boston was that he had boasted—yes,

boasted—that he could break the record in a sweatsuit, that he was accustomed to running 66-second quarter miles when he warmed up.

He did just that. With only Joe McCluskey as a potential, but in the race ever-fading, rival, Cunningham reeled off consecutive 66-second quarter miles (mile in 4:25) topped off by a 64-second final quarter, setting a world record of 6:34 and beating Nurmi's old mark by more than eight seconds. McCluskey, who had held a slight lead at the quarter-mile mark, finished second, 110 yards behind.

The next race where record-breaking times were predicted was at the 1500-meter run in the fiftieth annual A.A.U. track championship held at Marquette Stadium in Wisconsin, July 3, 1937. It was to be a duel between Cunningham and San Romani. It was, right up to the last lap. But with Cunningham trailing San Romani by a step beginning the last lap of the race, San Romani stumbled on the curbing and fell. In so doing he spiked Cunningham in the left leg. Archie got up and was even able to pass two runners, finishing fourth to a great ovation. To a similarly enthusiastic cheer Cunningham finished in 3:51.8, short of his own record, the spiking and its consequent interference with rhythm and pace no doubt slowing him. He was twenty-two yards ahead of Jimmy Smith, mentioned as an "Indiana Negro."

As if to settle a score, Cunningham and San Romani were set to meet a week later at the second annual World Labor Athletic Carnival held on the Randall's Island track. Another entrant of interest was John Woodruff, who had been running a 4:19 mile as a schoolboy but had given that up for the 800-meter race, an event he won in the 1936 Olympics. Advertised in the press was his estimated stride of ten feet.

Woodruff finished a disappointing fourth. But his appearance so spooked San Romani that he went out too fast, with Cunningham laying back just behind him. Then came the inevitable Cunningham driving burst down the homestretch to a winning time of 4:11.4. It was a hot day, and mention was made of "the heat, which loosened up his aging muscles." In third place was Gene Venzke.

The headlines actually alluded more to the half-mile winner, Elroy Robinson. He had broken Eastman's three-year-old record by three-tenths of a second and Cunningham's unofficial record by one-tenth of a second. His time was 1:49.6. Robinson's only regret was that Woodruff had not competed in the event.

But Woodruff would comply with Robinson's wishes a week later at Dallas's Cotton Bowl for the Pan-American Games. The headliners for the games included Elroy Robinson, Cunningham, and San Romani. In the 800 meters it was Woodruff who would set a world mark of 1:47.8. At the second turn of the last lap, with long loping strides, Woodruff passed Robinson, then increased his lead on the homestretch. And in the 1500-meter run, this time not the event in the headlines, Cunningham, with a hundred meters to go, shook off Chuck Fenske who had managed to stay right at Glenn's elbow until the homestretch, only to finish ten yards behind. Cunningham's time was 3:56.4, far from any record.

17

1938

I was at New York University working on my Ph.D. degree. Now out on the ranch they know that as a "posthole digger."

Ever-darkening war clouds were gathering. On January 3 President Roosevelt warned Congress of the need for military strength because of the international tensions requiring the United States to defend itself. (His warnings would go unheeded.) Not only war clouds, but also signs of a worsening recession since the middle of 1937 were accumulating. Another two million workers joined the unemployed ranks. But that tide would be stemmed, and by late summer there were some signs of economic recovery; Congress complied with Roosevelt's call for finance relief measures and public work projects.

Joe Louis, now world heavyweight champion, knocked out Max Schmeling in one round, successfully defending his title and avenging his only defeat at the hands of the German two years earlier. In the entertainment world, in a radio adaptation, Orson Welles so convincingly narrated H. G. Wells's *War of the Worlds* that thousands of listeners called that radio station, even called the police and newspapers, in a state of hysteria. There were anecdotal accounts of people fleeing their homes. A hurricane hit New England, causing extensive damage and taking six hundred lives. Notable deaths included Associate Justice of the Supreme Court,

Benjamin Cardozo, 68, and novelist Thomas Wolfe, 37. On June 25, in Bonners Ferry Idaho, Glenn's oldest living brother, Raymond, 31, was killed in a multi-car crash. He and their parents had been living in Idaho since the early 1930s in a home that Glenn had bought for them.

On November 1, at Baltimore's Pimlico Racecourse, Seabiscuit defeated the 4:1 favorite, War Admiral, in an epic match race.

Before that, in June, Glenn Cunningham had graduated from N.Y.U. with a doctorate in biology, health and physical education. The subject of his thesis was "The Relation of Selected

Glenn at his 1938 NYU graduation. Brutus Hamilton on left.

Cardiovascular and Strength Measures to Physical Fitness of Trained Athletes." It was a study of respiratory and pulse rate along with grip strength, before and after workouts.

He had been working by day in a stock brokerage firm and going to school at night. He now had his Ph.D. He rarely called himself "doctor" and never used the title "Dr." in any correspondence or conversation. When one of his daughters was little she had heard someone refer to him as a doctor. So she asked her dad if he was a doctor, why couldn't he treat them rather than have them going to one in town? Glenn told her it was because he was "the kind of doctor that did nobody no good!" In fact when he spoke to us in 1987 at our Boston banquet he alluded to his doctorate this way: "I was at New York University working on my Ph.D. degree. Now out on the ranch they know that as a 'post-hole digger.'"

Glenn during his brief stint as a stockbroker.

A month before the New Year of 1938, Cunningham, along with his wife and baby, had come to Sarasota, Florida, so that Glenn could train and the family could stay with "Doc" Roland "Kickapoo" Logan, his old trainer and friend and now Boston Red Sox trainer.

At the New Year's Sugar Bowl event, Glenn began the 1938 track year winning the mile in 4:13.2. That time broke the old Sugar Bowl record by eight-tenths of a second. Again it was his burst of speed coming down the home stretch to win by two yards. San Romani, no slouch at finishing drives, was second, Don Lash third, Chuck Fenske fourth. The New York newspaper headline read: DURABLE KANSAN, LIKE OL' MAN RIVER, JEST KEEPS ROLLIN' ALONG. The first paragraph said: "Ole Man River and Glenn Cunningham—they just keep rollin' and they don't say nothin'."

He did, however, say more than the song title implied telling that he would quit "When I can't keep up with the rest of the boys."

Another theme, oft repeated, the meaning of *Ad Astra per Aspera*, was spelled out in the same AP Ol' Man River article: "It was a Kansas boyhood—with cows to milk, wood to chop, wheat to harvest and other farm tasks—that built his phenomenal endurance." His endurance would help gain even more records in 1938.

The hook for the press this year was the purported rivalry between Glenn Cunningham and Archie San Romani. They were both Kansans. Both had suffered severe leg injuries in childhood, and both were now running for the New York Curb Exchange. San Romani, said to pattern himself after Cunningham, was heralded as heir apparent, the one who would become "King of the Milers."

The premier milers in the world now were Cunningham, San Romani, Don Lash, and Sydney Wooderson of England. Wooderson had bested Cunningham's world outdoor mile record of 4:06.7 by two tenths of a second the summer before.

Cunningham had his own predictions for the projected 1940 Olympics. He had high praise for Chuck Fenske. He said that Fenske was capable of a 4:06. He could foresee Leslie MacMitchell, then a New York schoolboy, as a member of the 1940 team. Although he thought highly of San Romani's abilities, he had to take into consideration Archie's new responsibilities as a family man and so omitted him in his crystal ball gazing. As for himself, Cunningham left it to the newspapers. Here his steadiness and consistency were highlighted, as was "his enthusiasm for the sport [that] has not waned."

Glenn was also working as a speaker for the Lecture Course Bureau of the Extension Service of the University of Kansas through 1939. Since about 1915 they had been furnishing programs to schools and communities in Kansas and Oklahoma. It would be the forerunner of what he would do for the rest of his life: to give—for lack of a more suitable term—inspirational talks, telling of sportsmanship and comparing values of the training athlete to everyday living.

The *Abilene Reflector* noted: "The University of Kansas never did a smarter thing than to send out Glenn Cunningham as an ambassador of good will for the athletic department."

The dramatic phase of the track competition for 1938 began with the Prout Memorial Games at Boston Garden, set for the end of January. Here Cunningham's opposition would be San Romani, with some suspense over whether Lash would enter the mile race. He would likely serve as pacemaker, helping to assure fans of a fast mile.

Despite the press ballyhoo it was almost a nonevent. The "barrel-chested Kansan," now representing the New York A.C., bested San Romani by ten yards, winning in 4:13.8. Running second to Norman Bright for part of the way, then behind San Romani for the latter part of the contest, Cunningham accelerated the last lap and a half, making it a no-contest affair. Gene Venzke, finishing strong, nevertheless placed third.

In the Wanamaker Mile of the Millrose Games scheduled for Saturday, February 7, the cast, besides Cunningham, would include the "Italian cornet tooter," Archie San Romani, who seemed to be Cunningham's equal out of doors, but not yet so indoors.

Cunningham's indoor victories in particular were born not only from sheer physical power, but also from mental power. It was knowing when to time his sprint, knowing how to take the forty odd turns on the indoor track as compared with sixteen out of doors. Board track racing always requires not only shrewd judgment of pace but also an instinctive sense of timing the drive for the tape. Cunningham was said to have owned a sixth sense of when to make his victory bid on the boards.

Anytime Venzke, Mangan, or San Romani did win over Cunningham, it came about by somehow forcing him to set the pace, usually against his will. It was generally thought that pacemaking itself takes a nervous toll. Furthermore the runner behind has a target to aim at and can better rate his finishing effort.

Those who studied Cunningham's Madison Square Garden strategy noted that he would make his final burst with 120 yards to go—when rounding the Ninth Avenue curve on the last lap. From his burn injuries, Cunningham, lacking the sprinter's lift, needed the inside track, the "pole," in order to launch his finishing drive. What he seemed to do was swing around on the banked turn and accelerate going downhill off that turn. This nevertheless was a true skill, and it could be disaster, with a runner losing his stride and pace if he did not maneuver the turns properly.

For this Wanamaker classic, Fred Schmertz who directed the Millrose Games was leaning toward Don Lash. He described him as "strong as a bull." This time Lash would have at least seventy minutes of rest compared with the twenty minutes or so in Boston. To add more suspense, San Romani was figured also to be stronger after Boston, Venzke still had the speed, and Fenske, only twenty years old, was on the upgrade and was the "miler of the future."

An article in the *New York Post* by Arch Murray, written on the eve of the 1938 Wanamaker Mile, transcends the mechanistic in explaining Cunningham's competitive drive. He quotes ". . . an old timer, in town for the meet." The old-timer explains, "It's the killer instinct. Cunningham came up the hard way, you know. The burns that almost cost him his life . . . were in the end his greatest asset. They taught him the value of working for what you want; they added a certain fiber of hardness to his soul."

Described as "the ruddy-cheeked old fellow, his face hidden in a cloud of smoke," the old-timer compared Cunningham to Jack Dempsey, Ty Cobb, and Bill Tilden. "Watch Cunningham tonight. You'll see what I mean. Win, lose or draw, he never lets up."

In other words, *Ad Astra per Aspera*.

Those "old-timer" observations don't tell a complete story. Nor does the following explanation from this particular writer-psychiatrist-old-timer, but combined they might make a more complete picture. For what was unique in this unique man was his appreciation for, and ability to, play.

NEW YORK POST, SATURDAY, FEBRUARY 5, 1938

'Killer Instinct' Has Kept Cunningham on Top of Mile Pack

MANGAN ONLY RIVAL SINCE 1932 TO HALT GLENN IN WANAMAKER

Millrose Games Test for Champion Will Come from San Romani and Lash Before Full House at Garden

By ARCH MURRAY

Anything can happen in the flaming fire of competition that is the Millrose Games, but the same thing usually does. The dice have rolled the same way four out of the five past years. Since 1932 only one man—now retired to the shadows beyond the banked rim of the wooden trail—has been able to halt Glenn Cunningham's string of triumphs in the Wanamaker Mile, classic event of the glittering games that usher in the Garden track season tonight.

That man was Joe Mangan, poker-faced Cornellian, and he had his night of destiny in 1936. But nobody else has been able to do it. They all have tried—mighty monarchs of the mile such as Blazing Bill Bonthron, Gene Venzke, Luigi Beccali, Archie San Romani and Don Lash. All have tried—but only Mangan found the secret formula of triumph.

Now another Wanamaker Mile rolls around, and once again the old master is going to the post a heavy pre-race favorite. Up in Boston last week he proved that he still possesses all of his old drive and power, his blasting kick on ageless battle-scarred legs. It would be a daring soul who would wager anything against him.

Fans Ask Many Questions

How does he do it? What is the answer to his constant flaunting of the burden of increasing years? Doesn't he ever tire of the incessant grind? How does he keep his incentive, that vital will to win? These are just some of the questions the 16,000-odd fans will be asking as they jam their way through the portals of the Garden.

Glenn himself will simply shrug away those questions. All he ever says is: "There's no secret. Steady training and an intense love of competition have kept me going. Maybe they'll have to cut my shoes off some day. But until the crowd stops roaring, I guess I'll be out there."

But there's more to it than that. And high up in a hotel skyscraper this morning, an old-timer, in town for the meet, seemed to come closer than any one to hitting the nail on the head.

"It's the killer instinct. Cunningham came up the hard way, you know," the ruddy-cheeked old fellow was saying; his face hidden in a cloud of swirling smoke. "The burns that almost cost him his life, when a Kansan youngster, were in the end his greatest asset. They taught him the value of working for what you want; they added a certain fiber of hardness to his soul.

"Great champions have been that way before him. All of them—the Dempseys, the Cobbs, the Shores, the Ching Johnsons, the Tildens, the Hagens and the Franks—were all killers in this sense of the word. They knew what they wanted and nothing would stop them. They never eased off the pace. They kept punching. Watch Cunningham tonight. You'll see what I mean. Win, lose or draw, he never lets up."

Hits Upon Basic Reason

He had something there—the basic reason why Cunningham is so hard to beat. He has that vital "meanness" when he gets out there, affable as he is off the track. And thus it is that he is always able to pack them in. Great as the other athletes are—the Herberts, 'San Romanis, Meadowses, Townses and the rest — the fight for pasteboards wouldn't be the same without Cunningham. He fills the Big House.

Perhaps his string of triumphs will be ended tonight. It's got to come some time, and the feeling persists that Archie San Romani is due for a top effort. He was all grimness yesterday—grimmer than ever before. Or Don Lash, hitting his crest, might race the field into the ground.

But whether the end does or does not come tonight, the fact remains that it is this killer instinct that has made Cunningham the champion he has been.

The king — and keeper — of the gate.

258

Play is a serious matter. So wrote Johann Huizinga in his classic *Homo Ludens: A Study of the Play Element in Culture*. In Glenn's competition, for the most part, it was the race itself that counted, not his time. And *that* race conformed to the essence of play, which Huizinga defined as ". . . an activity which proceeds within certain limits of time and space, in a visible order, according to rules freely accepted, and outside the sphere of necessity and material utility." I think the ideas of boundaries, limits, discipline, structure, and rules all appealed to Glenn, resonating and harmoniously blending with his way of life.

Furthermore, the activity must be performed "utterly" and "intensely." Finally, to do play really right, ". . . a man must play like a child." Huizinga also added: "The play-mood is one of rapture and enthusiasm." This harks back to Cunningham's Boston 1987 talk: "I never ran a race and won in my life because I was better than anyone else was. I think a lot of it is enthusiasm. If a bee ever stung you you'll understand what I mean. You know it isn't the size of the sting that makes it effective is it? It's the enthusiasm which the bee uses that counts."

I contend that Cunningham's affinity for children and animals, both of whom intuitively play, was born, and part and parcel, of his unique native ability to communicate with young people and horses, dogs, and other assorted creatures. In his play, he was expressing a basic human drive, a theme that will be returned to later. Cunningham, children, and animals were all bonded in their expression of play.

Back to the 1938 Madison Square Garden track, whose premier event was the Wanamaker Mile.

The capacity crowd saw Glenn allowing San Romani and Lash to assume the lead for the first three laps, then take over, never relinquishing the front spot, capping his win with a 59-second last quarter. Cunningham achieved his fifth Wanamaker win in six years. His time of 4:11 equaled the meet record. San Romani and Fenske were distant followers. Lash dropped out with a lap to go.

Wirephoto: Cunningham Wins Mile

Copyright by the Associated Press.

Glenn Cunningham is shown here as he won the Wanamaker Mile in the Millrose Games in Madison Square Garden last night. It was his fifth Wanamaker victory in six years. He equaled the meet record of 4:11. Archie San Romani and Charlie Fenske are shown far behind.

New York Times.

SUNDAY, FEBRUARY 6, 1938.

CUNNINGHAM TAKES WANAMAKER MILE AT GARDEN IN 4:11

Ties Millrose Meet Figures as He Beats San Romani Easily by 12 Yards

16,000 PACK THE ARENA

Herbert Retires 600 Trophy by Outrunning Miller—N. Y. U. Ace Timed in 1:12.6

WORLD RECORDS ARE SET

Johnson Excels in Dash, Towns and Tolmich in Hurdles— Woodruff Last in Half

By ARTHUR J. DALEY

In a race that was hand-tailored for him, Glenn Cunningham won the Wanamaker Mile before a capacity gathering of 16,000 at the thrill-packed Millrose A. A. carnival at Madison Square Garden last night with another of his highly efficient jobs.

The transplanted Kansan made it look so easy with a magnificent twelve-yard victory over his arch-foe, Archie San Romani, that the crowd even overlooked the fact his winning time of 4:11 never has been beaten in the history of the meet. Once Cunningham himself galloped the distance in 4:11 and once Joe Mangan did it, and until some one goes faster those figures will stand as the carnival record.

The race was cut to the Cunningham pattern from the opening gun and, once he took command seven and a half laps from the taut red worsted, it was all over. Hardly a person in the crowd, exhausted from a series of record-smashing sprint and hurdle tests, could expect anything but what actually happened.

Lash Sets Early Pace

The Old Master could not have planned the classic Wanamaker Mile better than it actually was run. He allowed the unpredictable Don Lash to set an early pace that was a dawdling jog that ruined all record-breaking possibilities and let the bottom drop right out of the Wanamaker Mile bag.

When the time at the end of the first quarter was announced as 63 seconds there was a low groan of disappointment and when the half was covered in 2:07 a speedy mile patently was out of the question.

But Cunningham apparently was satisfied to let it stay that way. He went past the three-quarters in 3:12 with no one in the field daring to take the play away from him. So, when he was good and ready, the Curb Exchange flier let go a lap from the finish and snapped the worsted twelve yards in front of his clubmate and friend, with Charlie Fenske of Wisconsin a step back, a thin black whisker ahead of Gene Venzke.

As for Lash, the villain in the piece dropped out a circuit from the end, more interested at the moment in what was going to happen in the two-mile run later in the program than in the eight-furlong feature. Cunningham's victory was his fifth in the race and gave him the initial leg on the new Rodman Wanamaker Trophy.

Nevertheless Glenn was disappointed with his performance. The Garden clock was five minutes slow, he explained, throwing off the timing of his warm-up. He did not feel comfortable in this race until the second half. He had thought he could have run a better time. Right after the race he was heard cursing under his breath, and, as if it was a revelation, was even quoted as having said "hell" and "damn." Accustomed to long days and hours working with laborers in the fields, from his vocal cords four-letter words always flowed freely; they were a regular part of his everyday vocabulary although he usually avoided these expressions whenever quoted.

Next followed lesser-publicized but no less dramatic runs. For example, he won on the old flat board track in the Seventh Regiment Armory meet in the old Park Avenue drill shed. Again, his last half was the faster. He set the pace early and was never really challenged. His time of 4:15.2 broke the old record of 4:18.2 set by Abel Kiviat back in 1913. Kiviat was among the three thousand spectators.

Jimmy Herbert won the 600, and Joe McCluskey won the two-mile run.

Cunningham won Boston's Hunter Mile a week later before thirteen thousand, his 4:10 then the fourth fastest indoor mile ever run. Venzke was second. Jimmy Herbert ran the fastest 600-yard run in Boston history, winning in 1:12.3.

Next would be the twenty-seventh running of the Baxter Mile, featuring Cunningham, San Romani, Gene Venzke, now of the New York A.C., and Blaine Rideout of North Texas State Teacher's College. The only hook sportswriters could fasten on to was that the year before, San Romani's plane was grounded and he missed the race, plus a spike wound had healed and he was ready to compete with Glenn Cunningham.

(A historical note: Abel Kiviat had won the Baxter event from 1910 through 1913. How would he have done against this 1930s generation of milers? Discussion was made that constant-speed running was a postwar innovation. That's post World War I. Milers were shooting for a 4:20 mile in Kiviat's era. And running against the clock in training wasn't emphasized.)

In the 1938 Baxter run, Venzke was shadowing Cunningham right up to the last quarter of a mile. Then Glenn turned it on with a race against the clock. The clock won. Cunningham's time was 4:08.6, twenty yards ahead of Venzke but two-tenths of a second behind his own world indoor mile record. At the gun, Cunningham was last getting off the mark, perhaps accounting for at least a fifth of a second, one newspaper speculated. The crowd had had some excitement at the three-quarter mark when Venzke, breathing heavily, had pulled up to within a stride of Cunningham. San Romani was a distant third.

Up to this time, a tabulation of Glenn's main races since entering college found him in sixty-two major events, winning fifty-one times, placing second eight times, and no worse than third in the remaining races.

Writing in the *Times* about Cunningham's Baxter performance, Arthur Daley commented that Glenn had "at last" captured the enthusiasm of track followers at large. He could not really explain this lag, "because there is not a finer character or sportsman in the footracing game than Glenn Cunningham." He did opine that Glenn's stellar participation in the relays, particularly his 0:50.2 quarter mile that had brought victory to his team, was maybe something fans truly appreciated.

Writers were now taking more notice of Cunningham's sportsmanship. One article cited his sending an autographed card to a young admirer, a fifteen-year-old boy, who was then recovering from surgery. A card saying "Best Wishes" from Glenn Cunningham buoyed the lad's uneasy two-week recovery stay.

Around this time, too, writers were taking more note of Glenn's humanity as expressed in his sportsmanship. Of one subtle but significantly sensitive encounter, here were the headlines:

DRAMA IN THE LOCKER ROOM

DOCTOR WARNS SAN ROMANI

GLENN CHEERS FELLOW KANSAN

The significance of this moment is best appreciated given its setting. It was on February 26, 1938, before a near capacity crowd of fifteen thousand at Madison Square Garden that Glenn Cunningham won the 1500-meter indoor run in 3:48.4, breaking Gene Venzke's 1937 world indoor record by one and a half

Start of the Famous Cunningham Sprint. The "Kansas flyer" is shown here heading into the last lap of the National A.A.U. indoor 1,500-meter race at Madison Square Garden, New York, in February this year. His finishing sprint pulled him ahead of the pack, enabled him to win in the record time of 3 minutes, 48.4 seconds. Cunningham runs with an easy, rhythmic stride which lengthens amazingly when he "turns on the gas."

seconds. Venzke was second in this race, almost four seconds behind. Archie San Romani finished a distant fourth. And now the real story began. Drew Middleton, the sports columnist, noticed a doctor examining San Romani with a stethoscope. Hearing what was going on in Archie's lungs, the doctor told the crestfallen runner that his lung was badly congested and that he should go home and get a good rest. The doctor gave him a prescription and an appointment to see him three days later.

Up to that point, for the press it was all Cunningham. San Romani was just sitting alone, prescription in one hand, battered spikes in another. Cunningham pushed through a crowd of admirers to get to San Romani and whispered something in Archie's ear. Then he went out of the locker room to ready himself to anchor the 2900-meter New York Curb Exchange relay. Which they won. But what had he whispered to Archie San Romani? Maybe it was something like "Your turn next time," or "Keep punching." We'll never know, but Drew Middleton caught the effect of Glenn's message. Whatever were the words, "When Cunningham went out from the dressing room you could tell what he had whispered had made everybody feel good."

Track teammate and K.U. classmate, Paul Borel, now ninety-three (in 2005) and in good health living in North Carolina, told a similar story at the fifty-year reunion of the Class of '34:

"I thought too of less exhilarating moments. One time, at the Drake Relays, our medley relay team was fielded. As the race proceeded, the quarter miler passed the baton to the half miler, who passed it to me, the three-quarter-miler. At the end of my distance, spent, I thrust forward the stick, and, unpardonable, let go before Cunningham had it firmly in his grasp. The neutral baton followed laws of its own and fell to the cinderpath, only to be kicked off the track by a subsequent runner. Cunningham stopped, retrieved the stick, and now, last in the field, resumed the chase. Yes, he caught up, and came in first. But having had to step off the cinders disqualified the team and we were denied the prize. A dark moment for me. All Cunningham said, as he put his arm around my shoulder, was 'Forget it, we'll take 'em next time.'"

The next race for 1938 was a week after the Baxter run. Dartmouth University had invited Cunningham to try for a world record on a new, high-banked indoor track. A brief local newspaper article mentioned that Glenn had arrived, by train, at 4:05 PM. Was this an omen that he would do a 4:05 mile and break the world record? It was to be a special race where six Dartmouth runners would pace Glenn Cunningham. The Dartmouth track had six and two-thirds laps to the mile, less than the eleven laps he had been used to. This alone would make for a faster mile. Talk of a world record was rife. CUNNINGHAM SET FOR RECORD RACE and other similar headlines invaded sports pages.

To give this competition the official look and status of a meet, two other events with Dartmouth runners were included. But the real focus was Cunningham running on a track with longer straightaways in quest of a world record. Cunningham had asked that there be no smoking. His wish was granted. He would have a smoke-free atmosphere.

No other name milers were participating. Instead six Dartmouth runners were given handicaps varying from five to six hundred yards. Their real role was as pacers. For example, the runner given the largest handicap merely jogged until Cunningham was astride him in the last quarter, then went as fast as he could to spur on Cunningham's last drive. The runner with the five-yard advantage dropped out at the half-mile mark.

The quarter-mile times were announced. Glenn traversed the first of them in the very fast 58.5 seconds. Realizing the pace as too torrid, he slowed to close his half-mile at 2:02.5 (64 seconds for the second quarter). The third quarter of a mile was run faster than the second, giving him a clocking of 3:04.2 at the three-quarter mark. By now the crowd, sensing history in the making, was delirious, their cheers inspiring him to a 60.2-second final quarter and a world record of 4:04.4.

Although generally considered the fastest mile ever run until then, whether indoors or out, a time that was not bested indoors until 1955, the International Amateur Athletic Federation never really recognized this as a record. They did not consider it to have been run in sanctioned competition, and the presence of pacers, particularly with all but one dropping out, was looked upon not too kindly. Nonetheless no one would disagree that at that moment, Glenn Cunningham had run the fastest mile ever.

First it was a 4:10 mile that was thought to be virtually beyond human capabilities. And now that he had broken 4:05, previously considered out of reach, a 4:00-minute mile was now considered in reach. Cunningham's bettering of these mileposts was attributed to better running tracks, better coaching, and better training methods. But there was a "something else" that at least one writer cited: "Reared on the high plains of Kansas, Cunningham has the heritage of courage of the pioneer ranch and farm folk who defied every rigor of nature to bring civilization to the short grass country. This heritage has translated itself into an unquenchable flame in the Kansas runner, that is still carrying him to new records after eleven years of the most rigorous competition the world could offer."

It was another variation on the theme of *Ad Astra per Aspera*.

Returning to New York he was interviewed the next night on a radio station. He said, "Someday, somewhere, somebody will run a 4-minute mile." He remarked that the hardest part of running a mile race "was the hours before it starts and the day afterward talking about it." What helped a runner was the cheering; what hindered a runner was smoking by spectators in a closed arena, something, he contended, that should be banned. Cunningham had taken into account all the intangibles, all the nuances, something his erstwhile coach Brutus Hamilton did not figure in when, based on his sophisticated formula, Hamilton calculated that the fastest the human body was capable of running the mile in was 4:01.66.

Another footnote was a March 8, 1938, *New York World Telegram* article telling of Glenn's longing for the never-received "shiny medal" he should have been given when he won the mile at the Elkhart Fair when he was thirteen years old.

The next race of note was the nineteenth annual Knights of Columbus games. At this point in 1938 Glenn had won all twelve races he had competed in. The journalistic hook for these games was that Glenn would be facing a healthy San Romani; he would be also running the 600-yard event against Jimmy Herbert and Howard Borck. In the mile he would face his regular shadower, Gene Venzke.

It was a typical Cunningham race—except as the press put it, "slightly faster." His winning time of 4:07.4 was now the fastest *unpaced* mile ever run indoors. He had run the second half slightly slower than the first (2:03.2). Gene Venzke, although second, was thirty-two yards behind, and twenty yards behind him was Peter Bradley of Princeton. Lou Burns of Manhattan "who had the temerity to lead Cunningham through the second lap," dropped out at the start of the last quarter. And San Romani, having pulled a groin muscle coming off the first turn, immediately dropped out. In the 600-yard run, Glenn finished third behind Herbert and Borck. Herbert had run the race in 1:11.1 shaving two-tenths of a second from Hornbostel's record three years earlier. Cunningham had a powerful finish but just ran out of space.

(In the 600, Cunningham made two false starts. He was trying to anticipate the takeoff so that he would be in front at the first turn. Conventional wisdom dictated that to win in the 600, you had to be in front at that first turn. He wasn't. Herbert and Raymond of Boston U. reached there at the same time. But the main point was Cunningham's two false starts. Normally this meant automatic disqualification. But the judges, without even conferring among themselves, ignored this rule. Obviously the spectators had come to see how Glenn would do in the 600, and the judges weren't about to disappoint anyone.)

The same night, Joe McCluskey, competing in the two-mile event, had advised Norman Bright how to beat Don Lash by timing his final spurt. His counsel proved fruitful. Bright edged Lash at the finish. "Maybe I ought to charge a fee for my tips," quipped McCluskey. As to his formula for beating Cunningham, "Why that's simple. Get a motorcycle!"

Around this time Glenn was beginning his role as a speaker for the Extension Service of the University of Kansas. He would speak on clean living and clean athletics. Despite the pedestrian titles, he "is packing them in with the excellence of his speeches," said the Kansas lecture bureau.

Following the Dartmouth—as it was now termed—"exhibition," there were a few unspectacular and relatively slow wins at races at New Jersey indoor meets in Elizabeth and Jersey City.

What was in the air now, however, was the possibility of the four-minute mile. The place would be the "brand new springy spruce track in the Chicago relays."

A newly developed seven-eights-inch special spruce track had been installed, built by the "master track builder," Herrick E. Horner of Philadelphia. The thinner boards were supposed to give extra spring. They wouldn't last as long as the thicker inch-and-a-quarter boards of Madison Square Garden, but they would be faster. On the other hand, it was still going to be eleven laps, no long straightaways. Glenn's main competition for the Bankers Mile of the Chicago Relays would be the 22-year-old Charles Fenske who had run a 4:08.9 mile a week earlier. Also competing would be Archie San Romani and Gene Venzke. The date of the Chicago event, also marking the end of the indoor season, was March 28, 1938.

If not a record, the Bankers Mile was a real barnburner. Cunningham remained well off any really fast pace for ten of the eleven laps. Whereas Fenske and Jimmy Smith of the University of Indiana traded the front spots, Cunningham remained content in the second or third slot with Venzke last. Then for the eleventh lap he really turned it on. "Pulling the spectators out of their seats," Glenn, 4:09.9, won by inches from Fenske, and Venzke's spurt pushed him past the fading Smith for third place.

Cunningham praised the track, almost apologized for running no faster. He did mention having a cold. The torrid schedule of racing and his very busy off-the-track schedule of speaking engagements had to be stressful, with breakdowns coming in the form of colds, fatigue, and weight loss.

But again I suspect that he preferred the come-from-behind, seize-victory-from-the-jaws-of-defeat role. Although he seemed to eschew record making, we can speculate about the times he could have done had there been faster milers in his day.

He had sometimes been lecturing five days a week and running on the sixth. Glenn Cunningham won all of his one-mile runs in 1938, and except for that third place in the 600-yard run, he won all of his other distance races. In December the A.A.U. certified that he had established the *American* record for the indoor, one-mile run in 4:04.4. It was truly his peak year. And it was still fun.

Here in 1938 is what William J. Bingham, director of physical education and athletics at Harvard wrote in *Famous American Athletes of Today*:

"No athlete ever loved competition more than Glenn Cunningham. . . . I have known many athletes who tire of competition, but I really think Glenn enjoys running today more than he did ten years ago. No runner has ever approached his record for consistency over so long a stretch of time. . . ."

18

EUGENE GEORGE VENZKE
(1908~1992)

Chust for so.

To appreciate any Cunningham legacy, understand the story of
Gene Venzke. In many ways they were alike, particularly in their
philosophies and attitudes toward life. The lives they led were
parallel in many ways. And Glenn and Gene had become lifelong
dear friends.

Ruth and Glenn, Gene and Peg, during a visit in the 1980s.

Eugene George Venzke was born in Leaf Valley, Minnesota.
The family later moved to eastern Pennsylvania. He had dropped
out of high school in order to work, something many boys his

age had to do, given the times. But when he was laid off from his job he returned to high school at age 23. That very year, 1932, he set the world record for the indoor mile at the Millrose Games. He would also graduate from Pottsdown High School

To Glenn—
A Great Athlete—
A Great Guy—
Gene Venzke

Gene Venzke circa 1936.

with honors. That fall he entered the school of education at the University of Pennsylvania as a 24-year-old freshman. As a senior, at which time he was holding the world record for 1500-meters, he received an award as "that member of the senior class who most closely approaches the ideal University of Pennsylvania athlete." That annual award was made on the basis of character, personality, scholastic standing, and athletic ability.

Gene Venzke married Margaret Mary Eisenhower of Reading Pennsylvania, in June 1938. He was 29, she 22. At the time he was "in the insurance business." They were married in Hollywood, California, and were to make their home in New York City. Two children would be born of the marriage: a son Gene M., and a daughter, Joan.

Gene's track career continued past Glenn's. He retired in 1943 at age 35. He had had the most success against Cunningham in the latter's last track year, 1940. In 1940 when he sought the Democratic nomination as a candidate for the Pennsylvania Legislature, he was listed as a business insurance salesman.

During the war he worked in a defense plant turning out gun mounts. In 1943, in one of his last competitions, he ran in the Millrose Games. Somewhere in that time he bought 23 acres of land in Reiffton, Pennsylvania, having earlier made some shrewd stock investments. There in Reiffton, he was known for his golf driving range and miniature golf courses, not remembered as much—to his chagrin—as the old runner. He was eminently successful financially.

In 1966, in a follow-up examination as part of that longitudinal study of sixteen champion runners, Venzke mentioned that the present day sub-four-minute mile runners train about three times as much as the runners of his day did. "Since 1943, the year I quit running, I have spent more energy per day in my driv-

VICTOR BY A FOOT IN MILE RACE AT BOSTON
Gene Venzke (right) beating Glenn Cunningham in invitation special at the Veterans of Foreign Wars meet on Saturday night. The
time for the event was 4:13.1.   Associated Press

Glenn and Gene in 1940.

ing range business, in its maintenance and development than I
did in training during my running days.

"I am on my feet about twelve hours per day doing such work
as cutting grass and picking up golf balls, also handling over a ton

of balls per day—twenty years of this, six months a year.' "

As to the off season: "I did a lot of pick and shovel work and stone masonry plus running about twenty miles per month."

His diet: "I eat a lot of good food—avoiding sugars and fats (saturated) to a great extent, and I have never been ill."

In 1966 Myra Brown wrote to him asking for information about Glenn Cunningham. In a handwritten response dated August 6, 1966, he wrote:

"I am very sorry to state that it will be impossible for me to compile the material you asked for on your story about Glenn Cunningham. Time is a factor. My hours in the golf business are from about 7:00 AM till 12:00 midnight—seven days a week. To do the proper job on writing about my wonderful experiences with Glenn would entail extensive time—I have no tape recorder.

"After November, when we will be closed, I will be able to spend time on this story."

True to his word, he then wrote back, his handwritten letter here duplicated:

November 23, 1966
To: Myra Brown
Enclosed you will find my very short "Glenn Cunningham story." I think it pretty well portrays my involvement with this guy.

If you want some further data on some of the factors discussed, I will be only too glad to oblige.

I wish you very well in your work with your very fine subject, Glenn Cunningham. His background is very valuable to future youth.

Sincerely yours,
Gene Venzke

About Glenn Cunningham:

The final round in the dining room. John Pennypacker, Captain of the football team, answered the call. A girl at the other end of the line asked where she could find Gene Venzke. Pennypacker said, "Find Glenn Cunningham, look ten yards back of him—there you will find Venzke." This brought a roar of laughter from all the athletes eating in the dining room for athletes at the University of Pennsylvania in 1936.

These incidents pretty well illustrate my track fortunes in the mile run against Glenn from 1933 to 1940. We competed against each other without let-up for seven years all over this dear old U.S.A. My victories over him were so rare that whenever I did win over him it was a national news item and a tremendous thrill for me.

From my first race against him to the last one, I was without let-up for seven years constantly tormented with an almost impossible task of trying to beat him. Cunningham was always in good condition, which was the quality that made him so great. He could run a quarter-mile in about 48 seconds, I in about 50; as a result he would give me a sort of "nightmare" toward the end of each race.

I spent a lot of time with Glenn in many of our travels. He always impressed me, "the guy never does anything wrong, how can he go wrong!" If only he would dissipate now and then it would be a big assist in my being able to beat him a few more times. That is what made the task so torturous.

Faced with the virtual insurmountable task of winning races against Cunningham, I resolved each year with renewed enthusiasm on a new training program to overcome his advantage. The pressure created by my faithful "underdog" fans certainly did create a solid new base of vigor and enthusiasm each year—it made me really fear the potential shame of a poor performance. Looking back over these eventful years, I have often said, "It is a shame it had to come to an end." As in all phases of life—each takes it terminal turn.

The relative temporary thrill provided for the fan at an athletic contest is soon forgotten. That is why a "seasoned" athlete is not too much upset by defeat. However, the "seasoned" athlete of stature is very conscious of what he can contribute to the future athlete who will be taking his place.

Being a "good example" is the lasting, but not so thrilling, quality of a great athlete. Glenn Cunningham was a shining example of that virtue. The only way anything in life progresses is through the process of the older person's experience and knowledge being passed on to the younger ones.

Glenn Cunningham has done a tremendous job since his running days in passing on the good patterns of life through the hundreds of lectures he has made throughout this country. He is still the fine example of clean and vigorous living. My wife once said, "The one thing I always saw this guy do that was bad was to put too much catsup on his food." To this day he is still very much in my mind—that of not letting him maintain a much better physical condition than I—not for running, but as they say in Pennsylvania Dutch, "Chust for so."

Like expressions in other languages that lose their intangible meaning and nuance when put into other words, *Chust for so* also defies translation. But you kind of know what it means, and you see and feel what it means, when you meet a Gene Venzke or a Glenn Cunningham.

I did meet Gene Venzke, albeit briefly, in November 1988. The occasion was the New York City Marathon. Our group, the American Medical Athletic Association, was holding our then annual sports medicine seminar. Gene Venzke and Ruth

Cunningham were honored guests. Venzke came with his son Gene, an attorney, who as I remember was even taller than his tall father. As part of the overall program, the video from the 1936 Olympiad's 1500-meter was shown. Venzke had been in it. He was thrilled seeing the scene over again. He said that it gave him the feeling of it all happening once more. He was bubbling over with excitement. Later, he spoke to us briefly and spontaneously, full of his characteristic vigor and enthusiasm.

He had had open-heart surgery twelve years earlier. When told he needed the procedure, he informed the doctors that "when you cut me open, fix whatever you see wrong—I have a lot to do yet." He had been, and remained, a busy man. Over the years he had developed patents on a golf ball dispenser and a grass cutter and had designed a stitch ripper for parachutes used by the government. He also wrote articles for the *Saturday Evening Post*.

After the surgery, among other things, he designed and installed a solar system in his home and built a stone wall along his drive.

By his own definition he was "a butter-and-egg boy from the country" who, in a eulogy written by Terry Brickhart in the *Reading Times*, "rubbed shoulders with the rich and famous without acquiring any of their bad habits."

Gene Venzke said this: "If the spirit is right, no amount of work will kill you." Glenn Cunningham could have said the same thing, so similar were their attitudes toward life. I think you could say that both Venzke and Cunningham did almost everything "chust for so."

19

1939

But I don't want to say anything. I was too intent on running my own race to analyze what was going on.

In his opening message to Congress, President Roosevelt, ever watchful of a world totalitarian threat, asked for approval of a defense budget of nearly one and a half billion dollars. The country was just beginning to listen to the president as it watched in dismay the fall of Spain's republic to fascist forces aided by Germany and Italy. The world watched, too, as Germany moved into Czechoslovakia. Roosevelt naively sought assurance from Hitler and Mussolini that they would not attack any additional countries. The New York World's Fair opened in Queens, New York. Among the promised scientific wonders of the future was television. In baseball the Yankees would win the pennant and the World Series for the fourth time in a row. But on July 4, Lou Gehrig, dying of amyotrophic lateral sclerosis, delivered his valedictory to a capacity crowd, speaking before microphones at Yankee Stadium's home plate.

Food stamp plans began in Rochester, New York, allowing those on relief to obtain free surplus commodities to supplement their regular food budget. Patients were more and more paying cash for my father's dental services, rather than bartering products grown in backyard gardens.

On September 1, Germany invaded Poland from the West while Russia did the same from the East. On September 3, France and England, honoring their treaties, declared war on Germany. I can remember that Sunday morning and my father saying simply "It's another World War." Only two decades after the "War to End All Wars," the powers that be were at it again.

As if to symbolize the grotesque and monstrous state of the world soon to be, on New Year's Day, 1939, there is a photo of Glenn Cunningham crossing the finish line at New Orleans' Sugar Bowl. He appears to have two left feet; the front left foot is inches away from the back left foot. He shows two left arms, one whose forearm comes off at three o'clock and the other a stub of a forearm and a hand appearing at four o'clock. On his left shoulder is another head, expressionless as if in a trance. Cunningham's countenance, too, reflects a state of altered consciousness.

This apparition came about when Blaine Rideout of the running Rideout twins put on a Cunningham-like spurt down the last straightaway, a drive that Cunningham held off as Rideout ran out of room. He finished close enough to lend Cunningham a second head that sprouted out of his left shoulder. The two-headed hydra partially resembling Glenn finished in 4:10.7, breaking Cunningham's previous 4:13.1 record for one-mile runs in the South. Don Lash, now an FBI man, was third.

Cunningham had flown in from Colorado where he had been engaged in a lecture tour for the Extension Service of the University of Kansas. Then right after the Sugar Bowl run he spoke in Sherman, Texas, at a Boy Scout program where thirty-seven scouts received awards. The title of his talk before the scouts and their parents was "Running Around the World."

Glenn and Blaine Rideout at the Sugar Bowl on New Year's Day 1939.

Actually he was now also gaining a positive reputation as a speaker. "We want him back next year," wrote the director of physical education in Camden, New Jersey. Cunningham had appeared before at least ten thousand students in South Jersey. The general secretary of an Ohio YMCA said that "Cunningham held the audience in the palm of his hand . . . his talking is as excellent as his running."

His ability to hold an audience "in the palm of his hand" never left him; certainly it was very evident as late as 1987, a year before he died. The titles of his talks, "Clean Living" and "Clean Athletics"—however pedestrian sounding, were nevertheless timeless. He would continue with speaking engagements through 1939 and into early 1940. And for the rest of his life, he remained in demand for his talks. They would also be his principal source of income.

For much of 1939 he would lecture Monday, Tuesday, and Wednesday, then take a train on a Thursday to the scene of a weekend race. Finally he'd do a little training or maybe just rest on the day before the Saturday race. He was having less control and less choice of schedule, less choice of where and what to eat. And less opportunity to schedule rest.

For the remainder of the 1939 track season, John Lardner predicted that "Gene Venzke will pass Glenn Cunningham as though he were standing still. . . ." The 1939 indoor track season began with the Knights of Columbus track meet held in Brooklyn's 245th Coast Artillery Armory on January 7. Among the outstanding regulars besides Cunningham were San Romani, Lash, Jimmy Herbert, Gene Venzke, and "young" Leslie MacMitchell. Venzke and Cunningham would run against each other in the 800-meter event. The year before, Venzke had won in 1:55 with Glenn falling down and not even finishing.

If either Gene or Glenn read Lardner's prediction of three days earlier, or even cared about it, we do not know. We do know that their race was a thriller.

Everything was whirlwind. Glenn had arrived in New York at noon for the race and was back in Kansas the next morning, courtesy of a midnight flight. He had requested, and was granted, an earlier place on the program for his 800-meter race. In the race itself there was the usual jockeying for the lead, then Glenn dropped in behind Venzke until three-quarters of the last lap remained. Here he made his bid, passing Venzke with only about a quarter of the lap to go. He won in 1:53, two seconds better than Venzke's 1:55 a year earlier.

Now it was a matter of demonstrating how his way of life, that is, "clean living," was reflected in his track victories. His training motto was "Early to bed and early to rise and you'll keep ahead of the rest of the guys." Still, he had credibility when he would tell thousands of high school pupils what to do and what not to do if they wanted to grow up "to be endurance citizens instead of citizens to endure."

Associated Press writer James Martin wrote this on January 8: "Cunningham's modesty, his minding-my-own-business attitude, and his refusal to alibi or say anything belittling of his rivals add to the halo over this greatest of all milers." Unlike many of today's athletes he was always mindful of the example he set.

(He was scornful of our contemporary crop of athletes. Audiotaped sometime in the 1980s, he said that "most of them are a bunch of bums.")

In early 1939 there were persistent rumors that he would retire. These were neutralized by the observation that at age 29 he was running as well as he ever did. I imagine that his talks and living up to what he said in his talks—his running a metaphor for a way of life—motivated and inspired him to continue to run and win over his competition. Thereby he could also win over his audiences.

As one writer put it in the January 10, 1939, *Coffeyville Daily Journal*: "His manner, his modesty, and his ideals of clean sportsmanship leave one refreshed with the impression that here is a man who preaches clean living and at the same time lives up to his own advice."

His advice was featured in an article that appeared in the Wednesday evening *Missouri Springfield Leader and Press*. Cunningham had addressed the students at the state teacher's college. It was a January 1939 date but the message was well ahead of his time, surely appropriate in today's fitness and health quest.

In his talk he was severe and categorical about smoking and drinking, and drinking even included soft drinks. (He was probably aware at the time of the drawbacks associated with refined sugars.) These substances "pull you down physically and mentally," he declared. An athlete who indulges "will always lay down sometimes during the competition . . . and when it takes every ounce of energy possible—then he's licked. He gives up." He pointed out that the athlete who smokes or drinks is always detected in the team sports and that "he can lay down nine-tenths of the time and then with one brilliant play fool the people." He added that he was able to establish the record at Dartmouth because the crowd of thirty-eight hundred had acceded to his request: "Please refrain from smoking." (Note: His dietary habits have been earlier described by Coach Hargiss. Cunningham advocated simple and wholesome foods. The only thing anyone could argue with today was his penchant for a well-done steak some hours before a competition.)

Physical training, he told them, was an essential part of education, as was mental training. He called sports a "healthy interest," but didn't recommend everyone seek strenuous sporting activities. "If you don't enjoy it, don't do it." But here he had to qualify, saying that every boy ought to enjoy some sort of physical activity. (He didn't spell it out but he was here speaking of the "rapture" of the play scene.)

The main point, I think, was his statement that it was vitally important for men to continue some sort of activity—enough to keep fit—after college. He alluded to so many businessmen who had become "just big blobs of flesh."

He contended that these same business people would feel better, accomplish more work in less time if they engaged in regular physical activity. Supposed lack of time was no excuse. Employers, he contended, should realize the value of physical activity and both encourage and allow the time for their employees to participate. It would be at least another thirty years, not until the "aerobic age," before these ideas and thoughts were put into general practice.

Cunningham's days were filled with travel to lecture sites and weekend races. On February 4 he ran the Wanamaker Mile. Glenn had won in five of the six times he had competed. This, his seventh appearance, would be a mixture of the typical and of the atypical for Cunningham. Atypical in that he did not let others set the pace. Rather it was Cunningham who took the lead at the sixth lap. There were five to go. He held the lead for another three laps. Then Chuck Fenske surged from third place to take the lead with Cunningham hanging on his heels. As they approached the last lap, typically Glenn cut loose passing Fenske. But Fenske was not giving up. Down the backstretch they were close together with Fenske right at Cunningham's shoulder as they rounded into the final turn. Glenn "made a supreme effort down the homestretch" and won two yards ahead of Fenske. His time was 4:13.

Wayne Rideout's late sprint permitted him to come in third.

He was followed by San Romani. Wayne's brother, Blaine, finished fifth.

Less than a week after the Wanamaker Mile he won the Penn A.C. Mile at Philadelphia and a day later the Hunter Mile in Boston in 4:10.8. Three days later he added a win in Providence, Rhode Island, in a slow time of 4:16. Then it was back to New York City to win the Baxter Mile in 4:12.6. Two days later he lost to John Borican in the 1000-yard run at the Seton Hall Games in Newark, New Jersey. Three days later he won the Veterans of Foreign Wars Mile in the Boston Armory. His time was 4:15.5. Two days after that he won the National A.A.U. indoor 1500-meter run in 3:54.6. He was winning but his times were slower. The hectic working and racing schedule was no doubt wearing him down.

But now he had a bit of a vacation. He had nine days of rest before meeting Don Lash. For whatever reasons, he wanted to take a rest from the mile. He was thinking that he could set a world record in the two-miler. He did win the I.C. 4-A two-mile run with a sensational ending lap and a quarter sprint, but his time of 9:11.8 was hardly world record

A week later, his next race was typical—though with a denouement that was anything but typical.

It was a 1000-yard race at Madison Square Garden, the annual Knights of Columbus meet. Typical was Glenn's pacing until near the end when he would have his surge. The pace setter, John Borican, who both "annoyed" (zigzagging and getting in front of the surging Cunningham) and "thrilled the crowd of 15,000" (he won by a stride, holding off Cunningham), cutting both indoor and outdoor record times previously held by Cunningham. What was not typical was the confused aftermath. Johnny McHugh, veteran starter, claimed Borican had jumped the gun.

What he should have done was shoot off the gun again once he realized what had happened. For some reason he didn't, and he couldn't explain why. Cunningham said nothing. McHugh would not sign off on Borican's apparent record performance. And Cunningham, who had also beaten the record couldn't get credit for breaking his previous record because only two timers were assigned to him. He said nothing. Later in the same meet he ran last in the mile event, won by Chuck Fenske in 4:11.1. As per Cunningham's earlier prediction, Fenske was now coming to the forefront.

Such was the case in the March 25 Chicago Relays. In a close "photo finish" Fenske edged Cunningham by a foot in a winning time of 4:12.8. A step behind him in third place was Venzke. But a week later Glenn did win the "Cunningham Mile" at Portland, Oregon, in 4:24.4; then he won the mile in the Kansas Relays on April 22nd in 4:29.2.

There were several more mile races scheduled in the spring. He did lose again to Fenske in the Crump Mile at the Cotton Carnival held in the Crump Stadium in Memphis, Tennessee. Again, Chuck Fenske of Wisconsin, the heir apparent . . . the "dark haired bespectacled kid pumped his sturdy legs not only past Cunningham, but away from Archie San Romani, Don Lash and William Southworth." He won in 4:11.5. San Romani had finished two yards behind Fenske. The headlines read: GREAT GLENN POOR THIRD. Actually he was only six yards back from Archie, but it was apparent that Cunningham's reign among the milers was slowly coming to an end. At least that's what many of the sportswriters were saying.

His work and run pace was frenzied. Now as assistant professor of physical education he doubtless felt an obligation to practice what he preached, to show that his clean living helped generate the endurance that allowed him to lecture, to compete, to travel, and to fulfill his obligations as a husband and father.

One more thing: Although all of the races were A.A.U. (Amateur Athletic Union) sanctioned, meaning that the runners were amateurs—engaging in the sport for the love of it and, God forbid, not receiving any money; in truth they did get money from the race promoters, who, in turn, were making the big bucks. That the athletes got paid was a well-known open secret.

He was also in demand as a speaker, usually receiving great ovations. One writer said he had a brilliant sense of humor; he was a willing speaker and his audiences were often enthralled with him. But the grind of the speaking events and the frequent races was taking its toll, which is why he felt like he did before the upcoming June mile race at Princeton's Palmer Stadium.

He didn't feel up to racing England's Sydney Wooderson, who was coming here for what was billed as a showdown race. Wooderson's 4:06.4 was now the world record for the outdoor mile. There was, however, even some controversy over this time. Several of the timers had clocked him in 4:06.7, a time that would have equaled Glenn's 1934 Princeton world-record performance. That the judging minority had prevailed cast a dark cloud on Wooderson's record setting the stage for not only a showdown, but possibly a 4:03 mile. Such was the ballyhoo for this race.

At first Glenn had declined the invitation. He was tired, he had raced too much, and he had driven in his car too much. He felt himself out of condition, his back and legs weary and sore from too many miles of auto travel. In an exclusive to the *New York Times* he said, "I'm in no shape and I'll compete only at the insistence of Princeton officials.'" His best time that spring for the mile was 4:15.4. Furthermore, a three-quarter-mile run on a track in Cornwall, New York, yielded a disappointing 3:12. Wooderson, on the other hand, had recently run the same distance in 2:59.5, breaking Blaine Rideout's record mark.

Despite Cunningham's statement that he was in poor condition and despite his belief that it would be unfair to the public and to himself to compete at less than his best, those Princeton officials *did* insist. So along with Chuck Fenske, Archie San Romani, and Blaine Rideout, Glenn Cunningham was going to participate in what was anticipated to be a world-record 4:04 mile run by Wooderson. Wooderson, despite the headlines to that effect, demurred. He realized that Cunningham would not set the pace. As for his setting the pace he declared, "I shan't. My main purpose in coming to America is to beat Cunningham. Hang the time." A headline from the *New York Sun* read: SCENE SET FOR PERFECT MILE.

The June 17, 1939, Princeton Invitational was billed as the "Mile of the Century." There were great expectations. There were also great rumors of an American cabal to "gang up" on Wooderson by the U.S. runners to deny him any semblance of success. Reports of such a thing came from the London newspapers. Belittling of any Cunningham pre-race "alibi" arose, too, from the same quarter.

The day for the event was bright and clear; the track was dry and fast. The first quarter mile found Wooderson in the lead, a lead he had immediately sprung to from his middle starting position. The other runners were content to let him assume the front position. At the quarter-mile mark, maintaining the lead, he was timed in 64 seconds, dampening any thoughts of a record. Cunningham, Rideout, Fenske, and San Romani were in single file just behind. And if there were any lingering notions from the spectators of the "perfect mile," they were dashed when his leading half-mile time of 2:08 was announced. If there were concerns or doubts also about any maneuvering applied to Wooderson, these, too, were quelled since his lead allowed him to escape any jostling. The three-quarter time, with Wooderson still in the lead, was 3:14 flat—"very flat indeed," wrote John Kieran two days later.

So far it was a decidedly uninspiring, if not dull, race. But soon the real drama would unfold. Here is the setting at the three-quarter mark: Wooderson leads Fenske, the latter just to his right by half a stride. Each is about to land on the left foot with the right foot flung to the rear. A stride behind, hugging the inside pole, is Cunningham, and running alongside him is Blaine Rideout. They two are entrained, their right feet taking a bite out of the track, their left feet flung backward. San Romani brings up the rear.

Then . . . reaching the turn for the backstretch, as if sensing Wooderson's weakening, Rideout shoots out and is at Wooderson's right arm. There is some contact. Wooderson reaches out with his right arm and does touch Rideout. Wooderson stumbles momentarily. At the very same moment, caught in the cramped quarters of four milers reaching for the inside pole, Cunningham's left foot hits the inside pole and he, too, stumbles. Rideout's lead is short lived as Fenske pounds past Wooderson and then sets out for Rideout, catching him at the start of the final stretch and sprinting the last hundred yards.

If Wooderson wanted to beat Cunningham, it would be a matter of which one could unstumble and regain his rhythm. Those close up described Wooderson as now being out of sync, "disoriented." He would never regain his rhythm or pace. Cunningham did. Caught in the vacuum of Fenske's spurt, he, too, picked up momentum, passing Wooderson seventy-five yards from home. San Romani, with fifty yards to go, also breezed by Wooderson. But Wooderson was mounting a surge of his own and caught Rideout coming into the homestretch. It was a catch he couldn't hold on to, and twenty-five yards from the tape Rideout, too, passed Wooderson.

Fenske won in 4:11. Cunningham was second, four yards in back of Fenske. San Romani finished ten feet later, beating Rideout by three yards. Rideout beat Wooderson by a foot.

Later it would be a *Rashomon* interpretation of what had happened. The British press cried "foul." Wooderson at first said he was fouled, later said he was misinterpreted, that it was an "unfortunate accident" and that Rideout had apologized. Rideout denied he apologized, but said he was sorry, too, that they had bumped. The American press referred to Wooderson as an "invader." Cunningham said that he saw what happened, "But I don't want to say anything. I was too intent on running my own race to analyze what was going on."

The matter of the "Mile of the Century" would soon die down. Wooderson visited relatives in the United States, said something about meeting Fenske at an August international race in London, and that was that, at least for the time being.

Lost in the tussle were the results of the three-quarter-mile race, a race that had truly thrilled the 28,000 spectators. It was won by Blaine Rideout's brother, Wayne. The thrill of that race was Gene Venzke's running. In the five-man field he was last most of the way. Then with 220 yards to go, he started his bid from his fifth-place position, reaching fourth, then third, then second place as he passed Leslie MacMitchell ten yards from the tape, only to run out of space as Rideout finished first.

The next contest of note, scheduled at the end of June, was marked by Cunningham's ineligibility. No longer a New York

Sydney Wooderson, British mile record holder, came over in June to run one race against the pick of America's milers in the Princeton invitation meet. He led for most of the race, but on the back stretch of the last lap Blaine Rideout attempted to pass him. No. 1, Rideout, in white suit, comes abreast of Wooderson, No. 28; Chuck Fenske, No. 10, the eventual winner, is third, and Glenn Cunningham fourth; No. 2, shoulder to shoulder the leaders streak along and Archie San Romani, No. 24, appears trailing the field; No. 3, Rideout has passed Wooderson, who apparently has been thrown off stride; No. 4, Wooderson steps on concrete curb which lines the track; No. 5, he comes down off the curb but has not regained his balance; No. 6, Wooderson's arm is thrown in air as he seeks to regain his balance, with Rideout definitely ahead and Fenske about to cut out and go into the lead.

That B-U-M-P!

(News of the Day—From International)

① Final lap of the Princeton Mile. .R to l.: Rideout, Wooderson (28) and Fenske. Now, watch this closely...

② Cunningham (6) and San Romani (24) are shown as Rideout nudges Wooderson. This...

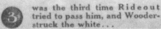

③ was the third time Rideout tried to pass him, and Wooderstruck the white...

④ curbing, lost stride and almost fell. Wooderson then bumped Rideout (see it?) and...

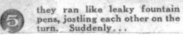
they ran like leaky fountain pens, jostling each other on the turn. Suddenly...

Wooderson lifts his arm, turns Rideout almost sidewards. But Sydney...

lost his balance, and the race. Fenske (10) went on to win. Now, who bumped who?

What Movies Showed!

High lights of Wooderson movies:—

(1) Wooderson and Rideout running shoulder to shoulder.

(2) Rideout cutting in without racing room (six-feet) but—

(3) Wooderson putting on a burst of speed and running into trouble on the inside.

(4) Wooderson's left foot hitting the rail, breaking his stride.

(5) Wooderson's right hand going out to clutch Rideout's shoulder.

(6) Fenske making his great homestretch finish.

(7) Wooderson overtaking Rideout again, then fading to last.

resident, he was barred from competing in the Senior Metropolitan championships, held to dedicate the opening of Jersey City's Lincoln Park. Nevertheless, not to lose his presence as a drawing card, a special handicap three-quarter-mile race was set up. In it he would chase five or six "guinea pigs" with graduated handicaps placed along the way. His time would be considered official, and the press heralded it as a try at breaking Wooderson's record of 2:59.5.

Cunningham outran by one yard the "limit man" who had a 125-yard head start and finished in 3:01. Given the slow track and the hot sun it was considered a remarkable performance. So, too, was the performance of San Romani. His 4:13.7 one-mile win broke Cunningham's old mark (Yonkers, 1937) by four-tenths of a second. San Romani had taken a page out of his fellow Kansan's playbook by running the first half in 2:11.7 and the second half in 2:02. Leslie MacMitchell was second in 4:16.9.

The specially staged handicap event was a tune-up for Glenn, prelude to the National A.A.U. Track and Field Championships early in July in Lincoln, Nebraska. In the field for some of the events were runners of old like Joe McCluskey and Howard Borck. Of historical note was the presence of Jackie Robinson's brother, Mack Robinson, who had medaled on the track in the 1936 Olympiad.

In the 1500-meter event, besides Cunningham there were Chuck Fenske, Archie San Romani, Blaine Rideout and Louis Zamperini. Zamperini, who had run in the 1936 Olympics, had a solid track career but was more noted for mistakenly being listed as killed in action in World War II. With his B-24 shot down in the Pacific, he had survived forty-seven days adrift on a raft. Picked up by a Japanese patrol boat, he would suffer in their prison camps for two years. At war's end he managed to be able to attend his own memorial track meet.

As for the 1500-meter race, Blaine Rideout won in 3:51.5. Chuck Fenske was second, followed by Zamperini and then Glenn Cunningham. Rideout's unexpected win carried with it the right to go abroad and meet Wooderson a month later at the annual Bank Holiday Meet at London. His performance also vindicated him. He had been accused by the British press of having been put in the Princeton competition only to harass Wooderson. But now he had to be recognized as a very good runner and a legitimate contender.

At around the very same time Wooderson won the mile at the British A.A.A. Track and Field Championships in the time of 4:11.8. A week later he won a 1500-meter race in 3:54.8. On the same day Cunningham lost to Blaine Rideout in a special mile invitational at Mahanoy City in Pennsylvania. Rideout won by two yards in a homestretch duel. (The seemingly slow time of 4:26 was probably a product of a slow track.) Barney Ewell won the 100-yard dash in 9.6 seconds. Nine years later, at age 30, he would take second place in the 200-meter run in the London Olympiad.

Meanwhile, back in London, Wooderson was fourth in a 1000-yard handicap race. At the same time the English footracing enthusiasts were less than enthusiastic about a Wooderson-Rideout clash. They would have preferred their man to have been matched against either Cunningham, San Romani, or Fenske, all medalists at that Princeton "bumping." But by late July the matter was moot. The London, July 28 AP headline read: WOODERSON INJURED; WON'T MEET RIDEOUT.

Wooderson, small, bespectacled, bookish looking, a solicitor —which is the term in England for a lawyer who prepares cases but only argues in lower court—was disappointed. He had felt ashamed of his Princeton showing and said, "It was my chance to make up for my miserable showing in America." He would never have another chance to race against any of the runners who beat him that day.

Following the fireworks of the Princeton Invitational, a relative calm fell on Glenn's track life. Headlines were sparse, races few if any. A Wichita, Kansas, newspaper wrote of his birthday in August and said that he was quietly preparing himself for the 1940 U.S. Olympic Team. The beginnings of the world conflagration that would shatter any ideas of a 1940 Olympiad in Finland were still a month away. The Cunninghams were living in Peabody, Kansas. Glenn also owned an 840-acre farm in Cedar Point, Kansas, operated by his brother-in-law D. F. Morgan, married to his sister Letha. (Letha was the older sister who accompanied the brothers to school on the day of the fire, and it was she who had been able to open the door so they could get out of the blazing room.) Glenn was dividing his time between home and the farm.

His weight had fallen from 168 to 154 and with it some of his extraordinary strength. The traveling, the lecturing, the racing had bitten into his performances. He was now taking it easy planning to resume training on his return to Lawrence September 10.

(Paul Borel wrote me of "Glenn's strength and super coordination. Roughhousing with football players much larger than he, they were not equal to the task of pinning him down, the converse being so.")

All the while he was actively lecturing. He was variously described as a clever and entertaining speaker. A quote from a Kansas paper: "He is now known over the United States as a speaker on athletics and health. He is an interesting and forceful speaker."

In a talk to students at Northwestern State College he struck his usual impassioned themes: that athletes who used tobacco or alcohol in any form were "worthless to a coach." (He practiced what he preached; remember how he had told a coach to throw his brother John off the track team when he had caught him smoking.)

A week after that talk a second daughter Sandra was born on November 25. Her birth appears to mark the last, though not the least, bit of excitement for 1939. Certainly less exciting was a December 31 year-ending race that was a portent of things to come. At the New Orleans Sugar Bowl 1500-meter run, Archie San Romani, now the world-record holder at 2000-meters, beat Glenn with a Cunningham-like finish. So did Blaine Rideout, and by inches. Atypically, Cunningham had taken an early lead and had still been leading with seventy-five yards to go.

20

1940

Wotta man, that Glenn Cunningham!

There were some notable firsts in the year 1940. First of all, Cunningham converted all rumors of retirement to reality. Ironically he made the announcement on the sports program of the spinner of tall sports yarns, Bill Stern.

He retired in the spring, continued lecturing but under the auspices of a new employer, Cornell College in Mount Vernon, Iowa, where he was hired as the new student health director. The position was created for him. In 1941 he was made athletic director as well.

For the first time a President sought a third term. Franklin D. Roosevelt ran against Wendell Wilkie in the November election and won handily. The New York Yankees for the first time in five seasons failed to win the pennant and World Series. The viewing of sports events on television was six or seven years away. But a promise of things to come, another first—color television—was demonstrated by CBS in New York.

As for the Great Depression, it was just about over. President Roosevelt had successfully requisitioned Congress for defense spending. Defense plants had sprung up in the large industrial cities and with that appeared a migration of unemployed, seeking the newfound war factory jobs. With the migration, too, came a bit of a dividend for homeowners who had barely held on to their homes during the Depression but now could add to their incomes by renting rooms to members of the newly arrived workforce. And President Roosevelt asked for, and got, a peace-time selective service draft.

The press talks in early January centered on Cunningham's apparent loss of some speed. He was scheduled to run in the Knights of Columbus half-mile. Any loss of speed would show up more in the 880 than, for example, in a two-mile race. In the press, the two-miler was thought to be an alternative for Glenn, for here speed was not quite as critical. Another thought was that Glenn would hang up his spikes this year. Whatever would be, eyes were focused on how he would fare in the 880 where his opponents would include the Olympic champion John Woodruff, also Gene Venzke, and new faces such as Charley Beetham, the national 880 champion, Curtis Giddings, Joe Zeitler, Sanford Goldberg, and Jim Kehoe. Kehoe was a 4:15 University of Maryland miler who had beaten Cunningham in the mile a year earlier.

Four thousand pairs of eyes at Brooklyn's Thirteenth Regiment Armory witnessed a familiar Cunningham race and Cunningham finish. He waited until the last lap to unfurl his habitual spurt, coming up from fifth place to win and finishing in 1:56.1. Kehoe was second, Goldberg third. The Olympic winner, Woodruff, was last. He even had to hurdle over Gene Venzke who had tripped and fallen. Although knocked off stride, Woodruff was already well in the rear. Jimmy Herbert won the Columbus 500 and Don Lash won a razor-sharp-close two-miler in 9:08.6, just a yard ahead of his old Indiana roommate, Tommy Deckard. Nineteen-year-old Leslie MacMitchell was another yard behind, coming in third. Lash's time was a record for two miles for that armory track. MacMitchell surprised many writers and onlookers by keeping up the brutal pace set by the first two finishers, giving the crowd something to cheer for and to remember.

Jesse Abramson, writing in the *New York Herald Tribune,* said that Cunningham, unknown to the spectators, had come to New York "with a three-day attack of ptomaine poisoning." He called Cunningham "the old complainer." Still he added that Glenn had run "with all his verve and aplomb."

The "old complainer" label merits some discussion. From way back, either before or after a race, there would be reports of his swollen tonsils, his swollen ankle, his infected teeth, his fatigue, and his inability to train. I doubt that any of these were alibis or exaggerations. But he did need some type of handicap to over-come, to spur him on, to let him snatch the proverbial victory from the jaws of certain defeat. Even when he had no handicap he raced best from behind. Allowing that it was smarter to let the other guy do the pacing, to be the hunter rather than the hunt-ed, he apparently needed to replay some kind of against-the-odds scenario that allowed him to run, time and time again, "with all his verve and aplomb."

Right around this time Cunningham spoke of his great ambi-tion to teach and to attain a teaching post somewhere. He was quoted in newspapers on January 8, only two days after that 880-yard win. The papers told of a radio interview the night before when he announced his retirement. He said that he was "more and more anxious to enter my chosen professional field." What he was aiming for was "a teaching position in a department of health and physical education preferably somewhere in the Midwest."

But there was more to it. It was now obvious that there would be no Olympics at Helsinki, Finland. Not only was a world war being waged, but Finland too had been invaded by Russia and was even labeled as a "belligerent country." Lewis Burton, writing in the *New York Journal* and *American Sports,* spoke of Cunningham being distraught over the upcoming cancellation of the Olympic games for 1940. Even in his radio address he had said: "I've continued in competition these past two years mainly with the hope of trying for my third successive Olympic team. Now conditions on the other side have made the holding of the Olympic games impossible. So why go on?"

But what he said further to Lewis Burton about the whole situation reflected narrowness and perhaps a naïveté, a shortsightedness shared by most of the athletes of that time: "I'm sorry about what's happening to the Olympics for a world of reasons,' he said with a genuine sadness. "and especially because of how it will injure the cause of athletics. It is going to hurt some people deeply. As for me, I'm ready to turn to other things. I want to get a teaching job in physical education, and that will take me away from competition. I had hoped to try out for the Olympic team, but I guess that's done with."

Especially because of how it will injure the cause of athletics. History would prove that the cause of athletics was little hurt. The hurt and injury would reach out infinitely beyond. Glenn's viewpoint, however disappointing and narrowly centered, was nevertheless typical of the time.

Still, he had miles to go before he would put his running career to sleep. Next on the schedule was the Veterans of Foreign Wars annual track meet at the Boston Garden, the first major indoor event of the year. For the first time Gene Venzke, now almost a forgotten name, was refused a place in the mile event. Rather he was designated for the half-miler. He refused. It would be the mile or nothing. He argued and he prevailed. He was allowed to enter the mile. For Venzke it would prove to be more than nothing.

Also entered and running in order of appearance were Chuck Fenske, Glenn Cunningham, Wayne Rideout, Archie San Romani, and Luigi Beccali. Venzke was lurking in the rear, dressed in his usual white track suit. That suit and his beautiful, if not flawless, style of running always captured the eyes of the crowd.

A crowd of eighty-five hundred was stunned to see a tall runner in white in the backstretch bolting out of last place. It took the tall runner, Venzke, sixty yards to go from sixth to first place. Was it too soon? And could he hold it? If one were taking odds, based on past experience and based on this field of runners, the answer would be in the negative. The rest of the field now set out in hot pursuit of this interloper.

Venzke was still leading Fenske and Cunningham into the tenth lap. Then Cunningham accelerated past Fenske, coming to Venzke's heels, trailing him by no more than two yards with Chuck Fenske barely in back of Cunningham. The trio continued in the same formation. Finally, in the homestretch, Cunningham gained a little more ground, coming to a foot behind Venzke at the tape. Venzke had won in 4:13.1, a time considered good for this early in the season.

It was yet another 1940 "first." It was the first time in seven years and nine runs that Cunningham had lost a mile race in Boston. And it was the first time in a long time that Venzke had bested Cunningham in a mile race.

Afterward, Venzke explained to the press how he had shortened his stride, chopping off two inches. This, he said, allowed a faster pickup. "Glenn has beaten me consistently since 1936," he told reporters, "because I lacked a quick pickup."

There was now speculation that Cunningham, having done so well, might reconsider his retirement decision. There was another story, perhaps apocryphal, written by John Lardner in the *New York Times*. It could have been tongue in cheek, yet I suspect there was much truth to it. It goes something like this: Venzke was resigned to running the half-mile that night. Then an idea occurred to him. He asked Cunningham how he was feeling. Cunningham said he was feeling fine. This response inspired Venzke to lobby himself into the mile run. Because if Cunningham had no ailment, he was licked from the start. The week before when he had complained of intermittent shooting pain here and there in his body, purportedly due to ptomaine poisoning from the tuna or the pie he had eaten earlier in the day, it could only mean one thing. Cunningham would be invincible. (Not only did he beat Venzke in that race, but Venzke had fallen down and had to be helped from the track.) But here in Boston where Glenn said he felt fine, it meant to Venzke that then Cunningham could be taken.

There would be races just before and a few races just after. But I'd prefer to have his racing career end where it really began. And that is with the Wanamaker Mile of the Millrose Games.

In the program for this early-February 1940 classic, Glenn's racing career and the personal ingredients he brought to the running scene were memorialized in a page of that program titled HAIL AND FAREWELL!

A great champion announces that this will be his last year of competition. The sports world suddenly stops to realize what Glenn Cunningham has meant to sports and particularly to his chosen athletic field.

It is not only that Glenn Cunningham is a world-renowned record-holder with eight years of glorious triumphs behind him; it is not alone that he ran the fastest mile ever paced by man; it is not only that he ran more fast miles than any runner, past or present; it is not alone that he has won this title or that title so many times; it is not only that his racing greatness encompassed all distances from a quarter mile to two miles, that has made him such an outstanding figure in the world of sport.

All these feats brought fame to Cunningham and glory to those he represented. But they did not make Glenn Cunningham the popular athletic idol that he is today. His own personality and fine character did that. Track and field athletics can well afford to hold up Glenn Cunningham as the No. 1 representative of the sport.

Cunningham was not always the popular idol he is today. When he first came East for competition, the fans thought his warm-up tactics were those of a show-off. They had never seen a runner warm up so thoroughly or conscientiously. They had never seen a runner warm up by bobbing his head like a racehorse to loosen his neck muscles. However, the fans learned in time that Glenn had definite ideas on preparing for his races. They saw him deliver, again and again. They came to understand him. They appreciated his modesty in victory, his grace in defeat, and his fine sportsmanship. They appreciated the fact that here was a champion without airs, who gave his best at all times, whether he was running on a relay for his team or for himself. Who can forget the competitive fire he poured into a handicap club relay at the Millrose Games here at the Garden, pulling his team from eighth to third place, after he had already won another great mile? Who can forget his patience with kids and unknowns who sought his autograph and advice everywhere?

All these qualities of the champion,—his clean living, his inspiration and influence on the youth of the land, his earning college and graduate degrees, while competing,—have been recognized by the sports tribunal that voted him the James E. Sullivan Memorial Trophy.

The Millrose Athletic Association, in sincere appreciation, adds its voice to the many tributes to Glenn Cunningham. We have a particular interest in Glenn. It was in the Millrose meet of 1933 that the Kansan made his Eastern debut. He has performed in our meet every year since then. He has won our Wanamaker Mile six of the seven starts. Tonight he will run his eighth and last Wanamaker Mile. The sport world cannot fail to miss a champion, a competitor, and a man such as Glenn Cunningham. The Millrose Athletic Association joins all track fans in saying: Hail and Farewell!

That program was printed for the meet and obviously before the Wanamaker Mile was run. Obviously, too, it had no way of knowing what was in store for the fans that night. But it did know who would be in the field. Besides Cunningham there was—you guessed it—Gene Venzke. And there were Chuck Fenske, Lou Zamperini, Leslie MacMitchell, and Blaine Rideout.

The sentimental favorite was Gene Venzke. Favored by the younger generation was Leslie MacMitchell. The odds, however, were on Fenske. He had beaten Glenn by three yards a week before in Boston, finishing in 4:10.3.

Before a hushed crowd of eighteen thousand plus S.R.O. they lined up. There was Leslie MacMitchell, the nineteen-year-old college sophomore. In another lane was the "Kansas Cyclone," Glenn Cunningham. A lane over, "conqueror of the great Cunningham" who had run the fastest mile ever recorded in January was Chuck Fenske. Ready to go, ". . . at the age of thirty-one, staging a spectacular comeback. . . . That fine veteran of the boards and cinders—Gene Venzke." Making his first Wanamaker Mile was ". . . that fine runner with a terrific punch at the finish—Louis Zamperini." To round out the pack was ". . . the outdoor 1,500-meter champion, one of the famous flying twins—Blaine Rideout."

(Clearly the above are partial quotes and are taken from a column in the February 3, 1940 *New York Herald Tribune* by Richard Vidmer titled DOWN IN FRONT. Vidmer imagined how Harry Balough—who handled the microphone at the Madison Square Garden boxing matches—would have introduced the runners. Vidmer, as Balough, described the color of their trunks, where they came from, what titles they held, what lane they were in, substituting "in this lane" for "in this corner." It wasn't all so far-fetched. Such was the hype, the interest, and the popularity of indoor track during the Cunningham years and even for some years beyond.)

Thus was their formation as off they ran, but not before two false starts from two different runners added to the suspense. Then came a clean start and they were off. From his outside lane, Blaine Rideout lurched over to the inside and quickly took the lead. He then ran the next four laps as if it were the whole race, accumulating a lead over the next man of more than twenty-five yards. He covered the first quarter mile in 0.56.8; at the half his time was 2:01. By then, however, he was starting to fall back to the single-file procession led by Fenske, then Cunningham, then Zamperini, who was followed closely by Venzke.

Near the end of the fifth lap, Fenske started to come on. With less than five laps remaining he passed Rideout, who was now in decrescendo mode. With four laps to go, Fenske was ahead of the field by ten yards. Cunningham meanwhile seemed to falter and dropped behind both Venzke and Zamperini. By now MacMitchell and Rideout were badly outdistanced.

Fenske, running smoothly, was increasing his lead. With three laps to go he was ahead of everyone by twenty-five yards. With two laps to go he was still twenty-five yards ahead but now Cunningham had found his feet and was reaching back into his past to summon up his reservoir of strength and speed. Glenn was able to cut the gap to seventeen yards at the end of the tenth lap. With one lap remaining, the crowd roaring in wild expectation, he opened up his throttle for a last charge.

Let Arthur Daley's *Times* reportage take over here:

"Chuck [Fenske] kept looking around as if fearing the worst. His lead dwindled like snow in a blast furnace.

"On whirled Cunningham, pulling Venzke and Zamperini along with him. Closer and closer he came. Fenske was tired and spent from the early going. His legs were heavy, and only his spirit was light and buoyant.

"But that was all he needed. A spent Fenske beat a gallant and driving Cunningham by three yards. Glenn had three on Venzke who was a foot in front of Zamperini. Rideout was lapped and MacMitchell, sick before the race, quit near the end."

Chuck Fenske Beating Cunningham in Second Fastest Mile Ever Run Indoors

4:07.4 FENSKE RUNS 4:07.4 MILE; GLENN SECOND, VENZKE THIRD

Wisconsin runner winning the Wanamaker Mile at Millrose Games at the Garden last night in 4:07.4, beating Cunningham by three yards with Gene Venzke, in white shirt, nosing out Louis Zamperini, of California, for third place. On extreme outside is Leslie MacMitchell, of N. Y. U., running his first big-time mile and being a lap behind the others. Blaine Rideout, of Texas, not shown, was fifth.

Fenske's quarter-mile times were 1:00, 2:03, 3:04, and 4:07.4 at the finish. It was then *the* fastest Wanamaker Mile time ever. And Cunningham had beaten his own best (and record) Wanamaker time by more than three seconds. Fenske's 4:07.4 equaled Glenn's Madison Square Garden record of 4:07.4 in 1938.

Cunningham felt he had delayed his finishing spurt just a bit too long. Twice he said, "I had too much left!"

Venzke was quite happy with his performance. It meant much to him: "I now know I'm in better shape than in five seasons."

Fenske, following a long apprenticeship, was now considered "Monarch of the Milers." And for the crowd it was the first race where four milers broke 4:09.

The Wanamaker Mile was not Glenn's last race. But it might be well to summarize his Wanamaker Mile record. In 2000 the late Stan Saplin encapsulated it. Here are portions of what he wrote:

THE MILLROSE STAR YOU DIDN'T KNOW

By Stan Saplin

Historical Editor, *Track & Field News*

Millrose Games Historian

Chances are, if you are a regular Millrose fan, that you have had the thrill of witnessing performances by all but one of the superb athletes entering the Millrose Hall of Fame in 2000.

But unless you are over the age that makes you eligible for Social Security, you never enjoyed the privilege of watching Glenn Cunningham majestically race around the eleven-lap track of Madison Square Garden. . . .

In Glenn's eight years on the boards, from 1933 to 1940, when there were other meets as well as Millrose at the Garden, he won 23 races there. He broke the world record indoors at 1500 meters three times and the world mark for the mile three times. . . .

Cunningham's six victories in the Wanamaker Mile were unmatched until Eamonn Coghlan won seven from 1977 through 1987. Glenn's first triumph came as a Kansas undergraduate in 1933 in a field that included defending champion and world record holder Gene Venzke and Ray Conger who had stunned the track world by defeating the legendary Finn, Paavo Nurmi, in the '29 Wanamaker. For the next few years, Cunningham vs. Venzke was like pitting Cone against Maddux in baseball last season. Glenn toppled Venzke every time, although in the '36 Wanamaker they both were defeated by the rocket-like last lap spring of Joe Mangan.

Cunningham did not confine his running to the 1500/mile. Twice he ran the anchor 440 leg on his club's mile relay at Millrose. At the Knights of Columbus meet in 1935 he won the mile and then doubled in the 1000, breaking the world record in the latter. In another double in '38 Cunningham broke the WR for the mile, running 4:07.4, and then ran third in the 600, equaling the listed world record; ahead of him, however, Jimmy Herbert won in world record time.

Wotta man, that Glenn Cunningham!

After the 1940 Wanamaker Mile it was all anticlimax. Here, anyway, is some of Cunningham's running history following that epic Wanamaker run—as the saying goes, "just for the record."

Merely a week later the site would be Philadelphia, the event the Penn A.C. Games. The cast, besides Cunninham, included Fenske, Blaine Rideout, Luigi Beccali. Cunningham had won in 4:15 the year before, but now the track world was looking for a sub-4:10. A crowd of eighty-five hundred saw Fenske and Cunningham duel the last two laps with Fenske maintaining his four-foot lead and matching Cunningham's spurt, snapping the tape four feet ahead of Glenn. His time was 4:13.5. Blaine Rideout, twelve yards in back, was third; Luigi Beccali dropped out two and half laps from home.

Glenn and Chuck met again only one night later in Boston. Fenske again won, this time in 4:11.2 before an overflow crowd of fifteen thousand, with Zamperini five yards behind for second place. Cunningham was another three yards farther back.

Next was the Baxter Mile at Madison Square Garden. A rejuvenated Gene Venzke with the shortened stride was the focus. After all, it was also the Baxter Mile where in 1932 Venzke had established the world indoor mark of 4:10, and now eight years later he had even bested that with his 4:08.2 in the Wanamaker Mile. Fenske was also entered, as were San Romani and Zamperini.

If Venzke's shortened stride was a potential factor, much was made of Fenske's lengthened stride. Abel Kiviat, the original Baxter Mile winner, related to the press how Fenske had borrowed the technique of the legendary Paavo Nurmi. Kiviat explained that Fenske gained added speed by generating greater power.

And the winner was . . . Fenske in 4:07.4. It broke Glenn's meet record of 4:08.6. Zamperini was half a second behind Fenske. Gene Venzke just nipped Glenn for third place though both were timed in 4:08.6. One writer said Glenn ran in labored fashion and had no finishing kick.

With only a day's rest he entered a 1000-yard run at the Newark (New Jersey) Armory. This was a "limited handicap" with Sanford Goldberg given a five-yard head start. Goldberg won followed by Fenske, then Venzke, with Cunningham finishing twenty yards behind him.

The trend was obvious. Glenn ascribed it to too little training in the winter and too much lecturing. He said this as a matter of fact, not as an alibi. He didn't expect to do well in the upcoming National Mile at Madison Square Garden. After all, as he put it, "I can't expect to run forever." I suspect he was now trying his best to fulfill commitments. His training consisted mainly of his races. And just before the National A.A.U. Mile he entered another 1000-yard event at New York City's 369th Regiment meet and won. His time, slower than he had once done, was 2:15.4. The flat track was considered slow and difficult, but he did win by forty yards.

That run was his training for the National A.A.U. Mile a few days later. The highlight of this evening was Greg Rice winning the three-mile race in record time. In the mile it was again a Fenske win. Cunningham was mounting a charge to overtake Fenske at the straightaway but then his foot hit the rail and down he went. Somewhat dazed, he still finished the race. All of the others reached the tape ahead of him.

The last scheduled run of the indoor season, the Knights of Columbus games at Madison Square Garden, March 9, 1940, was also billed as "last chance night" for all milers to beat Cunningham. It was written tongue in cheek because all of the writers recognized that Glenn's courage still burned brightly and that win or lose the loudest cheers would be for him that evening. He had won six out of the last seven years and his 4:07.4 time in 1938 was the record for the K. of C. mile.

It was all anticlimax. Fenske won, but his time was not nearly the hoped for record. It was a pedestrian 4:13.2. He had sprinted the last sixty yards. Glenn took second place, six yards behind Chuck Fenske. Zamperini and Venzke both trailed Cunningham. So again and just for the record:

His very last race was at the Kansas Relays in Lawrence Kansas. It was "Cunningham Day." In a special mile run he came in last but finished in striking distance of Blaine Rideout, whose 4:10.1 was a new Relays record. It broke Glenn's 1934 record. Blaine just edged his brother Wayne with Archie San Romani a few steps behind, and Glenn Cunningham a few steps in back of his fellow Kansan.

He had been leading at the halfway mark with a fast time of 2:03. What was missing was his finishing kick. He was given the gift of a blanket at day's end.

Effective September 1, Glenn Cunningham would become the new student health director at Cornell College, Mount Vernon, Iowa. He would also teach biology and personal hygiene. He would continue speaking to schools and service groups now under the public relations auspices of Cornell.

Cornell was a small liberal arts college with high standards. At the time its enrollment was restricted to about six hundred each year by entrance examination. He had turned down job offers in larger institutions that would have given him more prestige and more money, but at Cornell he saw the chance for some creativity on his part. "Cornell," he told the University of Kansas News Bureau, "seems to present opportunities that appeal to me."

However small was Cornell College, this would turn out to be the largest institution, and in fact the only organized institution—with the exception of the U.S. Navy during wartime—that he would ever be associated with.

21

A LIFE AFTER TRACK: 1941-1946

Those who work the hardest, who subject themselves to the strictest discipline, who give up certain pleasurable things in order to achieve a goal, are the happiest men

There's not much at all in the way of documentation to account for the three and a half years Cunningham worked at Cornell College. We do have his version, however, told almost fifty years later in that informal discussion following his 1987 post-banquet Boston Marathon talk. His description, subjective to be sure, nevertheless reflects an attitude he consistently applied to everything he did.

He was telling us how he handled two boys who were caught with drugs. (This happened years after Cornell, during the time he and Ruth were taking care of children from broken homes.) It was one of the few times he used corporal punishment. The moral of the story revolved about the relationship between authority and responsibility. To understand the context and the segue from his handling of the boys with the drugs and his handling of his job at Cornell College, it is well to quote the whole story as he related it. Here are his words as recorded on tape:

They had this boy from Florida that was heavily in drugs, was supposed to catch a flight but didn't catch it, his folks called and said he'd be there next day. Finally after three or four days he got a flight in. In the meantime he'd been in Miami picking up drugs. On the way in the plane from Memphis to Little Rock he robbed the stewardess's purse. So the security police and the city police at Little Rock got on the plane and brought him off. So I said I'm supposed to pick this boy up and they said you can't handle this kid and I said we had a lot worse. They finally released him to me. I took him home, it was late at night, I asked him if he had any drugs on him, he said 'no.' The next morning he went in to room with a doctor's son from Oklahoma City. And the doctor's son had been on drugs but he had been without them while he was there with us. And they both came down, they'd been taking drugs. And I suspected so I asked them; they denied it so I separated them and then I got the truth from them. And I said okay you know what the rules are. We don't allow the kids to smoke . . . use any kind of alcoholic beverages, any drugs. No boy/girl relationships because a lot of these girls have been on the streets. You can't have boy/girl relationships and have any discipline at all and I'll tell you, these are the rules, if you break them you pay for it with the skin off your rear end.

This one boy, the doctor's son, he's about six-feet, weighed about two-hundred pounds . . . he looked at me and said, 'you know I'm a black belt,' and I said you better start using it, you're going to need it. I said you get down or I'll put you down and get your ankles. Now if I put you down there you'll stay down there. And I meant it. He went down and got his ankles. I just took the rear end off of him . . . with a heavy leather belt. And he bawled like a baby. The other boy started bawling before I got a hold of him.

You're not supposed to do these things. But I will not assume responsibility without authority. Those two things cannot be sepa-

rated. *Responsibility and authority go together. And whenever you separate them . . . just like when I went and took this job at Cornell College. Organized the Student Health Service. They wanted to put me down in an old and moldy basement room that was covered with cobwebs. It was wet down there, it was damp down there. And I said how can you have a health department in a place like that? They said that's the only place we got. I said well you better start to look for something then. I said there's a room upstairs that would be ideal; it was large and divided up so we could have examination rooms and so forth. And they said well you can't have it, and I said well okay we won't have a health department then. And finally they found out they could let me have it.*

And I said what kind of a budget, and they said nobody has a budget here. How the hell can you organize a department without a budget. And they said, well you make a list of what you want and we'll decide what we can afford and we'll buy it. And I said there may be choices, if I can only buy one thing, I'd buy this one rather than that one but you may want this one because it's a little bit cheaper . . . and they weren't going to give me a budget. So I just sat there for two damn weeks waiting. And finally they gave me a budget.

After a year I got the health department organized and running. I became director of athletics and the head of the physical education department. No budget. And I said I won't schedule a game of football, basketball, wrestling or track or anything else until I have a budget. This lady in the office said well everybody's been operating here all these years without a budget, and I said how did they operate and she said just make a list. I said okay if I need, supposing I need three dozen jock straps and two dozen t-shirts. Oh she just blushed and turned and walked away. I got my budget.

You're either going to do a job or you don't do a job. We had peo-

ple from all across the country to see what we were doing in the health department, trying to copy it. We had lots of comments about the athletic department.

Besides reflecting his attitude in handling his position at Cornell, the additional moral of the story, as documented by studies, was that societies with strong fathers and discipline have very low juvenile delinquency rates, much lower than in this country.

Please indulge me to allow for a pause here to reflect upon Cunningham's prose. He was, to repeat, talking informally. His words flowed freely, for he was definite and unequivocal in what he espoused. But like most of us, we can write better than we talk. In the former you can always erase; if you have the luxury of a word processor you can cut and paste, use a thesaurus, and so on. When Cunningham dictated to a typewriter his sentence structure and punctuation were impeccable. Even his handwriting was quite legible.

When he spoke formally there was a cadence and rhythm to his delivery. He was plain-spoken and avoided big words. And like his races, he ended with a strong flourish. At least that was the pattern of his Boston talk.

Back now to the Cornell College years: However confrontational he may have sounded, his relationship with the administration and faculty was good. He always said that they were good people, dedicated and scholarly.

They learned and benefited from each other. By the time he left there in 1944, our country had been at war with the Axis Powers since December 1941. Men in ages up to their early forties had to sign up for selective service, and those 18 to 35 were being drafted into the army. Married and with two children, he must have been deferred for a while. By now he was 34 years old and about to be drafted. So he sought to enlist in the U.S. Navy. Mrs. Cox told a story about his induction. Apparently the examiners, noting his scars, told him that he'd be unable to withstand the rigors of basic training. Just as the time when a policeman had asked him to move out of the way when he was outside Madison Square Garden, he didn't announce who he was. Rather, he just let the scenario unfold. Here is her account:

They gave him a physical examination. He didn't tell them who he was or what he could do, what he had done or anything about it. And they came back and told Glenn that he just couldn't possibly pass to go into the Navy. He couldn't measure up, couldn't possibly do the things he'd be required to do. And while they were talking someone came in and spoke to him, called him by name, and they tumbled to the fact of who it was they had examined and completely reversed their opinion. Actually, they were very much put out about the mistake.

So in the spring of 1944, into the navy he went. He was based at the Great Lakes Naval Station in Illinois. Then he went to officers' training school at Princeton, New Jersey, in the summer of 1944; was stationed at San Diego until 1945; then returned to Great Lakes. He was discharged in 1946.

During his stint he visited burn-wounded hospitalized navy men. There are photos taken of him showing his burn wounds to the wounded patients.

At the Great Lakes Naval Station he established a physical fitness program. Impetus for the program had to do with his thoughts about the loss of life among sailors whose ships had been sunk. He considered that their inability to survive in cold water was a matter of poor physical conditioning. Whether physical conditioning made a difference in sub-fifty-degree

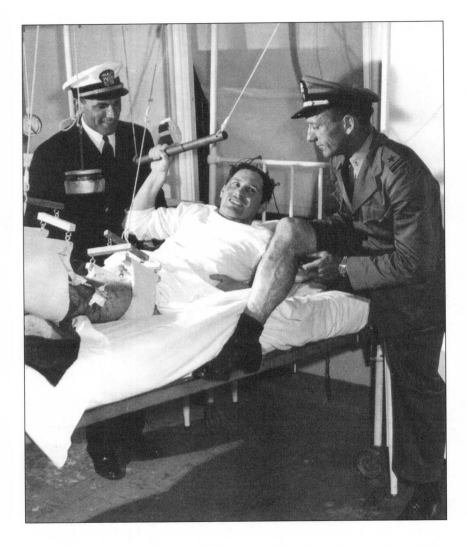

water, whether anyone could survive for more than a short period of time, is a matter of conjecture. Nevertheless, his thoughts
on the matter spurred him to design a successful fitness program
at Great Lakes.

Survival in other less than-optimal-war conditions was a matter of deep concern to Glenn. Over his lifetime he would jot
down his ideas, some quotes, aphorisms, rhetorical phrases,

homilies, sayings from the Bible and from the great thinkers on
scrap pieces of paper, on hotel stationery, even on the backs of
checks or receipts. His handwriting was small, economical, and
legible. He could get a ton of thoughts written in a small space.
Found on these scraps, among many other issues, are his
thoughts on prisoners of war. Here, to him, it was a matter not
so much of physical conditioning but of attitude.

He compared loss of life in the Korean War among
American prisoners, said to be 38 percent, to that in the
Revolutionary War when it was 33 percent. He opined that
selfishness was the main cause, the attitude "not what can I do
to help myself, but what can be done for me." He further cited
Turkey. Here he must have been talking about the First World
War, where Turkey was an ally of Germany. He wrote that
Turkey had 229 prisoners taken; some were wounded, but not
one was lost. He said that the Turks nursed each other back
to health.

Attitude, however essential and critical, could not possibly
explain these figures. What Cunningham did not consider, so
invested was he in the idea of attitude, was the relatively benign
prisoner-of-war treatment the Allies extended in the world wars,
and the British in the Revolutionary War, as compared to what
the North Koreans and the Communist Chinese inflicted on the
Americans in their custody.

Discharged from the navy in 1946, he returned to Emporia
Kansas. He and his wife Margaret divorced in August 1946. I
will pretty much skip over the reasons, for they are essentially
unknown and what "facts" exist are too vulnerable to the spin
machine. Margaret, from all accounts, was a lovely woman. She
died in 2001. She was intelligent, witty, attractive (described as

"comely" in the newspapers), sophisticated. Probably it was the unconventional life Glenn wanted to lead that was the major issue. I imagine very few women could adjust to his way of life.

But the lady he would marry a year later, Ruth Maxine Sheffield, was *the* one who could.

Born in 1923 and fourteen years younger than Glenn, she had entered Cornell College at age seventeen. It was the same time Glenn took his position there. She majored in physical education and had had a number of his classes. She also had worked a couple of semesters as his student secretary for her work/study program at Cornell.

After her graduation from Cornell in 1944, she taught school at Charles City, Iowa, 1944-1945, and Dixon, Illinois 1945-1946. Teaching, she told me, "wasn't my forte, and truthfully I wasn't that well prepared, being one of the first physical education majors from there, they didn't have the best program for it." She had studied piano from the second grade, with private lessons all through college, and gave a senior recital in 1944. She wanted to study with her uncle, Vernon Sheffield, who was a professor of piano at Emporia State Teacher's College, Emporia, Kansas.

So upon returning to Emporia in the fall of 1946 she met Glenn again.

Glenn was then in the process of moving a small house to an acre of land he had purchased, as he had several horses to bring there, and housing was very hard to get at that time.

One of Cunningham's scribbles, this one on a cutout sheet of paper about eight and a half inches long and three and a half wide, is titled GIRL WANTED. His handwriting is small and economical; there are about 224 words on thirty-eight lines filling one side. It is not dated. In it he describes the ideal woman:

GIRL WANTED

To fill an important position in any capacity
She must have a clean face, clean habits and a clean heart.

Need not know how to smoke a cigarette or how beer or liquor tastes and if she is not up to date on all the dirty jokes her ignorance will be overlooked.

She must be a girl who treats her mother and father and every other girl's mother and father with respect and does not refer to her mother or father as "the old woman or old man."

She need not be especially brilliant in school but she must be studious and persevering, never cheating on her examination or passing a problem until she has mastered it.

She must be truthful, prompt, obedient and industrious. She must make her employer's interests her interests and never be afraid to earn more than she is paid.

She is wanted to respond at once to any number of jobs. Merchants want her to sweep there [sic] stores for a few years and ultimately to take charge of the business.

Newspapers want her to start at the bottom and work to the top.

She is wanted everywhere—in the law, in medical practice, in the counting room and great public works. The people who pay big salaries are looking for her.

The people want her for judge in the court, member of Congress, senator and for President of the Greatest Country on earth, and the nicest boy in the world wants her for his wife.

(Note, too, a wry sense of humor, a steady paced cadence, and a strong finish.)

Obviously the meaning of his allegorical prose is open to interpretation. I contend again that he is describing what for him is the ideal woman. And as I know her, Ruth Sheffield Cunningham fits his mold.

They were married in Storm Lake, Iowa, on June 29, 1947.

In the photo of the wedding party, from left to right in the back row, are Mary Alice Walrod, her college roommate, Bill Morgan from Great Lakes, her sister Helen, and her brother Paul Sheffield. In the foreground are Glenn's daughters, Sandra and Sara.

After the wedding ceremony they spent only a couple of days at The Inn, a hotel at a resort area on Okaboji, one of a series of lakes about sixty miles north of Storm Lake. They returned to Storm Lake, gathered up the girls who had stayed with Ruth's parents, and on Wednesday drove back to Emporia.

They lived in Emporia for three years. While in Emporia, Glenn did at least a year of speaking for the University of Kansas Extension Service, receiving many other requests for talks as well. He took part in the "Temperance Tornado," a group that toured the state speaking against legalized liquor, as a vote was to come up in the fall of 1948.

Their life was uneventful, without much challenge. In today's vernacular you'd say that Glenn was trying to find himself. He wasn't sure what he wanted to do. One thing, though, he was certain of: Ruth related a well-remembered remark of his in which he declared that he'd rather be shoveling manure fifteen hours a day than have a nine-to-five job. And, she added, "he didn't say manure, either."

Again, in today's vernacular, he needed to "do his own thing." But *that* was still in the incubating stage. He was giving his talks on a way of life. In so doing he was making a living. Yet that was secondary. What was more important was to bring a message, one whose expression was an extension of him.

His way of life was also an expression of the typical personality of a runner. That personality was described in the 1970s by Dr. George Sheehan, cardiologist, author, and dedicated runner. He wrote that ". . . the runner is not made for the things and people and institutions that surround him." Sheehan noted that the runner's discipline, denial of satisfactions, and eschewing of the motivations that drive most men would seem to the casual observer as unnatural.

Another description, reflecting Glenn's makeup was formulated by Brutus Hamilton, Glenn's erstwhile coach—himself no slouch as a scholar and thinker: "It is one of the strange ironies of this strange life," he wrote, "that those who work the hardest, who subject themselves to the strictest discipline, who give up certain pleasurable things in order to achieve a goal, are the happiest men."

A good start in life.
July 13, 1952, at Cedar Point. Glenn, Glenn Drury, Lynn, Gene, and Ruth.

22

1950-1960

As long as there was room—and the question of room was a relative one since there always seemed to be room—they couldn't refuse anyone.

In the spring of 1950 Ruth and Glenn moved to the 840-acre ranch near Cedar Point, Kansas, about fifty miles west of Emporia. Glenn owned this ranch since the late 1930s. By that time he was relatively comfortable financially. How did that come about?

One source was expense money during the track years. Disciplined and Spartan in his needs, Glenn could consume less than he was allotted and so keep the change. Another had to do with his purchase of cheap land that later sprouted gas wells, with Glenn eventually accruing gas revenues. We can't forget, too, the matter of under-the-table money from the competitions. Finally there is the matter of his college fund. He did tell our group that during the Depression, he lost all the money he had saved. He probably did, but it was not all bank failure. Rather he had loaned money to farmers and businessmen who had, in turn, helped him at different junctures, but were then in dire financial straits. He had told them they could pay him back when and if there was an upturn in their financial lives. By the late 1930s, their fortunes restored, money flowed back to Glenn so that in 1938 he bought the 840-acre ranch.

The ranch itself included a twelve-room house, built in the early 1900s. It was once the setting of lavish social gatherings when owned by Charlie Topping, a wealthy uncle of the one-time Topping New York Yankee owners.

The Ranch: we should let Glenn's son Gene, now an ordained minister and missionary, describe it. His words are found in his composition "Nomad Tracks," a monograph that is "Free—not for sale." Originally meant as a diary of his thoughts, this narrative of the Cedar Creek country is dedicated to his parents. But in large part it is a paean to Glenn Cunningham, Gene's father, his hero:

To the north, the gravel road wound over the hill and down near the creek, where it disappeared on its way into Cedar Point. That little settlement on the Cottonwood River was nine miles away. Few cars traveled that road, leaving the summer days quiet save for the wind in the grass. Looking east, across the sheep pasture, the ground rose gradually to our boundary fence. Up there was a big shade tree where we kids liked to go for picnics and play cowboys and Indians. Turning south you saw the tenant house of the hired hand, and below it the corrals and big weathered barn. Sweeping your eyes from east to west you came to look across Cedar Creek, lined with tall, whispering cottonwood trees. Beyond the creek the land rose into prairie hills of bluestem grass. Near to a thousand acres of rolling prairie broken by river bottom fields of corn and alfalfa made up my little world. It was known as Cedar Creek Ranch.

This was my horizon if seen from the perspective of the large old rambling ranch house, which was home. Nearly a hundred years old, it had drawn county visitors from miles around when it was newly painted white in days of old. An old man told of how folks would come in their buggies on Sunday just to wheel up the long lane beneath the spreading elm trees and turn in to the circle drive for a visit. The ranch was situated in what had been wintering grounds for the nomadic buffalo and equally nomadic natives. They were known as "Kansa," the people of the south wind, or "Wind People." Their name has been given over 140 spellings. They called the wind their brother. They may have come from Mongolia. Among these hills the wallows of the buffalo could still be seen and along the river bottoms, the old campgrounds, now turned to fields, yielded up to excited boys following their father's plowing a treasure of flint spears, arrowheads, knives and axes. These were called the "flint hills."

This was the classroom of my early childhood. The land remains today, nearly fifty years later, engraved in my memory. All I have to do is close my eyes and I can hear the wind in the grass. I was very early absorbed by the study of weather and wildlife. As my maternal grandmother said with dismay, "They are growing up like wild Indians." That statement pleased us. My brothers and I hunted rabbit with throwing sticks. We heard the call of the great horned owl in the timber on cold winter nights, and the yapping of coyotes on the far hills. We ran down trails used for generations, some worn deep in the limestone outcrops.

The land and its history made a deep imprint also on my soul. Like the Kansa, I lived under the dome of the sky within the circle of the horizon. And I longed to follow the wind over the hill to see what lay beyond. In the course of time and according to plan, the Creator saw fit to fulfill this moving-hunger. This little journal, which I gratefully and lovingly dedicate to my father and mother, is a record of my road. If nothing else I pray to God, Who has lifted and led me, that it will be a heritage for our children.

Sara and Sandra would spend the summers at the ranch with Ruth and Glenn. They had friends who stayed for several weeks each summer. Glenn's main source of income was from his talks. He also farmed a lot of the land, raising alfalfa hay, oats, and some corn. He gained little if any income from the farming. What was harvested went mainly to feed his animals.

Around that time Glenn and Ruth had learned from the church of the need for locating displaced families from the war, and had applied to take a family. With the help of the church, they were assigned a family of Russian background to come and live in the tenant house. They were a family of five, a couple with two boys and a small girl. The parents spoke no English, but the boys had learned a bit in school. They stayed with the Cunninghams several years, eventually moving to New Jersey where there were others from their homeland. This venture, however, would become, as in the song line, "the start of something new."

Seeds of that new something began with Glenn's association as a speaker for the National Temperance League. Schedules were set up by the various states, and he would go for ten days to two weeks at a time, speaking several times a day at schools, churches, and civic clubs. Ruth would take him to Wichita Airport (about sixty miles away), and then pick him up on his return many days later, often late at night. By 1953 they had three children. They would go with him at times.

(Ruth, to me, was destined to follow in the footsteps of her biblical namesake, going where Glenn wanted to go, staying where he wanted to stay.)

During this time, too, Glenn began speaking for the Crippled Children and Adults organization, which became Easter Seals. He was also their board member for some years.

His talks were aimed mainly toward young people. He asked that his schedule be full; he disdained any "down time."

Sometimes he'd be gone for a week at a time and would call and write asking about things at home. He would go to different locations and travel long distances, always anxious, but frequently unable, to get home at night.

Here's a typical schedule during the week of April 16, 1956:

9:00 AM Waterloo High School (notation: $50)

11:00 AM Watertown High School

12.15 PM Rotary Club, Watertown

1:56 PM Oconomowce High School

2:50 PM Oconomowce Junior High School

6:30 PM Edgerton Methodist Church, Father & Son Banquet

The rest of the days of that week were equally packed. That Sunday he appeared in the morning at the First Methodist Church.

From his speaking in schools and meeting youngsters who by now learned of the ranch with its farm, its cattle, its many animals, written requests flowed from parents for their youngsters to come there for the summer. There was also a steady flow of parents whose kids were having problems, and Glenn would invite them to bring their children to the ranch for a while. Children would stay for days, weeks, months, even years. Even the courts became involved, albeit informally, asking the Cunninghams to take in a troubled child from a troubled family. As long as there was room—and the question of room was a relative one since there always seemed to be room—they couldn't refuse anyone. One time a church young people's group came for several days. Numbering eighty-eight, they camped out on the lawn and Ruth fed them three meals a day.

While Glenn did a lot of speaking during the winter, he was home all summer. Ruth would take their children and the kids visiting out to the fields; Glenn plowed or planted while they spent the day picnicking.

In the 1950s when there was little or no inflation, when a gallon of regular gas cost around twenty-five cents, their grocery bills could reach thirty-five dollars a day, just food for their growing family and the children who stayed with them.

As the number of kids who came to stay "for a while" increased each summer, Glenn and Ruth had to become more creative in planning activities. They often took the covered wagon, which was a Conestoga wagon Glenn had acquired from somewhere in Pennsylvania one summer, and drove out to the back pasture, while the kids rode their horses and camped, cooking their meals over a fire. In other evenings they would ride out across the creek and circle the pastures. During the day they had chores to do. In June it was the rodeo in Strong City on Highway 50 east of them, and for several years they took the Conestoga, and a truckload of the horses. The kids were in the parades and they all camped out near the rodeo grounds. One year they rode the horses to the rodeo. Ruth remembers frying chicken in the late hours of the night, getting ready for the next day's trek. It was, to say the very least, an unconventional, yet by no means aimless, way of life.

By December 21, 1959, when Nancy Jo was born, there were eight children. Sara and Sandra were gone by then. Sara had graduated with a nursing degree from the University of Iowa, and Sandra was a sophomore there. Sara was married sometime around then, but her husband died about a year later with cancer. She remarried several years later. (Sandra never married; she has a doctorate in occupational therapy, is retired, lives on the ranch today, and raises Arabian horses. Sara died of ovarian cancer in 1993.)

The boys, Glenn Drury 12, Lynn Sheffield, 11, and Gene

Alan, 10, were nearing junior high school age. Cedar Point, lacking a junior high, had only a very small high school, and even that was discontinued a few years later. Ruth and Glenn were concerned about the children's schooling.

And the Cedar Point house was old and in disrepair. They didn't have money to put into it. Actually, as part of the divorce agreement, it belonged to Sara and Sandra if something happened to Glenn.

And Glenn was always searching for something to bring in more income. As Ruth describes him, Glenn was not a businessman, not one to watch the details of finances or marketing. He did what he wanted to do always. Consideration of the fiscal right or wrong of it was anathema to him. Ruth paid the bills and kept the accounts, but Glenn made the decisions and Ruth followed along. His big extravagances, as she put it, were that ". . . he did love animals, and unfortunately that as well as with the kids, is where our money went."

Another time I wrote Ruth because I suspected Glenn may have been a student of Thoreau, or at least would have made Thoreau one of his idols. She wrote this to me:

"I don't know when or if Glenn read Thoreau, but I know he did have many of the same thoughts and attitudes. He loved nature, and animals and the simple things in life. I could hardly ever get him into a store to buy clothes. He wore the same jeans I patched to keep them, and only put on a new pair after I bought them and put them in the drawer for some time. He never spent money on himself, but we spent thousands on feed and care for the animals."

23

1960 TO 1973

Plays with the kids.

They found a forty-acre plot on Highway 54, about five miles east of Augusta, Kansas, and bought it, albeit with borrowed money. "Of course," Ruth adds, "we lived on borrowed money for the larger part of our lives. But it was all paid back in time. I finished the last payments after he died, but selling what was necessary to do it. He had an excellent credit with banks. If we couldn't make a payment, he always went in to talk to them, and made whatever arrangements were necessary. We knew all of the bankers in a fifty-mile radius! Being a banker's daughter myself, I had many anxious moments when bills couldn't be paid; you just weren't supposed to live that way! But somehow, we always managed to live—we never went without food or clothes."

On the plot they bought there was an old farmhouse. It had a large open upper floor, which accommodated bunk beds for the boys. On the first floor were two bedrooms and a bath, as well as a large screened-in front porch that they winterized and enclosed to make a third bedroom for the girls. Their last two children were born there (at the hospital in El Dorado): John in 1961, and Cheryl in 1963.

Their children went to Leon High School in Leon, Kansas, about five miles to the east. Glenn (Jr.) and Gene excelled in cross-country and track. Actually the high school lacked a cross-country team until Glenn Jr. started one when he was a sophomore. When he was a senior, Gene was also on the team, and they won the state cross-country meet for B schools. Jim Ryun was running at the same time for East High School of Wichita, a larger A school.

It was also easier for Glenn (Sr.) to go the twenty-five miles to the Wichita Airport from there. "And for the first time," Ruth wrote, "I could get his shirts laundered at the cleaners! Before, I usually had to wash, starch and iron about eight shirts every time he came home, to get ready for the next trip! Freedom for me. Not that I was at a loss for work, with ten children eventually, and at one time eight others with us for the whole year!

"I had no help, except for a lady that came once a week to help for one morning. The older girls basically took care of themselves, and even the older boys did their own laundry. I did all of the cooking, always having a snack for them when they came from school, but the girls usually did the cleaning up before they did their homework.

"I took care of most of Glenn's correspondence—I made the 'mistake' of saying soon after we were married that if he bought me a typewriter I could take care of the letters! But, I always enjoyed that part of it, enjoyed the contact with people, most of whom I never saw! He did not type, but always wrote in long hand any letters he did write."

At home his time was spent with the children, and they made no distinction between their children by birth and those who came from outside sources. In fact Glenn demanded more of his own children, wanting them to be examples to the children who came in from the outside. (This probably caused some resentment with his own kids.)

And he thought of animals as his friends; he would not hunt, saying he couldn't conceive of shooting his friends. For his children and the children who came for varying spans of time, he built a small "zoo." He filled it with animals they had as well as those he obtained. He knew practically every zoo in the area and spent a lot of time trading animals with them. The Cunninghams had some animals the zoos wanted and the zoos had extras they wanted to get rid of, so they both profited. "Well," Ruth wrote, "as with most of his ideas along those lines, it wasn't long before we just opened it [their home] up to anyone who wanted to stop by, spending our money feeding the animals, with no income coming in!"

Glenn and friends

Among his notes written on the back of letters and other scraps, one of the actual letters was from a V. A. Basgall, City Manager, Emporia, Kansas.

Mr. Basgall's first paragraph addressed the issue of an animal exchange. He heard that Glenn wanted to exchange "one female buffalo for one male buffalo, one male deer for three deer and provide us with one male sheep."

"This exchange," wrote Mr. Basgal, "would be agreeable to the City of Emporia."

Then the city manager added this request:

"I noted in your literature regarding your Youth Ranch, a picture of a llama. Do you have any for sale or exchange? Can they be placed in the enclosure we have for the other animals?"

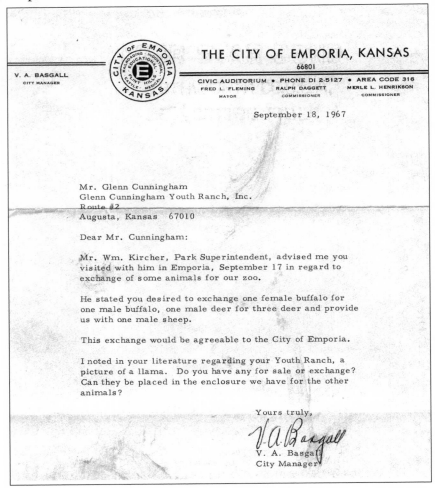

V. A. BASGALL
CITY MANAGER

THE CITY OF EMPORIA, KANSAS
66801

CIVIC AUDITORIUM • PHONE DI 2-5127 • AREA CODE 316
FRED L. FLEMING   RALPH DAGGETT   MERLE L. HENRIKSON
MAYOR   COMMISSIONER   COMMISSIONER

September 18, 1967

Mr. Glenn Cunningham
Glenn Cunningham Youth Ranch, Inc.
Route #2
Augusta, Kansas 67010

Dear Mr. Cunningham:

Mr. Wm. Kircher, Park Superintendent, advised me you visited with him in Emporia, September 17 in regard to exchange of some animals for our zoo.

He stated you desired to exchange one female buffalo for one male buffalo, one male deer for three deer and provide us with one male sheep.

This exchange would be agreeable to the City of Emporia.

I noted in your literature regarding your Youth Ranch, a picture of a llama. Do you have any for sale or exchange? Can they be placed in the enclosure we have for the other animals?

Yours truly,

V. A. Basgall
City Manager

Animal therapy was a staple of Glenn's approach to troubled children. Here is what he told us in April 1987:

"Animal therapy worked wonders for the kids. We gave them all a horse and they had other animals; they were always busy, they were always happy, just didn't have any problems. Of course I disciplined hard, didn't have to discipline often but I believe in discipline and without it you're going to have a generation just like we have today, committing crimes against society, just unbelievable; and it could all be ended in one generation if they could initiate discipline, a father in a family where he is the dominant one in that family. . . ."

At least thirty-five species made up the animal population at the farm. They ranged from bison and buffalo to monkeys and deer. He would try to add a new animal each year.

He knew that the youngsters "learn a great deal from their relationship with the animals." Animals he saw as "honest," and that they "respond to love and care." Out of the bond between child and animal he tried to teach that the trust and understanding between them led to better feelings for the youngster. "He learns compassion for others. Some even read up on the animals and learn all they can about them."

The bond that linked Cunningham with animals and children was his intuitive appreciation of play, akin to the Greeks' understanding of this basic need where they portrayed the god Eros as a child, giving him dominion over love and play. Cunningham never lost his ability to play. In the true sense of the word, he was, I contend, an erotic man.

There is poignant signature to Glenn Cunningham's identity, as he saw it, found in a 1966 scientific prospective study of sixteen former athletes ("A Longitudinal Study of 16 Champion Runners," *Journal of Applied Physiology,* 1251-1255, 1966). They had been followed over the years, measuring their blood pressure along with numerous blood chemistries, including cholesterol. Glenn had first been studied at the Harvard Fatigue Laboratory when he was there in 1936 or 1937 incidental to his presence at a Boston Garden competition. Studied at that same time were Fenske, Venzke, Lash, and San Romani. These five, along with eleven others studied elsewhere and at regular intervals, made up the total group. Glenn was listed as an "active farmer," and, fittingly, added to his official identity was, "plays with the kids."

(Fenske's competitive running career ended when he went into military service in March 1941. He was playing "a vigorous game of Racquet Ball a few times a week." Total blood cholesterol was somewhat elevated. Cardiogram was normal. San Romani's last race was in June 1940. Archie was smoking a pipe and a pack of cigarettes daily. He would wheeze when overheated with exercise or high humidity. Venzke was very active in his golf driving range but by then had an elevated blood pressure and signs of arteriosclerotic changes in the arteries of his retina. Lash had stayed active, mentioned that he had run a mile in 5:20 in February 1964, had retired from the FBI and exercised regularly. Cunningham's blood pressure was 100/60 in the left arm, 112/70 right arm. His total blood cholesterol level of 201 was then considered normal, as was his electrocardiogram. Resting pulse was now sixty. Charles Hornbostel had been smoking up to two packs of cigarettes a day for the past twenty-five years; his blood pressure was somewhat elevated.)

Glenn's "playing with the kids" took many forms. When they would work in the fields hauling hay, his son Gene told how Glenn would suddenly break out into song, or how he could convert grueling work into some form of play so that the day went much faster. And with the children under his care along with his own he would run and take long hikes.

Play was not only with the children. There came a day, February 13, 1964—the thirtieth anniversary of the Baxter Mile, when he would once more don a track suit and before a roaring crowd of 13,667 at Madison Square Garden, run a lap with Venzke and Bonthron. Myra Brown had asked Glenn about that meeting. "Mrs. Brown," he said, "Venzke wanted to run, to make a race of it, but Bonny was right beside me and he told me, he said, 'You fellows slow down, I'm not going to make it.'" They finally made it around the track. Glenn was quoted in the *Times'* write-up: "The public will have plenty of time to watch our lap." Bonthron had put on considerable weight by 1964. After the run a trainer had to spend much time rubbing down Bonthron's legs. Bonthron died in January 1983, "suddenly," according to the newspapers. He was ill with chronic lung disease at the time of his death.

But play and play therapy cost money. By now Glenn's debt was spiraling. As for income, his farming brought in a minimal harvest of cash. There he was mainly concerned with feed for the animals. His primary source of finances was from his talks. Here, too, he was no businessman. With some of the places where he lectured he was able to ask for their usual honorarium, about thirty dollars. In others he just asked for expense money and hoped they would pay him well. Sometimes they paid not at all. Among his papers is a "Disbursement Order" from Emporia Senior High School dated October 10, 1966. For his "Assembly Talk" there he received ten dollars. Nevertheless, in good weeks he'd make a thousand to fifteen hundred dollars. It was pretty good money for the 1960s but never enough to support the brood he was caring for at home.

By the mid-1960s, the reality of the imbalance between inflow and outflow became pressing. Glenn felt compelled to do what he must have hated to do. That was to seek help from the outside, something he had avoided for fear of external influence. It was the same, years earlier, when at college he had eschewed scholarship money.

So he incorporated as a not-for-profit organization, which would permit outside donations to be tax-deductible. Heretofore, promises and pledges of money from parents and from outside groups were frequently broken. With the incorporation there came booster groups, but with it, too, came the intricacies and petty minds of a small-town bureaucracy. Now under some scrutiny he was accused by a booster group of having a child under sixteen without a state health license. The Cunninghams always had written permission from the parents, but that did not satisfy the powers that be. He was fined. (The idiocy of all this: Glenn was found guilty, Ruth innocent, even though they worked together.) The judge never made him pay it, but the booster group now withdrew its support, as did other similar groups. More pledges and promises were withdrawn. There was another incident when local authorities accused him of starving some horses. These horses were all ill with swamp fever and Glenn had tried to avoid destroying them. Here was another fine, which the judge imposed but wouldn't let him pay. The courts that had asked him informally to take children had now tried to punish him.

Now, too, they had to turn down requests from parents. At times they had to sell parcels of his land to pay bills. The farm was described in one article ". . . with its seedy, run-down house, its broken, unpainted buildings and his children wearing worn hand-me-downs."

Still, by March 1971 there was a headline in the *Wichita Beacon* that read: CUNNINGHAM'S RANCH STILL DOING BUSINESS.

In the article there was a review of their goals and of their various problems. They were apparently just limping along in their work.

Something Glenn was quoted as saying in the March 1971 article deserves note: "People look at our operation and don't see the most important things. The facilities are probably one of the least important things as far as kids are concerned."

That obviously raises the important issue. What were the important things for kids, particularly troubled children? The first thing here to look at is the negative, the run-down facilities.

A young high school girl named Kathy had come from Chicago to study the whole project. This was 1967. Kathy had been at the farm for about a week. Myra Brown asked her this: "What did you first see when you first came? The clutter? The disorder? A lot of people would see that first. What did you think?"

Kathy answered: "Well—well, when I first stepped into the house I saw these kids and I didn't believe it. Everybody said 'Hello' to me. First thing I walked in—I didn't know anybody. This frightened me, 'cause all these people were around, but afterwards I discovered that all these children who needed this help, they would really help them."

Then she was asked, "How do you like it here?"

"Well," she began, "I think he's got a great thing going here . . . I hope he succeeds and I really think there should be more things like this and there's not many people like Glenn Cunningham. I think they have done a wonderful job here and, from what I have seen, I don't doubt that they have succeeded. I know they have succeeded in doing what they want to, but I hope they succeed even more, because things like this don't just happen every day. There are not many people like this at all.

"I think Glenn has an ambition for this place and he's willing to give his heart for anyone here, and both Glenn and Ruth love all the children here, their own and others, and I feel that they really can't do much more, even though they want to, they're just two people who give everything they have for others. People can be famous, and they can have money, and there are other people who make their lives nothing, but the Cunninghams have made something of life with the children and a happy home. I think they've done a wonderful job.

"Glenn and Ruth are as good as real parents. They're two wonderful people who love I think, everybody, no matter who they are or what they've done. And we all love them. The very first day I came here I loved them both. To give their hearts to people like that, especially children."

What Kathy was describing is what's today called cognitive behavioral therapy. Before it even had a name, this was what the Cunninghams were doing—this plus much more, but the approach was basically that of cognitive behavioral therapy, or CBT.

Its basic premise is that there is a continuum between thought and feeling. Out of this dynamic interplay comes an outlook, a view toward life—an attitude. Cunningham's philosophy (or psychology, or both) was a variation on a theme from the book of Proverbs, 23:7: "As a man thinks in his heart, so is he." Glenn's was a subtle deviation hinging on where you put the comma. But even here there were variations on the variations as he tried to fine-tune his thinking. Here are some of his notes, some with attributions, and others apparently aphorisms of his own creation.

1. You are not the person you think you are, but what you think, you are.

2. As a man thinks, so is he.

3. Belief influences action and action influences belief. Act as if it were impossible to fail.

4. Every great accomplishment started with a thought (Ben Sweetland).

5. The more you fail, the more you succeed.

6. He who subdues himself is strong (Lao Tse).

7. If you don't stand for something you'll fall for anything.

Number six translates to discipline. Add to that empathy, love, plus the interaction with animals, and you have all the ingredients of Glenn's prescription for life.

Ruth Cunningham wrote this to me:

"All of my children have burned into their brains the statement: 'Your attitudes will make you or break you,' and, 'It's not what you think you are, but what you think, you are,' and 'if you don't stand for something, you will fall for anything.' I think the country song writer stole that from him!"

Here are portions of the INTERVIEW WITH GLENN CUNNINGHAM, SUNDAY, JULY 16, 1967

Glenn Cunningham: "Well, you take a child that is abnormal. I'm thinking of behavior-wise. Attitudes are the important thing. Wherever you can change attitudes you can change people. Change their thoughts and then you change the individual. And that's all we can do here, primarily, just change their methods of thinking, the direction of their thinking."

As a follow-up he was asked if a certain boy was beyond help:

"No, I don't think so. Sometimes it takes a lot of convincing to get them to change their attitudes and thought-patterns, but that's one of the jobs you have to do when you work with these kids, of finding ways and means of making them want to change.

"It usually takes about two weeks. That is the usual time to see a definite change in a child. You get some of these kids that are just in here for a day, or for a short time, and then they go back. You can't usually do too much for them. But when they're here straight through for a period of weeks, then you can make a lot of change in them. Just like—they asked us to take a boy from El Dorado, from the Welfare Department down here at El Dorado. We took him and I got him going along under control while he was here, but he knew he didn't have to do anything permanently because he was going right back into the old situation. You can't help much in a situation like that. But if you can go right straight through over a period of time, you can—In two weeks time you can start making definite changes in the kid."

Asked if he made mistakes in his approach to troubled children:

"If I have I haven't been smart enough to detect it. I'm not saying that I don't make mistakes. It's like I was telling the kids last night. I make more mistakes than anyone. The person who doesn't make mistakes is the person who never does anything."

The following dialogue requires a more formal presentation:

Myra: "We'll get at it this way. In your opinion has any child had an injured spirit because of some punishment?"

Glenn: "No. Not that I know of. I think they gain spirit, rather than lose it."

Myra: "Well, sometimes sensitive children carry a hurt that doesn't show up but something happened that leaves a scar. I've known of children like that and they carried scars for years. Now you know the children. You know the scars that they carry on their souls. Their spirits."

Glenn: "I don't know whether I can express the things I want to here or not. But you know some people are extremely sensitive and always getting their feelings hurt because their feelings are always sticking out. The things we try to get these kids to know is that even though they are sensitive, they have to be capable of taking some blows and not letting it injure them too much. We have many children who come to us that are extremely sensitive."

Myra: "Yes. They have been hurt."

Glenn: "They have been hurt and they have been hurt very deeply. But I think when they know that when there is love in back of whatever treatment you give them, whether it is physical punishment or merely words, as long as they know there is love in back of it, that is the balm that soothes all the wounds and makes them realize that things are not quite as severe as they sometimes think they are."

Myra: "I think that mothers do sometimes misunderstand children, but in my experience it has been fathers who have most often erred in understanding. They just don't see the things as the child thought it was."

Glenn: "I think that is the problem with most people. That's one place where I really spend a lot of time and energy trying to remember back in my own childhood and remember how I felt at certain ages and how certain things affected me and why they affected me as they did. And things where I think my own parents could have handled me more wisely. And that's why I do certain things with these kids that people don't understand probably. And I talk to the kids about their feelings.

"I think the only way you can really get at all these problems is to have complete empathy. With the person you're dealing with. Just like I was talking with one of the girls last night. And she was talking about some of the problems. And I told her—She was talking about my deep feelings, and I told her I felt deeply every hurt these kids had. I feel each hurt that each one of these kids have felt and even though most people think that I'm just real rough and real severe with the kids, and all."

To further illustrate what he meant by empathy, let me fast forward briefly now to the late 1980's, to the making of the video entitled *The Iron Man of Kansas.* Near the end Glenn is sitting on a bench. He is dressed informally with open collar and sweater. He says: *The Lord allowed this for a purpose. I believe it has helped me to understand other people who are going through pain and suffering and difficulties better than the average person . . . I can just empathize with other people . . . those kids who came here, I can feel their hurt.* Then there is a pause—and the pause lasts at least ten seconds. He raises his arms as if searching for the upper body strength that propelled him to epic race finishes. This time his arms fail him. They drop limply to his side. Finally able to continue, he resumes with the theme of their pain—*that each one of them felt and I understood what they were going through, I could minister to them in a way that would help them to respond in a positive way and come out of that shell where they were constantly hurting.*

He could help them come out of the shell by creating a consistent, predictable environment. That goal was reached in part through discipline and work in the form of chores. He always used to tell the kids that until their chores were done, they didn't go anywhere else.

Kids were assigned tasks such as feeding the animals; each one was assigned an animal to care for. If the animal were a horse, any feeding neglect would be more obvious. Glenn said that there was something about the children working animals that made them very honest. Limits and boundaries and discipline were paramount. These were elements he embraced in his running

Images from *Iron Man of Kansas*

world. Even his relationship with the dog Jack: They ate out of the same plate, but when Jack transgressed by going outside his half of the plate, or—as Cunningham put it—"if he got across the line, all it took was a sharp whack on his nose." So, too, with the kids. Their main transgression—drugs—would be met with a trip out to the woodshed.

"Children want to be disciplined," he was quoted in the May 1968 *KU Alumni Magazine*. "If you make them mind they instinctively know that you love them. If you let them do anything they want to, they feel you don't really care about them."

He did really care. When he said in his talks "I never met a bad boy, I never met a bad girl, I never met a child I don't love," he meant it. He saw both animals and children as pure and innocent. Children became troubled because of their adult parents' inconsistencies and neglect. And those parental negatives, he believed—however simplistically—arose mainly from their abuse of alcohol and drugs.

What he was trying to bring about for the kids was that if you lived by the rules you could, as much as possible, create an environment that was predictable and consistent, and thereby they could feel a sense of security. Thus it was important to adhere to a regular schedule and have regular routines. So it then comes back to the primary importance of chores. Get the chores done: building fences, hauling in hay and grain, doing housework, cleaning up the yard, doing the dishes, making beds, doing laundry, preparing food for the next meal, feeding the animals. Then you can have your fun and you could play; he would often break out into song when they would haul hay, trying to unite work with play.

With children and with animals he, too, felt more secure. They were both bonded in expressing their need for discipline ("He who subdues himself is strong"—Lao-Tzu) and their love of play.

Cunningham was practicing, albeit informally, psychotherapy. In any form of psychological treatment, identification with the therapist will evolve. And the therapist, in this case Cunningham, becomes—okay I've got to use the term—the

Photo from the *KU Alumni Magazine*, May 1968

As dawn lights the eastern sky, a youngster at Glenn's ranch
goes about his chores, carrying water for the animals.

"role model." Or better yet, in his words, an example. One boy,
Johnnie, in a desperate quest to find someone to pattern himself
after, was enormously proud when Glenn gave his approval for
having charge of feeding the big animals: the horses, the deer, the
elk, the peafowl, a fox, and a coyote.

Glenn read a letter Johnnie, now (1967) in military service,
wrote him. He saved letters. He wanted affirmation, to know
that he had had made a difference in someone's life.
Characteristically, some of the recorded interview has him trying
to first find, amid the clutter, where he put the letter. Then he
quotes:

"He says: 'Dear Father, I was so glad to hear from you.'

"And then he goes on telling about this little girl he has been
dating here and how—I even sat down in the corner and

thought, and just about cried."

Myra asked him why he just about cried and he responded simply that it was the letter itself. Then he continues quoting from the letter:

"I'll tell you, I know I was loved and thought of and when you would say you could trust me with your car and money I felt as if my name was John Cunningham! As if I was your own. I still feel as if I was your own and you showed it."

Myra interrupts with "How fine!" and you can just about see her beaming. Then Glenn continues once more from the letter:

"Don't get me wrong, but I felt as if I were somebody. Even if it was by your name. I remember many times when people would come to the farm and say, 'Where's that boy that ate twenty-six eggs? And Mr. Cunningham trusted so well.' Well, I would say, it was me. And they would talk to me, and some people would say 'big deal, twenty-six eggs!' But to me it meant that I was somebody."

Myra then asks if Johnnie really ate twenty-six eggs. Glenn responds:

"Oh, yeah. For breakfast. He says, 'I wanted to haul animals, trade for you or be a foreman, so bad. Because you always said I was your right hand man. I wanted it so bad. Well, Father, I loved you and Mother so much. For what you have done for me. And a lot more for what you have done and are doing for other kids.'" Cunningham is noted here to choke back tears.

This is an extreme example of a young man needing and finding an identity.

Before going on we should pause and try to separate the relatively subjective from the relatively objective. This is always the danger of using anecdotal material. The Cunninghams kept scanty, if any, records. The recorder of the interview wanted to write a book about Glenn and was already enamored of the person and his work. So, too, the children he ministered to. So, too, was the girl Kathy. Even this writer who met him once and was indelibly impressed. Such is the subjective.

But what needs to be appraised is that which is relatively objective. *That*, in turn, refers to the principles behind his approach. Namely those principles of discipline, order, play, love. The force of his personality and his charisma certainly played a major role, both in dealing with the children and in his talks.

I contend that his principles were sound, basic and timeless. Who can argue with the need for discipline and the setting of limits. Who can argue with the need for order and regularity, all in fostering a sense of security. Who can argue with the need to love coupled with the need to play. It is similar to the training of a dog. I say this sans tongue in cheek but in all seriousness and sincerity. Both animals and children want to know what will please the parental figure. They want to know what to do and what not to do. Again I repeat that Glenn's intuitive understanding and ability to communicate with animals spilled over into his work with young children. He knew how to communicate with both.

The experience many of the troubled children had when exposed to the Cunninghams was likely to lead to positive changes in their lives. For what is it that changes someone, especially someone young and still impressionable? That *it* is found in a relationship.

Researchers, first at the University of Utah (Lambert et al.) and subsequently many other research groups, exploring the positive outcomes in formal psychotherapy, trace the success— where there is success, of course—mainly to the quality of the relationship. And it need not be with a professional therapist; it could be a coach, a teacher, a friend, a spouse, a clergyman, even the bartender, even—and I'm not kidding—a trusted animal.

The prime element in the relationship is empathy. This is something Cunningham also understood intuitively. He had a favorite poem on empathy. He was big on finding quotes, poems, and homilies. Such was part of his teaching (and preaching). First the poem whose author is missing:

Please don't make fun of the man who limps as he comes along the road
Unless you have worn the shoes he wears and struggled beneath his load.
Don't scoff at the man who's down today unless you have felt the blow
That caused his fall and know the shame that only the fallen know.
Don't be harsh with the one who sins, don't pelt him with wood or stone
Unless you are sure, yes doubly sure that you have no faults of your own.

He went on to explain: "I keep trying to give these little quotes because when you can tie something definite when the problem arises and I try to tie it into some of these things to give them a little quote to remember and give them a little encouragement, and I think if they realize, and I keep trying to make them know that I make more then my share of mistakes.

"I have made more mistakes than anyone. Like I was telling them last night, the only person who doesn't make mistakes is the one who never does anything.

"And, so I tell them, I make mistakes with them. I tell them I hope they will be able to forgive me for the mistakes I make, at least they've been honest mistakes. It isn't that I do things intentionally wrong to harm them.

"I think the thing we need as parents and as people working with youngsters is to make them know that we are just as human as they are, subject to the same frailties and all that they are, and if they can understand that they can open up and feel that here we are, just the same. Most kids look at their parents and think, well they never did anything wrong. I tell them, I made mistakes as a youngster, and probably over-emphasize those things, because I was just so darned busy working and had so many interests like my athletics and I loved school. I just couldn't get enough school. You know how I felt about Agnes Heueisen."

Agnes Heueisen has been mentioned earlier. She was his teacher. Here he illustrates the salutary impact a teacher can bring to bear.

"I loved her as I loved my mother, almost. She was such a tremendous person. She was one in ten million. As a teacher. I think it's all a matter of attitudes. Most of these kids coming out here come feeling that they are not as good as other people, that there's something about them that makes them lower then anybody else in every way, that they're just no good. Of course, they have been beaten down. I keep trying to build them up and encourage them,"

Glenn Cunningham was surely on to something.

But by October 1973 it was all over for the Augusta Ranch Farm and their work there. An article in the *Wichita Eagle* told of Glenn's plans to organize another youth ranch south of Plainview, Arkansas, "where he says facilities are better and people more cooperative." Ruth had remained behind a while so that six of their children could stay in school in Augusta.

Glenn addressing a youth group.

24

1973 ~ 1988

Only after he had done all his chores. . . .

Sometime in 1971, Glenn had spoken at a state Realtors meeting in Little Rock. There he heard about a place near Plainview, Arkansas, that had belonged to a man who was connected to the newspaper, the *Arkansas Democrat*. That man had used it to reward paperboys with a week of vacation there. It had a lodge, a swimming pool, a game building, and another building that housed small bunkrooms.

When the owner died, the relatives were anxious to sell it. With the difficulty they were having with the Kansas bureaucracy, Glenn saw another chance to continue his passion. At first he leased that land. He moved a lot of the animals to some pasture he had rented near Morillton, Arkansas, about twenty-five miles east of Hidden Valley. He also brought the horses down to another pasture in the same area. In the summer of 1973 the animals were settled in Hidden Valley at a bend in the road called Menifee. And around that time they bought the land they were leasing.

Their work with children continued but at a lesser pace. In a November 1988 *Reader's Digest* article titled UNFORGETTABLE GLENN CUNNINGHAM, Ken West, who had spent years with the Cunninghams, wrote that by 1976, "due to both finances and

Ruth's general health, the Cunninghams closed the doors of their ranch and purchased a home in a town nearby." Ruth added in a recent letter: "We had house parents come and take over the few kids we had and we moved to Conway [Arkansas]."

There were obvious reasons to stop. Glenn told us in 1987 that they received an average of sixty-eight dollars per child in outside help. They could no longer even pay the interest on their bank loans. In the Augusta Ranch and in this last one, at various times they would have to sell parcels of land to help lessen their burden of debt. He always implied, too, that they had given up the work because he knew Ruth needed to get away from it for her health. Ruth truly did have a heart condition. But Ruth thinks Glenn was tired, and ready to leave it. He was experiencing infrequent episodes of chest pain that he shrugged off. There were other signs, in retrospect, of incipient heart disease. Yet he would continue giving talks, continue taking care of the animals, and when some years later two couples reopened the ranch, he and Ruth agreed to serve as advisers.

In Ken West's article he tells this vignette: When he was living with them, West had been pilfering small-game traps from a box Glenn had told all not to touch. He was selling them at school for soda money. It bothered Ken enough that finally he confessed. "What did I tell you I'd do," Glenn asked, "if you were ever dishonest?"

"You said you'd whip my rear."

"So what do you think I should do now?"

"I guess you ought to start whipping."

Cunningham put his arm around him, told him he was punished enough already, said they should go in the house and talk.

"I've never forgotten that demonstration of forgiveness," Ken West wrote. Then he quoted Cunningham: "Honesty is the most important thing, Ken. Don't ever be too little to make a wrong right."

West would accompany Glenn on lecture tours and give a few talks of his own. He had studied the craft of custom knife making. Glenn had preached to him that "if you have a tune in your heart, you owe the world a song." With Glenn's help he had opened a shop in Conway. An epileptic, West died soon after the article was published, apparently during a seizure.

During the years that Cunningham was not formally doing his informal thing, he would find excuses to take children and his grandchildren to "Menifee," where they would see the water buffalo and other animals.

One time he had three of his grandchildren with him. Sara told the story of them playing around, and then about noon Glenn asked her if she was hungry. When she said she was, he told her to go look up in a tree for something to eat; she did and found a bunch of bananas there. A little girl then, she didn't know how they got there! He was apparently always doing things like that.

Another granddaughter, Jennifer, wrote an essay of how on one of their picnics with the animals nearby he gave her a stone. He told her it was magic, that it was a "worry-stone" and if you would rub it, it would make all your worries disappear. And, as a young girl, whenever she did rub it all her worries did indeed disappear. As she became older she learned the real moral of the story, that many things in life are out of our control and worrying only makes them worse. But the stone, which she has always kept, reminded her that some worries are less important.

And Glenn was a practical joker with children. His daughter Sue told of a time when she was young. She and friends took a walk down to a local graveyard. Knowing where they were going,

Glenn, and with him his brother John, drove to the cemetery ahead of the girls and suddenly materialized with sheets over their heads. The frightened girls fled. On their flight back home Glenn intercepted them in his truck and asked why they were running. When they told him, he drove them back to the cemetery and reassured them there were no ghosts. Finally back home he confessed to his folly and they all had a good laugh.

In a 1984 letter to Hank Brown, Glenn wrote this:

"While we do not keep children in our home anymore, I am never long without a group of children around me to play with and do all I can to instill in them a sense of integrity, honor and responsibility, and a desire to attain the highest goals in life that they can."

In 1984 he and Ruth also attended the fiftieth anniversary of the 1934 K.U. graduating class.

Paul Borel, his classmate and trackmate, wrote a letter to the alumni magazine telling of the visit he and his wife made to the Cunninghams sometime after the reunion while en route to the 1984 Los Angeles Olympics. He described their home as "modest, rich in love, surrounded by family members." He described attending a church service with Ruth playing the piano, one son welcoming worshippers, another reporting on his evangelical mission in Mexico, and even one more son preaching the sermon. The next morning after breakfast (he mentions Glenn eating four eggs) they went to feed the animals:

"We crowded into a truck of uncertain vintage. A grandson and one of his friends hopped in the back. We picked up hay and grain at the local feed store, and bounced over rough ground for some ten miles. There, we found a veritable zoo: water buffalo, llama, boar, goats, sheep, cattle, horses, jackasses, deer. Some 160 animals roamed the rolling wooded area. These, particularly the donkeys, form the basis for a business with zoos and other buyers of livestock. In earlier years the animals had played an essential role in the therapy designed to rehabilitate troubled youngsters, supplementing love, discipline and work.

"Our Class indeed had stars among its members, but none shown more brightly than did Glenn Cunningham."

Mrs. Paul Borel rides Sinbad the water buffalo, 1984, with Glenn alongside.

The years after his track career ended were not without more honors, not even without some running. In 1967, commemorating the last track meet to be held in Old Madison Square Garden, a famous name borne by four buildings, a panel of sports officials and sportswriters unanimously voted Glenn as the number one athlete in forty-two years of its operation. "In his eight years as a Garden Participant, no one could match Cunningham's achievements, records, consistency, range, and impacts," wrote Jesse Abramson of the *World Journal Tribune* in commenting on the honor. In 1974 Glenn became a charter member of the National Track and Field Hall of Fame now located in Indianapolis, Indiana. He made a point of inviting his old coach, Roy Varney, a man he loved not only for his coaching but also for the lessons in life he taught, to present his award at the induction. In 1979, in ceremonies spotlighting the hundredth anniversary of Madison Square Garden, Glenn was named the outstanding track performer in its history.

(The original elections to the Helms Hall Track and Field Hall of Fame were held in 1949. They were retroactive. Each year the foremost amateur in each of the earth's six continents is recognized. Glenn was named the Helms World Trophy winner for North America for 1933; his name appears on the trophy in Helms Hall, Los Angeles.)

When I had asked him in 1987 about human potential limits, in his response he told of some of the running he had done over the years and of his introduction into the modern track era:

"There is a limit, but we certainly haven't reached it yet. There's one big thing you have to consider when you compare yesterday's performance with that of today. We have improved our equipment. The shoes now are just designed so well. The University of Kansas, I believe, is the only university in the country that has three milers that have held the world's record: Jim Ryun, Wes Santee, and myself. They had us up there to jog around the track three or four years ago [it was actually the 1981 Kansas Relays]. I had been in an accident and could hardly walk. I had done nothing for a year, as far as running was concerned. In fact, I had a daughter and son in high school who had participated in track and other sports, and I would go out and run with them. I had no trouble keeping up with them, but after this accident I wasn't able to do anything as far as getting on my feet. I told them I might even have to walk around the track.

"It was even painful to walk. We started out on that track and Santee kept picking up the pace and we breezed through a pretty good quarter. I never drew a long breath. It was so easy and the track was so straight. I couldn't believe that track and those shoes. The shoes were so light. It was like they were filled with helium. I couldn't keep them on the track. It was unbelievable the difference in what I had to contend with when I was competing."

Jim Ryun, Wes Santee, and Glenn Cunningham at the 1981 KU Relays.

Photo courtesy of University Archives, Spencer Research Library, University of Kansas

I then asked him if he could have trained more rigorously. His response should be of interest to running scholars:

"Talking about the four-minute mile, the biggest stumbling block in the way of the athletes were the coaches. There wasn't a coach in the country back in the early '30s that believed the four-minute mile was possible. In fact, most of them didn't believe it until it actually happened. But in the time trial in high school, I ran a sub four-minute mile. There was only one watch, but it was close enough that I knew it could be done.

"I was never able to do a lot of training as far as practice running was concerned. Most of today's athletes run from 75 to 150 miles a week, I never ran over five to seven miles and only went on the track three days a week: Monday, Tuesday and Wednesday. Tuesday, I would take my hard workout, but after the warm-up I would never run over a mile. I would only do that usually for short distances, like two 660's or three single quarters. Sometimes I'd just sprint 220's and walk 220's and sprint 220's, or maybe sprint a straightway and walk the turns."

The accident he mentioned that happened a year before running with Santee and Ryun—a severe upper back injury sustained in a motor vehicle accident—was obvious when I met him in April 1987; his neck was rigid and relatively immobile. It was also apparent in what would be his last-ever Madison Square Garden visit, on February 27, 1988.

It was the USA/Mobil Indoor Track and Field Championships at Madison Square Garden that marked the hundredth anniversary of these championships. To celebrate, before the 14,643 attending, there was held a relay manned by past champions. From Cunningham's era there were Jimmy Herbert, Joe McCluskey, Gene Venzke, and Glenn, who passed the baton to the 95-year-old Abel Kiviat. The loudest roar was when Cunningham took the baton, its crescendo peaking when he handed off to Kiviat who, seventy-five years earlier, had won the 600- and 1000-yard championships on the same night, the only time such a double victory was ever accomplished.

Stan Saplin assumed master-of-ceremonies duties here. For

A still from viedo footage: In his last appearance at Madison Square Garden, less than a month before his death, Glenn passes the baton to Abel Kiviat.

him it was truly a labor of love. The first runner was Horace Ashenfelter, Olympic steeplechase winner. A few runners later came one of Glenn's contemporaries, "Jimmy Herbert, a national champion at 600 yards and world record holder." He was soon followed by 77-year-old Joe McCluskey. "He runs masters," Saplin declared, "won more national championships than any other man in history in running, twenty-four." (McCluskey's running form at that moment was that of a much younger man.) A few more younger runners, then . . . "Here is the most remarkable Gene Venzke, 79 years old, this great man was first, second or third in the national indoor mile or 1500 for nine consecutive years; he broke Paavo Nurmi's record for the mile [Venzke wore number 1932 for the year he broke that record]. And here's his old foe, Glenn Cunningham, taking the stick from Gene Venzke; national champion four times, world record breaker three times,

Olympic silver medalist, the fabulous Glenn Cunningham! [Glenn was wearing number 1934, the year he established a world record for the mile.]

"Now put this in your treasure chest of memories, any moment now Glenn Cunningham is going to pass the baton to Abel Kiviat, 95 years old; he last won a championship here in 1914."

Ruth was absent from this event. She was in a hospital near home, having suffered a mild heart attack. But she did see the event on television. She noticed something in Glenn's countenance: "I felt that looking at his face as he ran in the Garden that it was an extreme effort, that he was hurting, but wasn't about to show it. I know that his knees gave him a lot of trouble, and were painful. Maybe it was them that gave him that look, but it is a look I have seen on him before, of straining to do something, but with no thought of quitting! To me he just looked as if he was straining against some difficulty and was giving it all he had."

That Friday morning, February 26, 1988, Bob Corrigan and his wife visited with Glenn and had breakfast with him in the Statler Hotel across Seventh Avenue from the Garden. It was then that he had said to Bob, "There is nothing as important as a child."

"We spent about two hours with him that morning," Bob wrote, then added parenthetically: "one of the great experiences of my life."

Then next day Glenn went back home, to his family, to his animals, to his chores.

Almost two weeks later, on the morning of March 10, 1988, he was getting ready to take some llama to a sale in Missouri. First, though, he had to get feed for the animals so they could be fed while he was gone. After kissing his wife good-bye, he went to get a load of hay—some forty-seven bales—which he loaded by himself. Then he went to do the chores, and also unloaded the bales, also by himself.

He was returning to the house to get a tank of water and then return to the animals. But he apparently had a seizure (heart arrest) on the way out of the pasture, and slowly veered off the road. Someone who was familiar with Glenn and his feeding schedules found him and called the sheriff. A patrolman went to the church Gene Cunningham was pastoring to tell him the news. Then the patrolman came to their house. Ruth had been hospitalized for two weeks and had had a pacemaker implanted. She had only been home a few days. When the neighbors saw the patrolman, they thought it was Ruth who had died.

Ruth elected not to see Glenn in death. "I knew where he was, not in that body," she wrote, "and I wanted to remember him as he was to me. I still maintain those vivid memories."

There are many scientific studies attesting to the protective benefits of vigorous exercise in relation to heart disease. While it has been shown that there is a small but statistically significant increase in the number of years the active person lives compared with the sedentary one, the real difference is in quality of life. Glenn had beaten the "morbidity curve." What must have been extensive heart disease failed to translate into any illness. Animals die in a similar fashion. They know little illness, usually die rapidly, their autopsies revealing rampant disease processes.

People in the field jokingly point out that the only way to avoid the most important risk factor in heart disease is to pick your parents wisely. Glenn's father died at the same age, in the same manner (sudden), as did his younger brother John, who succumbed four years later in 1992. John was never the exerciser Glenn was.

Gene Venzke had a poignant memory of Glenn. Devastated by the news of Glenn Cunningham's sudden death, he wrote to Ruth. His letter is dated March 17, 1988 and after the salutation he says:

When the local news reporter called me and told me about Glenn, it was real hard for me to believe him.

I must tell you about the last day I spent with Glenn. We all met and changed clothes in the same room. The whole room bubbled over with joy among all of us—the tenseness of competition which prevailed 50 years ago was entirely missing.

I walked over to Glenn and said, "Glenn you raskal (sic), I've been waiting for 50 years to be on the same team with you—when I hand you the baton on our relay team I'm going to give you a nice shove to help you on your way"—it was a thrilling moment.

Right after the exhibition Glenn and I watched the mile race. We stood side by side discussing the merits of all the runners competing for the championship—what a wonderful way for both of us to wind up our competitive careers on the floor of Madison Square Garden!!!

You know, what makes this event all the more valuable—my son and two grandsons watched the whole show—little did I ever dream 50 years ago that this would happen. My wife, Peg, wasn't feeling well and couldn't make it.

About a half hour later as I was leaving the Garden, I saw Glenn talking to someone—both in street clothes. Something told me to butt in and wish you and Glenn the very, very best—it was our final parting—very hard to believe!!

Peg & I both pray for you both and hope you're doing well.

Most sincerely yours,

Gene Venzke

When he died, Glenn Cunningham was wearing his jeans. Out of respect, he usually dressed impeccably whenever photos were taken of him other than at home—or as when he met our group of doctors, or even in his last television interview when he described his itinerant early beginnings. But that morning he was in his old signature jeans.

The local newspapers said he had died in Menifee, instead of Conway where they lived. Menifee was the little hamlet where the animals were kept. He was seventy-eight.

This little vignette is illustrative of his life and of his death: One time Clint, Glenn's grandson, then quite young, was out with Glenn, and they were doing the chores when the truck got stuck in the mud. They spent a lot of time trying to get it out— which of course they did. When they got home Ruth asked if Glenn had gotten done what he wanted to do, and he said, "If I hadn't I would still be out there."

"That was the core of his life," Ruth wrote. "He accomplished what he wanted to do, or he would still be working at it!"

When grandson Clint got home from the truck encounter he told his mother that "Granpa called that truck a lot of bad names!"

Glenn Cunningham was cremated and the ashes scattered near a tree. At his memorial service Gene Cunningham remarked joyfully that his father was on his way home when he died, and only after he had done all his chores.

The land.

25

AD ASTRA PER ASPERA

I think he lived with a lot of demons that no one knew about. He struggled against many emotions even as he rose above many others. He loved and he hated; he could be the best and the worst.

Ruth Cunningham sent me a letter dated December 14, 1998. It was in response to a manuscript I was toiling with, one of whose chapters was on Glenn Cunningham. I want to quote part of her letter here where she describes Glenn: "He was fiercely independent, aggressive and purposeful, yet extremely easy going. He had a huge ego, but was still a humble man. . . . The motto 'Ad Astra per Aspera,' which is the state motto of Kansas describes Glenn—he knew nothing but to go to the top, regardless of the cost. He often said he would rather be dead than be mediocre. And that he wasn't. He lived life with intensity and deep emotions. He was either right or he was wrong, nothing in between. At the same time, I think he lived with a lot of demons that no one knew about. He *struggled* [italics mine] against many emotions even as he rose above many others. He loved and he hated; he could be the best and the worst—what he did was done with gusto, even though it might be wrong. He truly wanted to be the best, even though he knew he failed often, and he always wanted the best for those who came his way. But he wanted it on the basis of honesty, not gotten shabbily."

I don't suppose he was always the easiest person to live with. But Ruth truly shared his values, loved and admired him. Yet at the same time she could be quite objective.

She has always wished there would be a book about his running career. At the same time she realized that his running was merely an extension of the man: "I want his running career to be the focus, and of course, to do that, you have to halfway understand the man, his philosophy, what drove him, and his outlook on life."

To understand the man . . . Much of it has already been alluded to, speculated upon, discussed, examined. What it needs now, however, is organizing. And the best place to begin to organize is at the beginning, in Morton County.

There is a book celebrating the hundredth Anniversary (1886-1986) of Morgan County ,of which Elkhart is the seat. The foreword speaks of the early settlers, that they *struggled* against the extremes of "Mother Nature." Cited are the freezing blizzards, the instant dust storms, the flash floods, the grasshopper invasion, the droughts and prairie fires. "They literally 'carved' homes out of the land, only to have their dreams destroyed by the elements . . . but still they stayed, and survived!"

In prose and in slogan the theme of struggle repeats and repeats. Struggle is also the leitmotif in the modern Olympic creed as articulated in 1896 by Baron Pierre de Coubertin. However distorted and diluted by international politics it has become—it is an ideal nevertheless worth striving for: "The important thing in the Olympic Games is not to win but to take part," he wrote, "just as the important thing in life is not the triumph but the *struggle*."

And this from an old professor of mine whose name, unfortunately, I have forgotten: "Life is really not the pursuit of happiness, rather happiness *is the pursuit.*"

Happiness is often a by-product of struggle. Remember the quote from Brutus Hamilton: ". . . those who work the hardest, who subject themselves to the strictest discipline, who give up certain pleasurable things in order to achieve a goal, are the happiest men."

Saying something similar and coming from a sports perspective, Pat Conroy wrote this in the prologue of his book *My Losing Season:* "I was never a very good player, but the sport [basketball] allowed me glimpses into the kind of man I was capable of becoming. I exulted in the pure physicality of that ceaseless, ever-moving sport . . . [and in] my chosen game, this love of my life, I was the happiest boy who ever lived."

And again, the words of the man who broke the four-minute mile, Roger Bannister, writing about running:

"It also does us good because it helps us do other things better. It gives a man or woman the chance to bring out the power that might otherwise remain locked inside. *The urge to struggle lies latent in everyone.*"

And "human emotions," the philosopher William James wrote, "seem to require the sight of the struggle going on."

Struggle is apparent in growing up, in meeting and overcoming the various challenges that come our way. Our bodies have been geared, and have evolved, to accept and struggle with challenges and thereby develop and grow stronger. Simple illustrations: We lift weights in the gym. Overcoming the stress of one weight, the body system overcompensates and builds muscle to lift a heavier weight. In disease prevention, vaccination with an attenuated form of the virus provokes physiologic processes to overcome the invading, potentially illness-creating, virus. So, too, is it with the oyster overcoming its outside irritants to produce the precious pearl.

Challenge means the everyday stresses, everyday struggles that by meeting we feel gratification, gain strength and confidence. As put by Dr. Hans Selye, scientist and popularizer of the concept of stress and distress: "Stress," he said, "is the spice of life." The absence of stress is death itself. (When he said that stress is the spice of life, Selye was alluding to the everyday challenges we meet, rather than the "distress" that implies stimuli too overwhelming to cope with.)

And what is the nature of people who would embrace struggle? We know that both Clint and Rosa Cunningham were physically strong, hardworking, and determined people. Lacking modern conveniences, their main mode of travel was running. They were of Scotch-Irish ancestry, and a little of this component went into Glenn's makeup.

In his book, *The Scotch-Irish in America*, Henry Jones Ford, quotes an estimate of the Scottish character by Heron, who said that the distinguishing features of the Scot were ". . . an economy and even a parsimony of words, which does not always betoken a poverty of ideas; an insuperable dislike to wear his heart upon his sleeve, or make a display of the deeper and more tender feelings of his nature; a quiet and undemonstrative deportment which may have great firmness and determination behind it; a dour exterior which may cover a really genial disposition and kindly heart; much caution, wariness, and reserve, but a decided practical faculty which has an eye on the main chance, but which may co-exist with a deep-lying fund of sentiment; a capacity for hard work and close application to business, which, with thrift and patient persistence, is apt to bear fruit in reliance, courage, and endurance which, when an emergency demands . . . may surprise the world."

These Kansas pioneers recapitulate the struggles over the span of eons inheriting bodies that survived the ice ages, survived the drought and swirling dust storms of the Pliocene age, survived famines, wild animals, floods, everything and anything Mother Nature has wrought. We are all beneficiaries of bodies that crave struggle. We have developed the inner attributes that are brought to bear in the struggle against Nature's more malevolent forces.

The success of the state of Kansas lies in its struggle with natural forces, a virtual "survival of the fittest," paralleling Darwin's theory of evolution.

Here there is a bit of practical irony and ambivalence that dwells in the *Ad Astra* motto of Kansas. For it was the 1999 Kansas state school board that decided to remove any reference to evolution in all of the science textbooks, leaving only creation theory or intelligent design, allowing also no questions about evolution to be asked on state assessment tests. But after signed petitions in 2003, the school board reinstated the teaching of evolution. Conservatives, nevertheless, have vowed to revive the issue. In November 2005 the board of education voted that students should be exposed to critiques of evolution like intelligent design.

Besides the external, there exist the inner forces that we struggle with. What are the "demons" Glenn may have struggled with, that all of us may have struggled with?

An apocryphal old Jewish tale that I will paraphrase asks the same question. It tells of an Eastern king who wanted to meet Moses, having heard such wonderful things about the man. So he sent his painters out to draw a picture of him, one which he then referred to his phrenologists and astrologers—the psychologists of the day. Their analysis was that Moses was a cruel, greedy, self-seeking,and dishonest man. His illusions shattered, the king had to find out for himself. He went to Moses hoping he would be told that his phrenologists and astrologers were wrong. But Moses agreed with their analysis saying that was indeed what he was made of: "I fought against it," he said, "and that's how I became what I am."

Of course there were no stenographers to take down the exact words of Moses, but he could just as easily have said that he *struggled against it*. Obviously, a mighty struggle must be inferred here.

Enter now the demons we all struggle with, each of us with our individual variations, each of us in our own ways, ways that stamp our uniqueness. Glenn Cunningham had his best runs when he was struggling with the pain of an injury. The demons Glenn struggled with we all did, but with Glenn he also had what that old-timer called a "killer instinct." Remember: "It's the killer instinct. Cunningham came up the hard way, you know. The burns that almost cost him his life . . . were in the end his greatest asset. They taught him the value of working for what you want; they added a certain fiber of hardness to his soul." How similar this is to Friedrich Nietzsche's "Whatever does not kill me makes me stronger" (*Twilight of the Idols*).

The developing "hardness" came during a growing phase that a boy struggles with from about five to a little past the age Glenn was when he was burned. The issue for the boy involves an attachment to the mother and feelings of rivalry and aggression toward the father, while at the same time fearing displeasure and punishment from the father. How the boy resolves this cauldron of conflicting emotions and needs is critical.

Glenn *was* apparently able to resolve his "quarrel" with his father, physically, at age twelve, when he challenged him, and later when he worked side by side with him, particularly the time Glenn helped him clean up the streets after Glenn's celebrated homecoming following a track triumph. And along the way, whatever hostile feelings he may have had toward his father and his "striking ways," he was able to channel into work, play, and the struggle to recover from severely damaged limbs. He said this to Mrs. Brown about his father: "Mrs. Brown, my father was a very patient, tender man when there was need."

And a most successful outcome for this struggle came when he would marry a girl "just like the girl that married dear old dad." From what I can tell Glenn's mother was a strong, steadfast woman, honest, plain speaking, and even a good runner. Ruth is like that. She was also athletic and someone Glenn could engage with in play. On their land, they would ride horseback together. Ruth was an expert equestrian.

Glenn and his favorite horse, Ishtar.

Gene Cunningham has told me that his father was the greatest horseman he knew. He could control the wildest of horses. Today he would be called a "horse whisperer." In all relationships, however, for better or for worse, he had to be in control. Self-mastery and discipline were critical for him. Gene spoke of this at the memorial service: Quoting his father, he said: "The greatest victory in track it's a man against himself—the cruelest of all opponents—the other runners are not the real enemies; his adversary lies deep within: his ability with brain and heart to control and master himself and his emotions. The Bible says 'he who masters himself is greater than he who takes a city.' [It is] master of self by denial of self."

Glenn Cunningham could not work for anyone; he had to be his own boss. It was as if he had made an inner personal vow to never let any capricious overpowering external force take control of him, overpower him, or even make him compromise. To some degree, he could be called in today's vernacular, a "control freak." He was a strict disciplinarian, particularly with his daughters, even dictating the minimum age they could marry. And he had to be in the playground, on a ranch or farm, out of doors as much as possible, in life's natural playpen. The New York City and the Los Angeles of his time were both anathema to him. He could never have settled in either type of locale. New York was where he competed and where he earned a Ph.D. Life in either place was too fast, too superficial, too meaningless. He had to be in the vast outdoors, with animals and children, those who instinctively came by play. He meant it; he was serious when he made an addendum to his occupation, penning that he "Plays with the kids."

He was fanatically intolerant of alcohol, nicotine, and drugs, or anything that could control a person. Simplistically perhaps, he ascribed most family disharmony and child abuse to parental alcohol indulgence. He was mistrustful of adults, perhaps beginning with the negligence of those who had left the gasoline in the kerosene cans. He viewed children and animals as pure, the children adulterated only by parental neglect, and that in turn because of alcohol or drugs.

Happiness to him was the pursuit; he aimed high and reached for lofty goals, falling many times short, literally and figuratively, but always questing.

But for better or for worse—and decidedly on balance it was for the better—he had accomplished his greatest goal, to be an example. And a pretty good one at that. Gene Cunningham relates this vignette: "I remember so many times as a small child traveling with my father he would tell a story of when I was too young to even remember this, when we were up at the ranch in Kansas, we were going out under a snowstorm and he was trudging through the snow and taking the big long strides that were so big for me and heard me say behind him: 'Dad, I'm walking in your footsteps,' and he said it had a phenomenal impact on him because he realized at the point that it's not how many you influence, it's how you influence."

He was unique. His preaching resonated well in the 1930s and 1940's when our mythical heroes were the Lone Ranger who left town before the townspeople could thank him for his heroic gestures, or Tom Mix and his Ralston Straight Shooters, or Jack Armstrong, the "All American Boy." Or "The Shadow" who fought against the "evil that dwells in the hearts of men." Or the comic strip hero who would modestly ascribe his success to "clean living."

Rather than mythical hero, however, how does Cunningham merit the title of a hero for all seasons? Dr. George Sheehan, mentioned in chapter 21 where he described the runner as not being made for the things and people and institutions that surround him, once wrote on the subject of the hero in his column appearing in the *Red Bank (New Jersey) Register*. There he quoted the Spanish philosopher José Ortega y Gasset, who wrote that "heroism is the will to be oneself." Then Sheehan added his own interpretation of the hero, saying: "His life is a resistance to what is customary and habitual, to business as usual. The hero," Sheehan penned on, "takes himself and his place in time and creates his own drama."

Cunningham was the itinerant lay preacher, the farmer who

"plays with the kids," the man who eschewed the customary conventional means of making a living and surviving—partly because he was also a poor manager of money—doing things the only way he trusted to be right, *his* way. And spending his money on those things he trusted: children and animals.

Some of our contemporary sports "heroes" give a bit of their many millions to their pet charities. Some give a little of their time. Yet there may never be another who gives every fiber of his being to the causes he espoused. The values Glenn championed were timeless. I doubt we'll ever find his like again in the world of sport.

Like Moses who on a grand-scale quest led his lost and confused people, so too was Cunningham, on a more local scale, seeking to lead lost and confused children. What then is the refined by-product of his inner dynamic struggle with the demons and angels that nested within his soul? What had Glenn Cunningham become?

He had become the person he deemed he was meant to be. And to many, particularly to his missionary son Gene who spoke most eloquently at his memorial, he was a hero: "I'm not ashamed," he declared, "to say that throughout my entire life my father was the greatest hero that I've ever had. He still is. It's an amazing thing, you know, in a family, that when you can see the best and the worst, the world has seen the best. In my family, the family and I have seen the worst. It doesn't change the fact that he was always a hero to me."

Years later, on October 13, 1995, Glenn Cunningham was inducted into the Cornell College Athletic Hall of Fame. Ruth and Glenn Jr. attended the ceremony. Ruth wrote some copy for the event. This is how she ended: "Glenn loved poetry, and Emily Dickinson wrote one of his favorites:

If I can stop one heart from breaking,
  I shall not live in vain;
If I can ease one life from aching,
  Or cool one pain,
Or help one lonely person
  Into happiness again
I shall not live in vain.
"To me, this was Glenn Cunningham."

EPILOGUE

The oldest of Glenn's running fraternity, Abel Kiviat, died in 1991 at age 99. Rediscovered sometime in the 1980s by Stan Saplin, he had reached sudden celebrity status. A quote from his obituary: "Today, you hear of high school kids running 50 to 60 miles a week. I never ran 5 miles in a week."

Gene Venzke, strong-willed to the last, went reluctantly into a nursing home in 1992. He wanted to be independent, but he needed the assistance of a nursing home. Shortly thereafter, he had kidney failure, probably general organ failure in the end, and refused dialysis. Like Cunningham, he didn't linger, but went all at once.

On August 31, 1990, Luigi Beccali, 83, died. He was in Rafaello, Italy, but had lived many years on Long Island where he had opened a wine company. In a letter to Ruth Cunningham after Glenn died he had written this: "I was indeed moved to hear of Glenn's death. We often competed together, including two Olympic Games. I always found Glenn to be a true sportsman. Please accept my heartfelt condolences along with my very best wishes for you."

In 1940 Jack Lovelock was thrown from a horse and was unconscious for days, suffering a concussion that left him with persisting double vision and spells of dizziness. He had married and settled in New York City, where he was assistant director of physical medicine at the Hospital for Special Surgery. On December 28, 1949, he called his wife, telling her that he would be coming home early. His double vision and dizziness particularly troubled him that day. He was standing on the southbound platform of Brooklyn's Church Street Station when he suddenly lurched forward and was instantly killed by an incoming train.

Bill Bonthron died in January 1983, as mention on page 343.

Roy Varney was a beloved high school math teacher, a track, basketball, and football coach. He left the school system in 1944 or 1945 to share in a local business until his death. Born in 1901 in northwest Kansas, he had been abandoned by his parents at the age of five; his foster parents died before he was 13 years. He died in December 1977.

Twins Blaine and Wayne Rideout, born in 1916, both graduated from the University of North Texas in 1940. Blaine Rideout, the brother who was involved in the Princeton Wooderson race incident, worked as a football trainer for his alma mater and for several universities. He died in the spring of 1981 at a V.A. hospital in Utah. Wayne became an athletic trainer at various Texas high schools over a thirty-year span. He was elected to the Helms Foundation National Hall of Fame as a track coach. Both Rideouts were elected to the N.A.I.A. Track and Field Hall of Fame in 1955. Wayne died July 24, 1994, after suffering several strokes.

Sydney Wooderson, as of early 2006, is living in England.

Homer Woodson "Bill" Hargiss had earned sixteen collegiate varsity letters, had coached football, and track and field at the University of Kansas, and—besides Glenn Cunningham—had coached four other world-record holders in track. He died in October 1978 at age 91.

Brutus Hamilton, who finished second in the 1920 Olympic decathlon and who had coached Cunningham in his first year of college competition, went on to the University of California at Berkeley where he coached track for thirty-three years. An assistant coach in both the 1932 and 1936 Olympiads, he was Olympic head coach in 1952. In December of 1970, at age 70, he died.

Forrest C. "Phog" Allen had had an illustrious career as a basketball player, having played under James Naismith (the inventor of the game), then as a basketball coach at K.U. where he was later named a Hall of Fame College Basketball Coach. He died in September 1974 two months shy of his eighty-ninth birthday.

World War II robbed many of the promising runners both of reaching their full potentials and of any further Olympic competition. Among them was Chuck Fenske. He had served as vice president of Oscar Mayer & Co. and died in June 2002. A daughter, Virginia Moede of Los Angeles, his only immediate survivor, had commented that missing the canceled 1940 Olympics was his biggest disappointment.

Fellow Kansan Archie San Romani, who like Glenn Cunningham had overcome a severe childhood accident (his right leg was run over by a truck at age 8), enjoyed a career as a musician and as a teacher. He died at a nursing home in California in 1994 at 82. He had placed fourth in that classic 1936 Olympic 1500-meter race. Archie's survivors included a wife, Lena, one son and four daughters. Cunningham and San Romani had raced each other on 28 occasions with each winning 14 times.

Jimmy Herbert and Joe McCluskey were two of the runners from days gone by who had appeared in Madison Square Garden along with Venzke and Cunningham that February night in 1988: Stan Saplin had dubbed Herbert as "the best man never selected to the Track and Field Hall of Fame." Herbert had received a B.S. degree from N.Y.U. in 1942 and later studied there for a law degree and a master's in public administration. He was in politics and was a delegate to the Democratic National Convention in 1968 and 1988. He died in 1997 at age 82 from kidney failure two weeks after surgery to remove a malignant tumor on his liver.

Joe McCluskey was still running masters events in 1988 when he was 77. He ran in an open two-mile race at Fordham when he was 84. He had married at age 42; within the next seven years the couple would have eight children. He had served for almost five years in the Navy during the second World War, was a New York stockbroker for thirty years, and coached the New York Athletic Club track team for fourteen years. McCluskey would downplay his natural ability; rather he attributed his success to desire: "When you can't stand at the end of a race you know you've given everything. I ran a lot of races," he was quoted, "when I couldn't stand at the end." One bitter note had to do with the with the miscounting of laps in the 3000-meter steeple-chase during the 1932 Olympiad, resulting in McCluskey's earning third, instead of second, place. He died in 2002 at age 91.

Ralph Metcalfe and Barney Ewell were sprinters who some-times appeared in the same meets as did Cunningham. Metcalfe was a member of the winning U.S. 1936 4x100m relay team. He was a silver medalist in the 200m run at the 1932 Olympiad and was second to Jesse Owens in the 1936 200m event. He had a master's degree from U.S.C. and much later was a U.S. con-gressman, representing an Illinois district from 1971 until his death in 1978 at age 68.

Barney Ewell's track career was interrupted by World War II. Thirty years old at the 1948 London Olympiad, in a photo fin-ish he placed second to teammate Harrison Dillard in the 100m and second to another teammate, Mel Patton, in the 200m. In the 4x100m relay he ran the first leg in an easy win for the U.S. team, whose first place would be reversed when an official ruled that Ewell had passed the baton to the second runner outside the passing zone. But this negative ruling was also reversed three days later by a jury of appeal and Ewell would get his gold medal. He died in 1996 at age 78.

Don Lash, Fred Wilt, and Leslie MacMitchell were competitors who entered the track scene during the latter stages of Cunningham's running career. Lash, who had held world indoor and outdoor records for the two-mile event, was a special agent for the FBI for twenty-one years. He had two sons, and had been married for fifty-six years when he died of cancer in 1994 at age 82.

Fred Wilt, also a two-miler, had won three national titles in cross-country competing for the New York Athletic Club. He ran the 10,000m events in both the 1948 and 1952 Olympics. In 1950 Wilt won the James E. Sullivan Memorial Award as the nation's outstanding amateur athlete, an award Cunningham received for 1933. Wilt died in 1994 at age 73.

Leslie MacMitchell had been national 1500m champion from 1939 through 1941 and would later win the Wanamaker Mile three times. When he was the vice president of the College Entrance Board Examination in 1976, Dr. T. Leslie MacMitchell was honored as New York's outstanding track and field performer at the 56th anniversary dinner of the Boys Athletic League. The honor bestowed upon him that night had earlier been awarded to other native born New York athletes such as Sid Luckman, Whitey Ford, and Sugar Ray Robinson. MacMitchell is alive and well as of early 2006.

Joe Mangan, one of Cunningham's cohorts in the infamous "slumber mile," was distance coach for the 1960 U.S. Olympic Team and twice coached the Southern California Striders to National A.A.U. titles. He was 75 when he died in 1986.

Jesse Owens ran into hard times after the 1936 Berlin Olympics, where he had won the 100m and 200m runs, the long jump, and was a member of the winning 4x100m relay team. In later years he did achieve modest success as an inspirational speaker and as a public relations man. A heavy smoker, he died in 1980 of lung cancer, six months short of his 67th birthday.

Paul Borel lives in North Carolina and recently, at age 92, scored a 92 for eighteen holes of golf.

Lou Zamperini, born in 1917, is still living and active. He ran the 5000m event in the 1936 Berlin Olympiad and in 1938 had set the best NCAA mile mark of 4:08.3, a collegiate record that lasted fifteen years. Returning to track following his horrific prisoner-of-war experiences, his attempts at a running comeback fell short. In 1954 he wrote an autobiography. Essentially updating and adding further details, his book—whose foreword was written by Senator John McCain and was first published in 1982—is titled *Devil at My Heels: A World War II Hero's Epic Saga of Torment, Survival, and Forgiveness.*

Gene Cunningham, essentially following in his father's footsteps, has been on a mission, literally, as a missionary. Until very recently he was the pastor of Crossroad Bible Church in Perth, Australia. Basic Training Bible Ministries is the ministry that he began in Conway, Arkansas, after leaving the local church there. He and Ruth have worked with groups in India, Africa, and various other places. They founded and funded a seminary in India that trains native pastors to go back into their own villages to teach. They have helped with mission work in New Guinea, Burma, Russia, Nepal, and more. With his wife, Gene still travels several weeks out of the year to these locales.

After almost three decades of work with son Gene's Basic Training Bible Ministries, Ruth Cunningham has moved from Hot Springs, Arkansas, to Tuscon, Arizona, and will be living near her daughter Sharon. A prolific reader and avid letter writer, independent and self-reliant, her only concern in the move was to be near a well-stocked public library.

Cunningham's first son, Glenn Drury, has done real estate work, also worked with mortgages, and buying houses and restoring them. Son Lynn has a small Bible group that he teaches a couple of times a week, and is also working in construction. One of his daughters is a firefighter with the Conway Fire Department, the first woman on the force.

Sara, Cunningham's daughter from his first marriage, died in 1993 or 1994 from ovarian cancer. His other daughter, Sandra, has a Ph.D. in occupational therapy, is retired, and living on the old ranch in Kansas. She never married and is raising Arabian horses. The girls and their dad had a falling out way back in 1962 or '63, and they never really reconciled, though Ruth and Glenn did see them in 1984. Sandra did come to Glenn's memorial service and stayed with Ruth. Margaret, his first wife, died in 2001.

Avery Brundage died in West Germany in May of 1975, at age 87. For twenty years he had been president of the International Olympic Committee. Red Smith penned an essay in the *New York Times* several days after Frank Litsky's official obituary had appeared there. Smith wrote of Brundage's righteousness, integrity, rigidity, and insensitivity. He closed his piece saying that ". . . with the news of Avery's passing, there comes to mind Dorothy Parker's epitaph for another rich man: 'He lies below, correct in cypress wood, and entertains the most exclusive worms.'"

It's likely that Brundage had a leading role in removing the two Jewish athletes, Sam Stoller and Marty Glickman, from the 4x100m 1936 U.S. relay entry. Conventional wisdom was that he did not want to "humiliate" Hitler any further, having earlier exposed the German leader to black athletes. Sam Stoller died in 1983. Marty Glickman, who also was a star Syracuse football player, did run well in the European tour following the 1936

Olympics. He later played some minor-league professional football and would soon embark on an illustrious career as a sports commentator, his last role as the radio announcer for the New York Jets before he retired in 1998. He always retained bitterness for what was indeed a taste of American anti-Semitism. He died in January 2001 at age 83, following complications from cardiac surgery.

But there was one bad rap pasted on Avery Brundage. A nonvoter in a suspension agreed upon by twenty American officials, he was the unfortunate spokesman who announced Eleanor Holm's Olympic team banishment. Eleanor Holm enjoyed mild celebrity status as a singer and actress—she appeared in the 1938 movie *Tarzan's Revenge*. She was divorced from Mr. Jarrett, married Billy Rose, divorced him, married retired oil executive Tom Whalen, and in February 2004, at age 90, she died.

Myra Brown, author, poet, and educator, had written extensively on the Kansas Flint Hills, and as quoted in her obituary, "she was motivated unfailingly by the loftiest of ideals." Mention too was made that for the past several years she had been working on a full-length biography of Glenn Cunningham. A closeness had developed between Myra and the Cunningham children, and when she entered the hospital, the family had stayed up until 11 PM. praying for her recovery. At age 81, in September 1970, she died.

ACKNOWLEDGEMENTS, SOURCES, NOTES, ANNOTATIONS, AND LACK THEREOF . . .

When you write about someone's life, objectivity and thoroughness arise as major issues. How much do you put in and how much do you leave out? How much can you document, and even more important—how much published documentation actually does exist?

Bubbling up and somewhat troubling, too, is that just about everything I heard about the subject was almost too good to be true. Gene Venzke's wife succinctly summed up the problem when she said that the only bad thing she saw Cunningham do ". . . was to put too much catsup on his food." Then add to the mix this writer's having been indelibly impressed after meeting the man.

Glenn Cunningham's pet phrase ran to the effect that he never met a bad boy, never met a bad girl, never met a child he didn't love. He acknowledged that his own children and the kids under his care sometimes did bad things, but he'd tell them he had done a few bad things himself. Do we need to know about those bad things? Maybe. Yet I will leave that to others. The thrust here was to illuminate how Glenn expressed and lived by time-honored values and led a life that in many ways was heroic. My answer was to focus on the legacy he left for those who knew him the best, his family. And the way to do that, for me, was to focus on Kansas and how his life reflected and resonated with *Ad Astra per Aspera,* the Kansas motto.

Who was the real person? That is a question we can ask of anyone. Philosopher, psychologist, physician William James in an 1878 letter to Mrs. James (*The Letters of William James,* Vol. 1, p. 199) said that the best way to define a man's character was to seek out the time he himself felt most deeply and intensely active and alive. At such moments he can say, "This is the real me!" Even though Glenn Cunningham was oftentimes rigid, too patriarchal, opinionated, and overly strict with his own children, especially his daughters, he nevertheless would do his thing with all his might; "with gusto." As earlier put by son Gene: "I'm not ashamed to say that throughout my entire life my father was the greatest hero that I've ever had. He still is. It's an amazing thing, you know, in a family, that when you can see the best and the worst, the world has seen the best. In my family, the family and I have seen the worst. It doesn't change the fact that he was always a hero to me."

If that's good enough for Gene, it surely is good enough for me, and I hope for everyone else.

Physicians would call this a clinical examination. By *clinical* is meant the diagnosis made at the "bedside," based on a focused history and physical examination. That history here is an oral history, told by the patient and in this book, by the people who were on the scene at the pivotal junctures of time.

An accomplished horseman, Glenn Cunningham would be pleased that the source of almost everything written here is directly "from the horse's mouth."

That means interviews with siblings, neighbors, coaches,

teachers, fellow runners—all present at critical moments. Newspaper articles found in a scrapbook covering Cunningham's track career from 1932 to 1940 make up the essential written documentary, as do the descriptions of Kansas history as outlined and noted by Mrs. Myra Brown, a friend of the Cunninghams and a writer with a penchant for accuracy and truth, who undertook the task of interviewing all of the main characters. Besides Glenn, she interviewed the people who knew him during his growing-up years—that is, the high school and college years— and his coaches and teachers from his grammar school years. She collected letters from them, including a letter from the widow of Dr. Hansen, the physician who treated Glenn and Floyd after the fire. In all, on parched, water-stained, yellowed papers, I had about two hundred thousand words of text covering these interviews that were taped and transcribed in the mid-1960s. Sadly, Myra Brown died before being able to organize much of her notes and transcribed interviews. Her work frequently served to distinguish fact from aprocrypha.

Many original newspaper photos have been scanned and attributions, where available, are included in the subheadings. There are many photos, too, from the Cunningham family collection.

In the category of honorable mention are the helpers without whose generous assistance I could have neither documented nor properly written many of the passages in this book.

For example, Howard Schmertz, son of Fred Schmertz, told me the history behind the Wanamaker Mile and the Millrose Games. In the epilogue, Ruth Rideout, now living in Byran, Texas, widow of Wayne Rideout, wrote me about the passing of her husband and of Blaine. Other historical data and archival material was discovered for me by Mark Gladstone, research librarian at the Clarence Dillon Library in Bedminster, New Jersey.

Historical facts also were both the product of my memory and that of standard textbooks. Helpful, too, was David Wallechinsky's *The Complete Book of the Olympics* (1988) and Peter Levine's *Ellis Island to Ebbets Field: Sport and the American Jewish Experience*, particularly with facts about Avery Brundage and the 1936 Olympics. A video documentary, *Hitler's Pawn*, further documented Brundage's agenda. Details about Moe Berg were gleaned from Nicholas Dawidoff's *The Catcher Was a Spy* (1994).

The Kansas Historical Society helped me obtain microfiche copies of the *Hugoton Hermes* that documented the schoolhouse fire and Glenn's recovery process.

Myrna Barnes, curator of the Morton County Historical Museum, sent me original photos taken as far back as 1913 that chronicled the growth and the hardships met in Elkhart's early days.

Editorial assistance was invaluable: Professor Frank Korn was supportive in organizing my ideas and approach. Professor Larry Lengle, a boyhood friend, gave me a most helpful and thorough lesson in basic English, especially by persuading me to painfully part with beloved sections of fluff that were masquerading as prose. Jurilei Lambert spent countless hours providing me with electronic copy. Her spontaneous feedback helped guide me all along the way. Dr. Jerome Abrams, who skillfully delivered our last two children and first grandchild, also skillfully helped cross t's and dot i's and correct errors where others had overlooked them. Dr. Charles Kiell skillfully produced scans that were difficult for me to do. And finally Bob Corrigan, the man who planted the seed of this undertaking, provided me with copies of newspaper clippings covering the hardships the Cunninghams faced in their quest to help troubled children.

CUNNINGHAM FAMILY

Henry Clinton Cunningham
Born: September 20, 1877
Married: April 14, 1901
Died: July 27, 1956
Father: Drury Cunningham
Mother: Nancy Catherine Kent

Rosa Agnes Moore
Born: December 05, 1882
Died: March 1, 1961
Father: Samuel Moore
Mother: Harriet Amanda Griffith

CHILDREN:
Name: Glenn Verniss Cunningham
Born: August 04, 1909   Atlanta, Kansas
Died: March 10, 1988   Conway, Arkansas

Name: Margerie Cunningham
Born: December 03, 1901
Died: November 5, 2004

Name: Floyd Cunningham
Born: December 27, 1903
Died: February 18, 1917

Name: Letha Cunningham
Born: March 25, 1905
Died: March 1992

Name: Raymond Cunningham
Born: April 26, 1907
Died: June 25, 1938

Name: Melvin Cunningham
Born: April 2, 1913
Died: May 1913

Name: Melva Cunningham
Born: April 2, 1913
Died: March, 1992

Name: John Cunningham
Born: April 23, 1914
Died: December 12, 1993

CUNNINGHAM CHILDREN

(From Glenn's marriage to Ruth; Sara and Sandra from his first marriage are documented in the text on pages 230, 300, 326, 334) and in the epilogue, p. 391)

Glenn Drury Cunningham, born April 14, 1948
Lynn Sheffield Cunningham, born November 15, 1949
Gene Alan Cunningham, born October 18, 1950
Sue Ann Cunningham, born May 2, 1953
Cindy Ruth Cunningham, born January 31, 1955
Cathy Lee Cunningham, born July 5, 1956
Sharon Kay Cunningham, born November 20, 1958
Nancy Jo Cunningham, born December 21, 1959
John Clint Cunningham, born April 8, 1961
Cheryl Louise Cunningham, born July 1, 1963

Glenn Cunningham mile times: 1932-1939

	1932	1933	1934	1935	1936	1937	1938	1939
Big Six Indoor	4.21.9	4.21.8	4.20.3					
Big Six Outdoor	4.14.3	4.18.4	4.23.3					
National Intercollegiate	4.11.1	4.09.8	4.08.9a					
Kansas-Missouri Dual	4.23.0	4.20.3	4.35.5					
Kansas-Kansas State	4.25.0							
Kansas-Nebraska			4.35.5					
Tulsa Athletic Club		4.29.9b	4.16.7					
Kansas-KSC-Nebraska Triangular		4.17.4						
Butler Relays			4.17.9					
Penn Relays			4.11.8					
Hunters Mile – Boston			4.18.4					
Bankers Mile – Chicago	4.19.2							
Columbian Mile – New York		4.12.0	4.08.4	4.14.4	4.46.8	4.29.0c	4.09.9	4.12.8k
Wanamaker Miles – Millrose Games		4.13.0	4.11.2	4.11.0	4.11d	4.08.7	4.07.4	4.13.0
Baxter Mile – New York		4.14.3	4.14e	4.09.8	4.10.2f	4.12.4	4.08.6	4.12.6
Highlander – Canada				4.16.6				
Canadian Mile				4.19.0				
Knights of Columbus – Boston				4.16.4				
Kansas Relays			4.12.7	4.17.5g		4.14.1h		4.29.2
Princeton Invitation			4.06.7	4.11.2i		4.07.2k		
Texas Relays				4.28.3				
Dartmouth Invitation						4.07.2j	4.04.4	
Prout Mile – Boston						4.11.9	4.13.8	
Sugar Bowls – New Orleans							4.13.1	
Providence K of C							4.14.8	
5th Regiment – Baltimore							4.15.0	

a – 2nd to Bonthron   b – 2nd to Dawson   c – 2nd to San Romani   d – 3rd to Mangan, Venzke   e – 2nd to Bonthron   f – 2nd to Venzke
g – 2nd to Dawson   h – 2nd to San Romani   i – 3rd to Lovelock, Bonthron   j – 3rd to San Romani, Lash   k – 2nd to Chuck Fenske

APPENDIX

Two Sermons by Gene Cunningham

IN MY FATHER'S HOUSE

Early lessons in the art of overcoming, or
"You're never beaten till you quit!"

We are sitting on a prairie hill in early spring. There is still a hint of winter past, but the sun is warm and the breeze soft over the waving wildflowers. My two older brothers and I sit in various postures of boredom. Nearby my mother is holding our little sister. We are silent, and every move to ease cramped legs is cautious and slow. The ground below us drops away into a shallow saddle and rises again to another low hill. The prairie grass blowing in the wind looks like the waves of an ocean. Nearby a meadowlark sings his happy song. My eyes are fixed on the little Shetland pony grazing there in the distance. Over the little mare's back lay my father—motionless save for occasional hand movements that guide the slow progress of the grazing pony.

Earlier, on our way into the ranch house from the pastures, we had seen the long slanting glide of a prairie hen going to her nest. Landing near it, she had then circled it cautiously before going to sit the eggs nestled there. Prairie chickens were not a common sight in the early fifties. Once they had been everywhere, but were gradually hunted near to extinction. My father wanted to catch that hen, and raise the young. He knew that the young would have only a 50/50 chance of survival because of the coyotes and other predators. Having mentally marked the spot of the nest, he had then caught the little mare and begun the stalk. If he could raise them he would keep a pair and release the others and restock the land.

During my life I have known and lived among many Indians. I never met anyone more Indian than my father. For him it was not a matter of blood but a way of thinking and a way of seeing things. He was a child of the plains with the tint of the sun on his face and the sound of the wind in his voice. He was brown as a walnut and lean as a whip. He could ride better than any man I've ever seen sit a horse. It seemed that all the forces of the prairies were compacted into him. He was like the elements. His nature could go from the gentleness of a spring day to the ferocity of a Kansas tornado in a split second. When he set his mind on something he would think of an unpredictable and unorthodox method then pursue it with an iron determination till it was accomplished. And he wanted that prairie hen!

The sudden lunge of his figure snapped us all to attention as we saw the brown fluttering bird captured in his big hands. I remember seeing the broad smile he flashed as he came walking through the waving grass. He had done what others would have called impossible. He was known for such feats. Yet it was his conviction that what appear to be insurmountable obstacles can be overcome by clear thinking, the will to achieve, and endurance.

In fact endurance was stamped on every aspect of his life. It was ingrained into every fiber of his being. He came by it at great cost. As a boy of eight he and his older brother were terribly burned in a fire that destroyed their one room country schoolhouse. After nine days his brother died. The doctors recommended amputation of my father's legs, but his parents refused. They were told he would never walk again. He said, "I will walk again," and after a long and painful recovery, he did. He not only walked; he ran his way into the history books as the "Iron Man of Kansas" and "The Kansas Cyclone." With those scarred and seared legs he claimed the world in the mile run. He spent his life teaching us that what he had done, any other boy or girl could do. It was all a matter of conviction, courage, and endurance. His athletic fame opened many doors to schools, civic clubs and sporting events.

He used to travel six to seven months a year, encouraging both young and old to see in every obstacle the opportunity to overcome. He believed that people only fail because they give up. To him only a quitter is a loser. As we heard him say many times, "I must have fallen hundreds of times trying to learn to walk again. Had I given up I would be an invalid today. You may fail many times before you achieve your goal. Get up and try again. Never quit!"

Seeing him accomplish the seemingly impossible was a common event. I remember one occasion when one of our Scottish Highlander bulls had bulled through the fence into a neighbor's herd of cows. His four cowboys had tried to herd him home and the big bull became violent, goring one of their horses. My father and I went to get him, riding the tough little Arabian horses he loved. When we arrived the fellow said, "Now Glenn, you ain't going to get that bull with them two little ponies." My father just smiled. He did not believe in talking about what you were going to do, you just did it. With an application of "horse sense," which he claimed with a grin was nothing more than stable thinking, a little bit of lariat magic and the job was soon done. I chuckle when I remember it. As we rode away I had the lead with a rope around the bull's horns dallied into my saddle-horn, my father had the tail of the bull dallied around his. He had nearly lifted the bull's hind end so he was walking like on tiptoes. As we rode away I heard the guy say to his hands, "By God, I never seen nothing like it!"

Father was a philosopher and teacher. In every incident he saw a lesson or an illustration. He was outspoken and opinionated. He used to say, "Have an opinion on everything. If you find you're wrong, then you can change it." His message and example has given hope to many broken lives. My father had great compassion for those whose lives had been scarred and broken by some misfortune. He and my mother opened our home to hundred of troubled boys and girls. Some lived with us for the summer months, others for years. Often groups of fifty to a hundred would come to the ranch to ride horses, camp along the streams, and listen to my father expound his philosophy of life. Over the years the numbers of young lives he touched ran into the thousands.

The mounting cost of caring for so many was staggering. In time my father began to sell off parcels of land to raise necessary funds. When the land was gone, we began to go deep into debt as he mortgaged everything of value. I recall an incident that occurred that left a deep impression on me. I was about seven or eight at the time. We were on one of our evening rides across the pastures. We would often do this with groups of kids that came out. As the day faded into brilliant prairie sunsets we would listen to the mourning doves cooing in the hollows. Often we would scare up a coyote, and everyone would give the little prairie wolf a chase. Twilight would give way to dark, and we would ride in awe under the glittering stars. We were sitting on a hill, admiring the surrounding glory. My father had his leg hooked over his saddle horn, letting his favorite stud, Ishtar, graze. He made a comment to my older brother Glenn and me about God's creation. My brother responded with something along the line that it would be good if God would help us with our mounting financial needs. I will never forget my father's response. To me it revealed the core of his way of life. As he looked up at the stars he said, "The Lord has been very good to us. All of you kids are healthy and strong. One of you could have been killed along the way in an accident. We are all able to see and hear and enjoy all of this" (as he looked around us). He then said, "We have the real riches. Never doubt God because of what you don't have."

Recalling that moment in later years, I wondered if he was thinking of the loss of his own brother at such an early age. No doubt for him the poverty and hardship of his family were suddenly put into perspective by that loss. The real wealth of life with all its opportunities was revealed. And for him, crippled and in terrible pain, a deeper meaning of life was found. That incident had deeply stamped itself into his remaining brothers and sisters. One of my aunts once recalled something my father said, as he laid in his bed of affliction in that poor and humble west Kansas home. "He said," she told us, "God has a purpose in this. Somehow I will find out what that purpose is!" I have no doubt that God's purpose was to teach a lesson in overcoming. And to give to the world a living example of the power of a life that refuses to give up when faced with obstacles.

THE EDUCATION OF THE ROAD
Travel as a course of study

"No matter where you travel,
human nature is basically the same."
—my father

As I have already said, during the winter months my father was gone much of the time. He devoted his time to audiences of young people in schools or churches, athletic banquets and civic clubs. His message was built on his own experience overcoming the terrible burns received as a boy and principles and disciplines that made him a champion miler. He would stand before the crowd with his erect posture and ringing voice and captivate young and old alike. No matter how many times I heard him speak, it always had the same effect on me. His message was strong medicine, but he was one of the most sought after speakers in schools and universities across America. He believed that life was seventy five percent attitude, and the rest untiring effort. He would mingle his rough country humor with stern exhortation in challenging his listeners to aim high in life. He used to say things like, "If you aim at nothing you'll hit it every time." He did not believe in setting a lot of rules and regulations before young people. Rather it was his way to strive to build fundamental principles into them. He did not speak at them, instead he spoke to them, as valuable individuals. Neither did he set himself up as one who had achieved, but rather as one who continued to press on in the race of life.

Whenever it was possible Father would take one or more of us along with him. His way of travel was never easy. He traveled fast and light. Most times he drove, sometimes taking the battered truck along to trade for unusual deer, sheep and cattle. As in everything he did, when you went with him you learned to endure. There were no stops except for gasoline or oil. We learned early that this was our only chance to answer nature's call, and you had better be back before he was ready to leave! A couple of times young fellows living with us thought his warnings were bluff, until they were left to walk many miles home. We seldom ate in a café because it was too expensive. Meals consisted of a sack of groceries including a loaf of bread, meat, cheese and milk. Often in summer he would get boxes of fruit. A real treat was a quart of ice cream, which had to be eaten with plastic spoons before it melted. I could not count the times we kids slept to the lights and noise of the road as he drove through the night to make a school appointment the next morning. I would wake up drowsy and bleary-eyed to look up and see him sitting like a sphinx behind the wheel, and be lulled back to slumber by the soft sound of his songs.

He loved to sing and he sang well. Looking back, I believe his songs were to him a type of therapy for a soul that was often burdened or lonely. Many of the songs he sang were old ballads or love songs you never hear anymore. Others were funny tunes about country life or working on the railroads. He had plenty of experience at both. One of our favorites was "Old Sheep." It reminded us of a collie dog we once had, and it always made us cry. As often as not he would sing old hymns. He put real meaning into them, singing them almost as a prayer. My father had a strong faith in the Bible, and often quoted it. He used to say to us kids, "Learn the Bible. It has the answer to every problem you'll face in life."

As we drove the long miles he would speak to us about everything under the sun. He never stopped teaching. He spoke to us as adults, and from him we developed a broad vocabulary. He coached us on things like how to give a firm handshake, and to stand with good posture. When we were introduced to people we were taught to look them in the eye and speak clearly. My father believed in swift and strong discipline, and disobedience was dealt with on the spot, regardless of who or how many were present. He was a keen student of human nature, and urged us to learn by watching others. While his convictions were unshakable, he would not ridicule others who differed. If he believed them to be wrong he stated it flatly and without hesitation. However he did not stoop to try to tear others down. He often said, "You never build yourself up by trying to destroy someone else. People only seek to destroy those greater than themselves." He strongly believed in individuality and the right to personal privacy.

Of the many things I learned while traveling with him, the thing that stands out most was his compassion for broken lives. He taught me that all of us are in one way or another "disabled," whether in body or in soul. Misfortune could just as quickly maim and scar one as well as the other. When his speech was over, he was often surrounded by people he had challenged. He never failed to notice the one sitting in a wheel chair at the back, or a withered leg in a brace, even the eyes and face that spoke of a tortured soul. He gave himself to these people in a special way, without making them uncomfortable. His life and message served to challenge them to tackle the hardships of their life with renewed hope. The cruelty of mankind was well known to him, and we were sternly warned never to take advantage of the misfortune or failure of others. Because of his fame and strong character, he and my mother were often the target of malicious gossip. We kids were not immune at school. When we would tell him of some hateful story making the rounds he would say, "Just consider the source. What kind of person would make up such a thing?" He did not retaliate, or even degrade those who maligned him. He simply ignored them. Knowing well the pain of both physical as well as mental injury gave him wisdom and insight into dealing with others whose lives were marked by tragedy.

It was his conviction that every life was created for a purpose. The real value of a life is not to be found in what we have, but in what we are. He was no stranger to human frailty, whether in himself or in others. One of his fundamental principles was that all failure could either be a stumbling block or a stepping stone. He would declare, "It is not what happens to you that makes a difference, it is how you choose to respond!" He saw life as a block of marble, which we were to chisel into shape according to what we saw in it. It went against his grain to see people simply give up because they had marred the life they had been given. To him the race was never over until the finish line. I saw a sequence of pictures once, I believe in an old *Life* magazine. It was during one of his races, and he was forced off the track and fell to the ground. The movie frames showed him roll, come to his feet, and charge back onto the track, far behind the other runners. He did not win that race. But as he would say, "I finished!" As I write I am reminded of Michelangelo, who was known for taking the spoiled blocks of marble cast off by those who had marred them, and turning them into a masterpiece. This was my father's philosophy and work in dealing with broken lives.

My father never charged for his speaking engagements. He would ask a modest allowance for travel. It was up to the recipients to judge the value of what he had to say. Often there was little or nothing. I recall one particular time when I had gone with him alone. Driving from one engagement to the next I remember him saying, "I hope this next group will give us something. I am out of money." To an eleven or twelve year old this sounded like alarming news. How could we get home without any money. How could we eat? I was not aware at that time that his esteem with the local banker was such that he could write a check on an empty account. There was no question that he would cover it. His message that night was as strong and confident as ever. He urged each listener to consider the effect our lives have on those around us. "Someone is looking up to you. They will follow where you go." To illustrate he told of a time when I was a small boy of four or five. We were going out to the barn through deep snow. Because it was waist deep for me I was stretching my little legs to step into the prints he made. From behind him I said proudly, "Daddy, I'm following in your steps!" He said that simple childish statement had brought home to him what responsibility is on us all. We never know who might be following in our steps, so we must live not only for ourselves, but also for those coming after. He closed his message with one of his favorite poems, "The Bridgebuilder." When finally the crowd dispersed we drove on. I never knew if he was given anything for coming, and he didn't mention it again.

My father loved to travel. In his athletic days he had traveled around the world. He had raced all over Europe, and the Orient. He always told us there was no place more beautiful than America. He preferred to drive and see the country roll by. In his travels he criss-crossed America many times. He often met and mingled with many great and famous people. He was quick to tell us that the two are not the same. Fame was only a matter of recognition. Greatness on the other hand was to him always a matter of character. It was his conviction that character was most often built by overcoming adversities and misfortunes. Fame is quick to draw attention, but greatness is often hidden in apparently ordinary lives.

My early travels with my father were an education in themselves. It was the beginning of a course of study, which he passed on to me. The world is a classroom designed for the study of the art of living. Every road, each stop along the way has its own lessons. Outside our common daily round, we see through different eyes, become a different person. Our minds are opened to other ways and perspectives. Without compromising our beliefs or convictions, we can learn the value of diversity in cultures and customs. These will differ, if only slightly, in the next town down the road. My father used to say, "Everyone you meet has a lesson to teach you. Never stop being teachable, try to learn something from everyone." Each life's experience can challenge or warn us. The road of life provides many opportunities to lend a helping hand or give a word of encouragement to those who have broken down along the way. The road today is no different than that ancient way on which the Samaritan found the beaten and battered man. That old story tells us that human nature never changes. There will always be those who live on the spoils of beating others into the roadside ditch. There will always be others who will pass by unmoved to help. Some will cast a stone of contempt, others will laugh. Some simply look the other way. But likewise there will always be modern Samaritans who do what they can. It has been my experience in this course of study that they who are moved with compassion for the plight of others do so because they have been there in a ditch. Not unlikely, there may have been no one to lift them in their time of travail.

Yet it is often the case, when we are on the road less traveled, that we come to our most memorable meeting. There on the roadside, with the wind in the grass, just when it seems there is no hope of aid, in great need and desperation we cry, to whom we know not. Suddenly looking up we see a stranger. The mark of the road is on him. We sense in him a gentle wisdom, a humble compassion. His eyes speak of experience too vast to be contained in a library of books. There is help and healing in the timbre of his voice, and from his mouth the simplest of words takes on a profound meaning. The help of this stranger is unorthodox. He does not change the punctured tire, nor repair the vehicle of our travel. It is not his way to offer us money for our needs. He holds all the wisdom of all the roads of history in his heart. His help is offered in quiet words, "Follow me!" He calls us to the education of the road. But it is a new way and it transforms all who take it. In that moment each of us must make our own choice. How we decide will determine our eternal destiny. When you meet him, take care which choice you make!

[From the program of the Vitalis/U.S. Olympic Invitational track meet, January 20, 1979]

OUTSTANDING MADISON SQUARE GARDEN ATHLETE IN 100 YEAR HISTORY

VITALIS/U.S. OLYMPIC INVITATIONAL
ELEVENTH ANNUAL
Saturday, January 20, 1979
Madison Square Garden, and NBC-TV

GLEN CUNNINGHAM SELECTED AS
TOP TRACK ATHLETE IN 100-YEAR HISTORY
OF MADISON SQUARE GARDEN

Glenn Cunningham, the dominant mile and 1,500 meter runner of the 1930's, has been selected as the outstanding track performer in the 100-year history of Madison Square Garden. The Garden, which observes its centennial in 1979, has played host to indoor track meets since 1888.

Cunningham, 69, a native of Elkhart, Kan., and now a rancher in Conway, Ark., received the Vitalis Award for Sports Excellence today at a ceremony at the Garden where he was joined by indoor world record-holder for the mile Dick Buerkle of Rochester, N.Y.; top high jumper Franklin Jacobs of Fairleigh Dickson University; and 800 meter stand-out Mark Belger, formerly of Villanova. The award to Cunninham was presented by Jack Krumpe, Executive Vice President of Madison Square Garden Corp.

Cunningham will be honored again at the inaugural track meet of the Garden's centennial year, the Vitalis/U.S. Olympic Invitational of Jan. 20, 1979. The ceremony on that date will be carried on NBC-TV, which will telecast the meet beginning at 11:30 P.M. EST.

In 1967, on the occasion of the final track meet at the former Madison Square Garden at Eight Ave. and 50th St., Cunningham was selected by a special panel as the top track performer to compete in that arena during its life span of 42 seasons. On that panel were the late Daniel J. Ferris, former secretary of the AAU; the late Fred Schmertz, long-time promoter of the Millrose Games; Pinky Sober, a long-time track and field official; the late Arthur Daley, sports columnist for the *New York Times;* and Jesse Abramson, a foremost track and field reporter since 1925, who wrote for the *New York Herald, Herald Tribune* and *World Journal Tribune* before becoming director of the Vitalis/U.S. Olympic Invitational 11 years ago.

The panel was unanimous in selecting Cunningham.

The choice for the Vitalis Award, emblematic of track excellence in all four Madison Square Gardens, was this time left solely to Abramson, an eyewitness to every indoor meet in New York in the last 53 years.

Abramson's opinion is no different now than it was in 1967. "In his eight years as a Garden participant," Abramson said, "no one could match Cunningham's achievements, records, consistency, range and impact."

From 1937 to 1940 Cunningham, a product of the University of Kansas, raced in 31 Garden miles or 1,500 meter races and won 21 of them. He established six world records at these distances and posted another for 1,000 yards. In 1935 he won all five of his Garden races: three at a mile, another at 1,500 meters and another at 1,000 yards. In 1937 he won all three of his races at the Garden, all at a mile. In 1938 he lowered the mile indoor mark to 4:07.4 in the fourth straight win of his New York season.

A versatile performer, he won his first three Garden races of 1939 at distances of a mile, 1,500 meters and two miles. One of his most memorable wins was the legendary "Typographical Mile" of 1936, an almost unbelievably slow but strategic battle against Gene Venzke and Joe Mangan which was timed in 4:46.8.

Cunningham is credited correctly with making the mile the glamour event in indoor track. He had style, talent and grace. He also had a courageous story. A school fire had burned Cunningham's legs when he was eight. He began running to strengthen the legs, and this therapy marked the beginning of a brilliant racing career.

In 1933 Cunningham was voted the Sullivan Award as the country's outstanding amateur athlete.

THE PHILOSOPHY OF GLENN CUNNINGHAM

From Glenn's phone interview with Paul Kiell in November 1986, and from his post-banquet talk to the American Medical Athletic Association in April 1987.

AMAA: Let me recreate the scene. It's 1934. Princeton's Palmer Stadium. Glenn Cunningham breaks the world record for the mile. But on that day you had a bad ankle.

Cunningham: Yes. I had warmed up. I was just taking a little spin on the grass and stepped in a hole and popped my ankle. They first told me I'd better just cancel out of the race.

AMAA: Your coach said later that it swelled up like a popcorn ball.

Cunningham: That's right. In fact, my trainer put on a basket weave. I went out and thought I'd give it a try anyway. My ankle was swelling so fast that it ripped that heavy taped ankle, just ripped the tape out during the race.

AMAA: And yet you broke a world record.

Cunningham: Yes. I was in pretty good shape then and was coming up to three different big races including the Princeton one. We got on a train and went out to California for a race out there. I couldn't even put my foot on the floor to walk. It was terribly painful. I wanted to withdraw from those next two races but the promoters insisted that I get on the track and start the race, go thirty yards and walk off the track. But I've never quit a race in my life and never intended to. I went ahead and entered, even though I hadn't been able to get on the track for a workout. In fact, I could hardly walk. I tried to run and lost those next two races.

AMAA: You hear about this often: For instance, as in your world record, where the athlete is either injured or ill and somehow this either takes the pressure off in some way, or the athlete relaxes and struggles less with himself. It's not unheard of that on a bad day an athlete will set a world record.

Cunningham: But I think it's the mental realization that he is going to have to really put everything into it that he possibly can that carries him through the mental state more than anything else, I never ran a race and won—in my life—because I was better than anyone else. I think a lot of it is *enthusiasm.*

You know, if you're stung by a bee you'll understand what I mean. It's not the size of the sting that makes it effective is it? It's the enthusiasm that the bee gives it. I think it's that way with our athletics, in fact in any field of endeavor

Records are made to be broken and I believe performance is more mental than physical, at least it was with me. My problem was that I was burned as a child and much of the circulation in my legs was destroyed. Chunks of flesh fell out of the muscles which were replaced by scar tissue. I had no legs, I had no feet, my legs were burned, circulation destroyed, muscles damaged, transverse arches on my feet—I used to be able to take my toes, all except the big toe and just lay it back on the top of my foot. So I had no drive and I think most coaches and trainers would say you had to have that transverse arch in order to run fast. But I didn't have it, so I just trusted the Lord for what I didn't have while still believing that I could run a little bit.

AMAA: Dr. Jack Lovelock spoke of a mental rehearsal, of creating an atmosphere of the mind, a mental-physical conditioning. The technique has become more systematized lately where an athlete pictures the race, the terrain, the crowd, etc., prepares mentally, going over the whole course picturing every step vividly. By the way, you had a friendship with Lovelock. Were you aware of his notions about mental preparation?

Cunningham: Not necessarily. But I think this is something that has been on the minds of people competing through the ages. It's just something that may have come out more recently. I'm sure that most outstanding athletes use this type of thing in one way or another.

AMAA: You had the race with Lovelock in 1935 at Princeton and it was one of your first losses. Then in 1936 in the Olympics, you and Lovelock would break the world's record, as would the first four men in the 1500m run. Lovelock was first and you were second. There's a picture of you and Lovelock shaking hands. You don't see much of that these days, the kind of things we used to call *good sportsmanship.*

Cunningham: That's the one thing about track. We were always friendly competitors. We were friendly off the track, but on the track we battled each other with everything we had. I think that's the real essence of sports, or supposed to be at least. I was just reading an article about how the fights they have, like after the World Series. Those things ought not to happen.

AMAA: The training in your day . . . well, let me quote Lovelock and then I'll quote you. Lovelock said that he himself began to contemplate the four-minute mile. He said he was unable to see that just as our knowledge of physiology and psychology increase, there could also be "no limit to the human capacity for speed." And you said that the human race wasn't getting any faster, "it's just beginning to realize its potentialities."

Cunningham: There is a limit, but we certainly haven't reached it yet. There's one big thing you have to consider when you compare yesterday's performance with that of today. We have improved our equipment. The shoes now are just designed so well. The University of Kansas, I believe is the only University in the country that has three milers that have held the world's record: Jim Ryun, Wes Santee and myself. They had us up there to jog around the track three or four years ago. I had been in an accident and could hardly walk. I had done nothing for a year, as far as running was concerned. In fact, I had a daughter and son in high school who had participated in track and other sports, and I would go out and run with them. I had no trouble keeping up with them, but after this accident I wasn't able to do anything as far as getting on my feet. I told them I might even have to walk around the track.

It was even painful to walk. We started out on that track and Santee kept picking up the pace and we breezed through a pretty good quarter. I never drew a long breath, it was so easy and the track was so straight. I couldn't believe that track and those shoes. The shoes were so light. It was like they were filled with helium. I couldn't keep them on the track. It was unbelievable the difference in what I had to contend with when I was competing.

AMAA: Did you feel that you could have been trained more rigorously?

Cunningham: Talking about the four-minute mile, the biggest stumbling block in the way of the athletes were the coaches. There wasn't a coach in the country back in the early 30s that believed the four-minute mile was possible. In fact, most of them didn't believe it until it actually happened. But in a time trial in high school, I ran a sub four-minute mile. There was only one watch, but it was close enough that I knew it could be done.

I was never able to do a lot of training as far as practice running was concerned. Most of today's athletes run from 75 to 150 miles a week. I never ran over five to seven miles and only went on the track three days a week: Monday, Tuesday and Wednesday. Tuesday, I would take my hard workout, but after the warmup I would never run over 3/4 of a mile. I would only do that usually for short distances, like two 660's or three single quarters. Sometimes I'd just sprint 220's and walk 220's and sprint 220's, or maybe sprint a straightway and walk the turns.

AMAA: You had to take an unusually long warm-up didn't you?

Cunningham: Yes I did because I had several things that were against me. If I didn't warm my legs up properly, the circulation not being good, they would naturally tie up. Then I had this neck injury which would tie up my shoulders and spread all over me if I didn't get it loosened up real good.

AMAA: Now, let's go back a little into your life which may illuminate that point some more. The 1500m in the 1936 Olympiad was a race you sorely wanted to win. You spoke of that as your toughest defeat but certainly not the toughest moment of your life. That goes back to the time you were seven years old when you were severely burned. Your brother was killed in the same fire. You were told you would never walk again. As I understand it, you would have more difficulty walking than you did running.

Cunningham: Part of this has been recorded incorrectly. Naturally, having walked at one time and then coming to a place where I couldn't walk, I had to learn to walk all over again, just like a tiny infant. After you are seven or eight years old and you try to get on your feet and fall, I knew the only way was to pick myself up and try one more time.

AMAA: Was there anything or any person in your life at the time who inspired you?

Cunningham: My parents were the greatest inspiration I had. They never knew what defeat meant. They never worried about anything. They would just do whatever they needed to do with whatever they had and let the consequences come. They were always very positive about everything.

AMAA: Your career ended about 1940. What did you do then? I know you've been a teacher, a lecturer, a lay preacher, and you and your wife have ten children.

Cunningham: I think athletics are wonderful—in their proper place. They were not everything to me by any means. I wanted an education, and I was at New York University working on my Ph.D. degree. Now out on the ranch they know that as a "posthole digger." I got the Ph.D. degree, went back to the University of Kansas for a time, then over to Cornell College, organized the Student Health. At first I was teaching, in fact I was head of the Health Department of Cornell College and took over as Director of the Physical Education Department. Then I went into the service, served in the Navy World War II, came out of the service and my wife Ruth and I decided we would do the thing we always wanted to—work with boys and girls who were having problems.

AMAA: Tell me more about that.

Cunningham: Well, we had a little ranch here in Kansas, 880 acres, with a beautiful view of the country. It's cattle raising country, just gentle, rolling country with two creeks running through the place. We started working with kids and were thinking of six to eight kids at a time which we could handle with the facilities we had. But my problem is that I never could say "no." The next thing we knew we had eighty-eight kids with us for a short period of time. There were times when we had only a few, but we often had many more. And, the kids at our place didn't do a lot of running around. Their friends would end up coming over and we'd have double the number of kids just from the towns and city around us. They'd spent the weekend, Thanksgiving, Christmas vacation, other holidays.

AMAA: I guess you've seen many of them grow up into adulthood and become successful. I know you've helped a lot of these youngsters. In fact, your quote about the human potential applies to some of the youngsters you've worked with as well. The human race maybe is just beginning to realize its potential. Can you talk about that?

Cunningham: I believe our young people are the greatest asset this nation has. We let them go down the drain, this nation goes down the drain.

I have never found a bad boy, I never found a bad girl. I've never seen a child I didn't love. We had over 9500 boys and girls through our home in a little more than thirty years, as many as eighty-eight at one time, never found a bad boy, never found a bad girl. Lots of kids have done a few bad things, but I told them I've done a few of those myself. I think we all have if we're honest enough to admit it. Kids came in there just as a part our family along with our own ten, and we just had a terrific experience.

We never had a child fail a course in school. I'd like to tell you about two kids that came to us. One came out of a mental institution in Ohio. She spent time, they were going to send her back. The mother called and said she thought the girl was experimenting with drugs. We took the young lady; she was supposedly not too sharp. She graduated from our high school, honor student of her graduating class. She represented the school in state contests in voice and in speech. I have never met a more talented young lady.

Then I had a letter from a woman in St. Louis: "Dr. Glenn Cunningham, please God put my heart on these pages for Glenn Cunningham to read. My son Johnny was born thirteen years ago," her letter began. When he cried she slapped him, he would cry more, then she would burn him with cigarettes to give him something to cry about; then when he started toddling around he would aggravate her so that she'd just haul off and hit him and knock him end over end around the room. She said she broke dinner plates, not over his head but over his face. When she broke his nose, she put him out with a foster family. They sent him back, said this child is absolutely incorrigible. She put him in school, they kicked him out of public school, he was so disruptive they said they couldn't carry on classes. She put him in a parochial school. After a while the sisters that taught first grade told her she had to take him out of school because they had the good children to think about. She put him in a school for the emotionally disturbed. They kicked him out. He came to us, fourteen years old that summer, had never passed a grade of school. What in the world can you do with a child fourteen years old that has never passed a grade in school? He fitted in size with the seventh graders; we put him in the seventh grade. His first examination was in his math course. He topped the class with a grade of ninety-seven. He breezed along, no problem, graduated the eighth grade. We always attended the activities. He came home with his diploma, when he received it he said, "Father and Mother, when I get my high school diploma I'm going back to St. Louis, to those doctors who said I'd never amount to anything, that I had brain damage and couldn't learn. I'm going to try and get a hold of those guys and I'll tell them, I'm going to go to college and I'm going to ask them what courses could I take in order to help *them*." Johnny graduated from college just a few years ago, got a letter from his mother saying that Johnny had graduated from college, a boy who supposedly could not learn, according to some of the people that worked with him—some of the psychiatrists.

Well, we found that animal therapy worked wonders with the kids. We gave them all a horse and other animals, and they were always busy, always happy, just didn't have any problems. Of course I disciplined hard, had to discipline often, and I believe in discipline because without it you're going to have a generation just as we have today committing crimes against society, just unbelievably, and it all could be ended in just one generation if we could initiate *discipline*. A father in a family works as the dominant one in the family. He rules the family, not that he's overbearing, I tried not to be, and my kids all respect me. If I say "jump" they say "how far?" and I'd like the world to be that way. But we had a wonderful experience. We had to give up our work. We were there for seventeen years and had over 8,000 boys and girls. We financed it pretty much ourselves with an average of $68.09 per year of outside help. Finally we got so heavy in debt we couldn't carry on our work. We had to close down because we couldn't even pay the interest on the debt. We have a young couple out there now, three younger couples doing the work, and thank God they are doing a good job with the young people who are in trouble today.

AMAA: The human potential. We've spoken about it in terms of performance. In any sense, you do consider discipline of paramount importance in the human equation. And, from what you've said, the example we set is critical in terms of our children, in terms of society in general.

Cunningham: Discipline is *the* thing. So many young people are growing up and families are so mobile now. Everybody is working, everybody is going their own way, kids really have no discipline imposed upon them. I was just reading notes from kids that I spoke to, I suppose a couple of hundred of them that wrote notes. The thing that they expressed was that they appreciated the things I said. I hit the drugs real hard. They commented about how that will help them to say "no" and to grow up to be drug-free person.

AMAA: The discipline to say "no." How do you explain drugs in sports now? It's so widespread.

Cunningham: These people actually have no objective in life. They're drifting. Life has no meaning. That's why teenagers are committing suicide by the thousands; because they can't face the future. Life has no meaning to them. They never really learned to do anything. This is one of the problems with many of the kids that come to us. They say, "I'll be thrown out on my own, I won't be able to earn a living, I won't be able to do anything, what's going to happen to me." The guilt and fear of all the things they have done, especially with drugs and sex, make them feel life is not worthwhile.

People say the problem is that kids won't talk. We didn't have any problem getting them to talk. They tell you something and say, "Don't you think I'm terrible?" You know, parents try to make their kids feel the parents never did anything wrong. Well, there's not a person living that hasn't done something that he shouldn't have. This is the thing that the kids need to hear. They need to hear that we're human, we make mistakes and we can overcome those things. But they also need to hear that we have to recognize them as mistakes, face up to them and determine to do differently from there on.

But so many of them try to avoid these things, and try to shove them behind them and say, "I didn't do that," or "It wasn't my fault. It was just some thing that happened that didn't involve me . . ."

AMAA: Perhaps we can sum it all up with your conception of setting an example, a "role model," already a clichéd term, but something you've taken seriously.

Cunningham: I think the example we set is the most important thing any of us do, because we determine the life of the individuals who look up to us. Each one of us is an example to many other people; at times we may not even know to whom.

INDEX

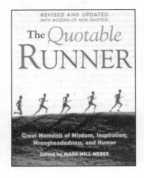
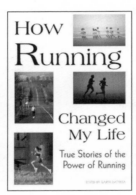

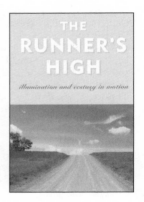
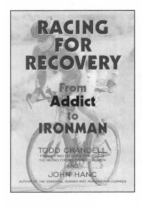

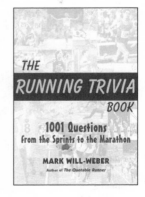